THE
EXPLORER
NATURALIST

Frontispiece. California sea otters. (Phyllis Thompson)

THE EXPLORER NATURALIST

By Vinson Brown

with illustrations by Judith Hennessey, Phyllis Thompson, Jerry Buzzell, William Carey Grimm, James Gordon Irving, and Rune Hapness

Cover photograph by Tom Brakefield

Stackpole Books

THE EXPLORER NATURALIST

Published by
STACKPOLE BOOKS
Cameron and Kelker Streets
Harrisburg, Pa. 17105

Printed in the U.S.A.

Library of Congress Cataloging in Publication Data

Brown, Vinson, 1912-
   The explorer naturalist.

   Includes index.
   1. Natural history—Technique.   2. Natural history.
I. Title.
QH60.B76   574.5'028   76-4871
ISBN 0-8117-0603-6

Contents

Part I

Fields of Study and Their Methods

1

LIVING WORLD OF THE NATURALIST

THE CHALLENGE

Most people look at the world around them and see it as a mass of meaningless objects. They do not look at a leaf and see its many meanings, particularly its absolute, vital importance as both oxygen producer and carbon-dioxide absorber, so necessary to the continuation of all life. They see a wasp simply as a wasp. They have no conception of its many, varied ways of living, the exciting adventures of its hunt for food, and the curious distinctiveness of its relations with other wasps and other living things. Most of all, they do not grasp the fact that all life on this earth, which is so small compared with other objects in our immense universe, forms a complex association and ecosystem (as an ecologist calls a complete environment), which is tied together in its past and future with living things in a delicate balance with each other and with the rocks, minerals, waters, atmosphere, sun, and moon.

To the explorer naturalist it is a tremendously interesting adventure to explore and try to understand all of this, endless in its fascinating pathways and vistas of sudden glory, but also in its discoveries of ugliness and waste produced by thoughtless humans. Indeed, his adventure has all the elements of a great challenge and drama, in which he can be one of the key figures. If he really understands and tries, he may be one of the heroes who helps save the world from destruction by pollution and waste and point it toward a new age where men are in harmony with nature and with each other, a future this once lovely, green earth, unique in our solar system, surely deserves.

NEW EXPLORERS

Fortunately there have been increasing numbers of new explorers of science, bringing us new concepts and changes, all with much promise for both the world's future and for your absorbing interest if you become a part of the new pathfinding. It is not necessary to be a professional naturalist to be part of this dramatic adventure. Today, in fact, many professionals are in need of the help of amateurs, provided that they indeed have trained themselves to be a help and not a burden. To give such training is one major function of this book.

A hundred years ago some of the great naturalists were also amateurs, such as Thomas Belt, Theodore Roosevelt, and William Henry Hudson. Like most naturalists of their time they were massive collectors of specimens, for the whole world was opening up like a newly hatched egg, and the naturalists were dragging in from all parts of the earth a wealth of strange new species. Collection and classification was the rage in those days, with not much interest in the deeper meanings of the plants' and animals' lives, their behavior and social qualities, or their positions in the world as a whole. Today the emphasis has changed and new elements of scientific seeking have entered in that were not even thought about in that past century or in the first years of this century.

Among these ideas is the concept of the conservation of natural resources, including all that lives, and the realization that we are living on a small planet with limited resources and a fragile system of life that could be easily upset and destroyed by industrial and commercial man if his appetite for power, wealth, and more production is not rechanneled constructively and intelligently into more creative work. Today we are slowly, perhaps too slowly, grasping the truth that each kind of animal and plant is a precious heritage, and an infinitely complex and interesting being about which we still know very little. Today a new kind of naturalist is trying to educate the bulk of mankind about the priceless value of almost all living things and their need to be kept in balance and harmony.

The new naturalists are learning to work together in unified and dynamic teams, more effective than the lone researcher, although some who seek alone still have their places. However, the old indifference to anything but one's own special field is being replaced by an understanding of the interdependence of science and life and an attempt to create bridges of understanding among the scientific disciplines so that many may contribute more effectively to the advancement of all knowledge. Even as we are learning with deeper insight that most animals are social beings and that social relations and interdependence between plants is very strong, so also mankind is belatedly learning how to produce new social organisms in which the quality of life becomes more important than its material aspects and in which the dangerously selfish habits of the past are redirected into creative channels for the betterment of all living things.

We are helped in this endeavor to understand ourselves and other living things better by many new inventions in the fields of electronics and microscopy; by new discoveries in atomic, molecular, and life structures; and by new chemical formulas that allow us to see as never before into the minds, the senses, and the moods of living creatures and plants, including ourselves. For example, scientists have studied with such aids the nerve impulses of a frog and are even able to see fairly exactly how the frog looks at the world. They understand now that the frog sees only the things essential to its existence and conserves the energies of its nervous system by ignoring nonessentials. How much better this helps us understand how a frog acts. This is just the beginning, for with every mystery that is explained, a dozen new ones may rise.

Another of the new concepts rapidly rising to prominence is that in the social lives of animals we can find the origins of the social lives of human beings and so can better understand not only the animals but ourselves as well. Thus, we may find the keys to unlock the cures for the present disharmony of man, which threatens the well-being of every one on earth.

The exploration of new knowledge about ourselves and all life, considering that we have similar cells and similar chemicals, enzymes, reactors, and even, conceivably, spirits and moods, has not only infinitely enriched the study of natural history, but has led to something that is both a danger and a challenge: More and more natural scientists are forced to work together in groups, where the submergence of the ego in the common cause and effort is vitally important. There is always the danger in groups that one person may try to dominate and in doing so inhibit or even destroy the creativeness of his compatriots. However, a new humbleness is being found, in which the leader himself knows how little he knows, and guides those who work with him as a good coach guides an athletic team, more by kindliness, understanding, and the dynamic action of his personality than by gruff orders, harsh criticisms, and sharp commands. In these teams, the amateur, starting alone as a general naturalist and perhaps not too effective as yet, although eager to learn, can eventually emerge as a true explorer naturalist, either partnered with professional scientists or perhaps eventually forming a team of amateurs of his own. The team, with its greater resources, can either have access to or own (or both) the technical facilities and instruments often so necessary for good scientific research today.

THE SCIENTIST: YESTERDAY, TODAY AND TOMORROW

Truly great scientists have always had this feeling of humbleness and dedication to seeking the truth no matter where the trail may lead. Charles Darwin, famous for his discovery of the theory of evolution by natural selection, found that another natural scientist, Alfred Wallace, had made the same discovery at practically the same time. Humbly and with a high sense of honor he made sure that Wallace's paper and his were published at the same time so that both could be announced as co-discoverers. He also acknowledged that their theory probably would have great changes made to it in the years ahead as new scientific discoveries were made, and he admitted that there were holes in it, with some questions left unanswered, just as they are today, although some too-dogmatic teachers of evolution seem to forget this. Sir Isaac Newton, the great genius of the science of physics in the eighteenth century, chided his admirers by saying he felt "like a little child wandering on a beach, picking up a few pretty stones, while the whole Ocean of Truth stretches before me still unknown!"

Modern science in this century, and particularly the biological sciences, has burst through so many barriers, and shown the falseness and misconceptions of so many past ideas about the reality of life and matter, that we not only find ourselves peering into totally new worlds of reality, thought, and concept, but can see the absolute necessity for all to keep an open mind. And how much greater is the joy and the thrill to grow with such an open mind and to explore these new fields, which open like secret kingdoms, leaving behind forever the blinders of custom, dogma, and prejudice that have for so long held back the human race. Think how, in just the past few decades, discoveries about both atom and cell, the bases of both matter and life, have caused us to lose both fixity and certainty about their true nature. The atom has changed before our amazed eyes, as scientists look through the electron microscopes, into a system of waves, impulses, and particles, far more complex and dynamic than in our earlier imagining, while the cell has proved to be such an even more complex little world of unseen forces and powers and combinations of infinitely wonderful molecules that we realize what we now know is only the start of a very long journey. Indeed, even the middle pathways of this journey are likely to be so far beyond our present comprehension that they may be reached only by human beings so far beyond our present wisdom and knowledge that we will seem like ants, nay, even worms, in comparison.

We are seeing a time when the amazing and infinite complexity of life and matter and their interrelations has become so great that a new sharing of knowledge and techniques, a new teamwork, is needed. This presents a challenge and even a danger, but it is likely to be the major if not the only way to break open the new eggs of knowledge. Fortunately, training to prepare oneself for such exciting work can start at any time in life, for one thing we now know about the human brain is that in nearly all human beings it has tremendous quantities of unused cells, so that most of us have potentials of creative work often far beyond our wildest dreams.

At first you should learn some of the basic knowledge of a naturalist as provided in this book, and then you will be able to do your own research intelligently, either alone or as part of a scientific team. Thus, you need to develop some good general knowledge of all that lives, and the interractions of living things with each other and their environment, for nowadays it is becoming increasingly clear that the specialist does not function with his greatest power if he does not see and understand himself as part of the whole.

TWO PROJECTS OF EXPLORER NATURALISTS IN ACTION

Let us watch two explorer naturalists, who obtained their preliminary knowledge and training and are now beginning some real exploration. While either of the following projects can be done alone, possibly simply as a part of early training, each is shown here in cooperation with others because of the greater values and results likely to be obtained. The explorers could be men or women of any race or age or nationality, for among true scientists there is no sex, race, national, or age discrimination. Though the work of the first explorer seems more complex than that of the second, the first job is actually, paradoxically, a training for the second.

Observe the first naturalist as he walks across some fields and into a small deciduous woods along a creek. He is tanned and healthy looking, of course, for he is by now used to wandering in the out-of-doors where wind and sun, walking and exploring, do wonders for all of us. He moves with sureness and quietness, making no hasty motions or loud noises to disturb wildlife, and alertly watches everything about him, his eyes alive with curiosity and wonder. He has a knapsack in which he carries a couple essential field books, a notebook, and some simple collecting equipment, though his aim is to collect only what is absolutely essential for a scientific project, realizing that the harmony and existence of living things should not be disturbed without extremely good reasons. He also has a pair of good binoculars, a magnifying glass, and a camera, as these are often essential tools of the naturalist. Besides these he carries some small stakes, a steel measuring tape, and some twine for this special project, which is one of the best for a beginning naturalist to start with because it gives him a picture of the wholeness and interrelatedness of life. In short he is involved in a classic project in ecology (the science of the interaction of living things with each other and their environment), and ecology usually involves in time all the other branches of biology in one way or another.

What is this project? It is to describe and measure accurately by number what scientists call an *ecosystem*, which is the combination of an ecologic community of plants and animals with its geologic and climatic base. An ecosystem can be very large, like a biotic province, comprising an area as big as a state or more, and with many smaller ecosystems within it, or it can be quite small like this one strip of streamside or riparian woods along a creek in western Pennsylvania. This particular amateur scientist is studying this wildlife area as part of a combined project of several scientists, looking into its statistics of number and kind and degree of life, its potential, and the possible hazards to its future.

The need for such studies is becoming more evident as civilization recklessly narrows the areas of wildlife, and these precious heritages of our past face greater danger of disappearing. By the comparison of two or more studies of the same area over a few years, scientists can see what is actually happening and so have ammunition to show the public and the government officials and politicians what needs to be done to preserve and enhance our environment for ourselves and for future generations. Also, such studies open new vistas of fascinating research and a beginning understanding of new secrets of the wild that will awaken interest in and appreciation of the treasures we have and how we can lose them.

Unfortunately many such studies in the past have been done too haphazardly, with biased viewpoints and far from accurate data. Astonishingly, modern scientists have found, in studying so-called "scientific" ecological reports of ecosystems in earlier years, that many workers at that time completely forgot even to pinpoint the exact location where a particular study was made. So the great potential value of such studies to be used in comparison with more recent investigations is often lost.

Fortunately our explorer naturalist has been well-grounded in what to do and he is proceeding methodically, although with a feeling of the excitement of adventurous discovery, to do each part of his job exactly right. He had first prepared a map of the area of the streamside or riparian woods he is exploring by taking a U.S. Geodetic Survey Map of the same area and enlarging the part he needed from 1 mile to the inch up to ⅛ mile to the inch photographically. (See Figure 1-1.) By use of the contours on the map and the line shown by the creek, he was then able to map for himself a fairly exact area covered by the riparian woodlands along the creek. Because of the change we are having to the metric system, he decided to translate the feet and yards of the map into meters. Then, using a large, rocky cliff by the creek as a major point of reference, he drove a steel stake into its top and used this as the base for a transect line through the middle of the woods. This line was not only marked on the map, but also marked with wooden stakes at every 100 meters, using a compass to bear on a straight course. To get the metric distances fairly accurately, but not take all the time needed by exact measurement, he had previously practiced his normal stride over a measured 100-meter course, numbering the strides until he was able to pace off the 100-meter distance fairly consistently.

With a blue pencil he then marked off on his map a number of 100-meter square areas that covered all of the area of the riparian woods. Each of these areas was numbered on the map (as shown),

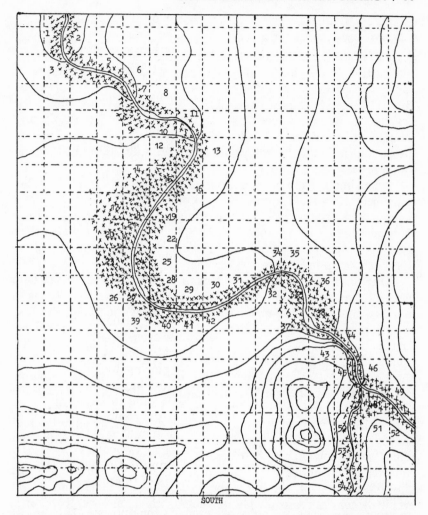

Figure 1–1. Map of riparian woods, charted for population count of plant and animal life. Only the creek, contours, tree symbols for the woodland, 100 meter squares, and the 54 numbered squares on this map are shown to keep it simple. The 54 numbers are each put on a piece of paper and the pieces put in a hat, from which seven numbers are selected. Suppose these are 5, 19, 23, 30, 31, 38, and 49; each of these squares is then carefully mapped, showing all trees and major shrubs, and observations of mammals, birds, reptiles, and amphibians are charted, for a population count. (Vinson Brown)

each number placed on a small piece of paper, and all the pieces of paper placed loosely in a box. From this box he had his sister, a disinterested person, draw seven of the numbers, which he then determined would be the numbers of the square metric areas on the map he would especially investigate. The reason for this was to have a random sampling of squares from the whole area, an area far too large to be studied systematically as a whole. From a close study of these seven squares he felt he would be able to get enough information to develop a fairly accurate picture of the wildlife in the whole ecosystem and determine animal and plant populations. Thus, if 7 metric squares were used and there were 49 100-meter squares in the whole woods or ecosystem, he could multiply any population statistics he developed by seven to produce a picture of the population and the relationships of wildlife and plants in the whole area.

Choosing a random sampling of squares was important because scientists have found that too often in the past naturalists making such studies of an ecosystem had chosen such squares from their own biased viewpoints, for example, because the squares they used were easy to approach or for some other personal reason, so that such samplings were not well-balanced.

Our naturalist has already staked out his squares in the field by careful measurement and run nylon lines between the stakes to mark each of the 7 100-meter squares he needed to study. But this is only part of the total effort on this one ecosystem, since these first squares are usable only in mapping and making population counts of the macrolife of the area, such as the large trees and shrubs, the birds, the mammals, the reptiles, and the amphibians. For the smaller or microlife, two other naturalists of the team have been assigned, one to study a random sampling of 10-meter square areas within the woods for such medium-sized plants as herbs and small bushes plus the larger insects and their relatives, while the other had undertaken to do research on samplings of single metric squares, small enough for close observation and counting of the tiny life of the soil, the bark, the wood, the leaf mold, and microscopic or near microscopic plants such as algae, mosses, liverworts, and fungi. Such a division of the job was based on the obvious fact that no single person could undertake the whole job as a spare-time effort and do it adequately. Then, besides the three field men, they had backup help from experts in such important specialties as mathematical statistics, taxonomists who could identify correctly difficult specimens brought in from the field, a climatologist, and a soil expert. All of these team members, of course, gave only part-time help to the project.

Our explorer naturalist, as his part of the project, also made a larger map, scale 10 meters to 2 centimeters, of each of his seven squares, in which he mapped the location of each large bush and tree, using a special symbol for each plant species, and a number for each mammal, bird, reptile, or amphibian seen or heard, or its tracks or other signs found in the area of the square.

Although our naturalist came to the area at different times of the day or night, in the night using a flashlight covered with red plastic to give a red light that disturbs few animals, and although he camouflaged his body and even his movements to appear as little as possible like a man, certain nocturnal mammals, reptiles, and amphibians were almost impossible to count by such methods. Thus, he carefully had to set out live traps of different sizes and types in their runways or near where he suspected they lived in order to capture and actually see them. Each animal was then immobilized or rendered unconscious if necessary by injection of a harmless chemical, photographed, and tagged or marked in such a way that any future scientist who examined the area would know that each marked animal was part of a previous counting and could use his own captures for comparison with earlier records. Then the animal, properly identified, was released unharmed. If vitally necessary for the project, some of the creatures trapped or seen were killed to be used as reference specimens, each to be kept in a museum with appropriate records if necessary to be examined by other scientists. (See chapters 2 and 3 for further details on these techniques.)

During all these wanderings in the woods, which our amateur can do in his spare time, a lot of things happen besides the counting of individuals of each species encountered. It would take a whole book to describe all his adventures, but a few can be hinted at here. For example, he sees that numerous willows grow both on land and in the water's edge, and so are not disturbed deeply by floods during times of heavy rains or snow melt, and that each species of willow has its own special niche in the streamside that it likes. This is a part of his increasing awareness of the dominant plants and animals of his study area and an enlargment of his understanding of why they are dominant. He observes the easy way the extremely common and successful white-footed mouse is camouflaged by its brownish- and whitish-color pattern merging with the similar colors of the ground, bark, and leaf mold, and how extremely fast are the reflexes of this bright-eyed little creature, so that when a hawk or owl dives for it, the mouse can dodge in a flash into the cover of brush or into a hole in the ground. Thus, each plant or animal becomes to him in time an individual with striking peculiarities of form or action and he begins to see all the interactions and close relationships of all the things of the woods, the plants giving shelter and food to the animals, while the animals help fertilize both plants and soil and aerate the soil for the plants' well-being by their digging in the ground and by their droppings. Then there are the many chains of life he learns about, such as plant eaten by insect, insect eaten by mouse, mouse eaten by weasel, weasel eaten by great horned owl, owl shot by man.

He learns more and more details about the behavior of living things, seeing that each species and even each individual of a species has special qualities. Thus, among shore birds, a sandpiper he sees scratches its head by reaching with its leg up in front of the body and under the wing, while a similar-looking plover scratches its head by reaching its leg up over the wing. Slave-making ants of the species *Formica sanguinea* (figure 1-2) march as armies through the woods to attack the communities or cities of other ants, killing off the adults and taking the pupae to enslave when they become adults. The slave-making ants attack boldly and ferociously. Some attacked ants fight back bravely but less effectively and with poorer organization of their army, while still other ants flee in fear or fight poorly.

It is natural that our naturalist in his work of gathering statistics on the ecotone also sees how many animals and plants are associated together, sometimes very loosely, as in the general plant-animal association of the riparian woodland; sometimes very closely, as in an ant city, a bird flock, or a mammal family, colony, or herd. He sees, for example, how the weasel family consists only

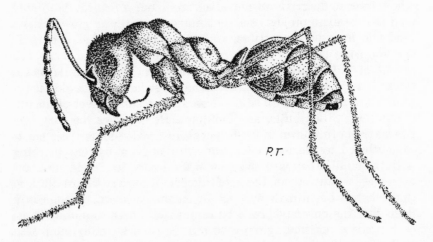

Figure 1–2. *Formica sanguinea*, the slave-making ant. (Phyllis Thompson)

of the mother and her children and that the father has nothing to do with them, even being attacked by the mother if he comes near, whereas the otter family is a very closely knit group, with father, mother, and children working together in constant cooperation and harmony. So he sees that social behavior can be very important in helping a species of animal be more or less successful in continuing to live and produce young. Even in plants, those that live closely together seem to protect and help one another, as do blackberry vines with their thickets heavily armed with spines.

All these observations are not only increasing his general knowledge and his feeling of increased understanding of all living things, but also they are preparing him for the time when he decides to specialize. Maybe he will make a special study of the social behavior of certain wasps, such as the white-faced hornet, or perhaps he may move into a special field of ecology such as observing the changes brought to life by the increasing pollution of a salt marsh. In every such case of specialization, he will try to find out everything previous scientists have done in this field and particularly what they have not done, for it is in the unexplored areas that he can most likely add what may be vital discoveries to human knowledge.

Let us briefly observe, for example, an explorer naturalist actually doing some research more specialized than the ecological study we just outlined. Suppose he has been so fortunate as to discover an isolated beach below some cliffs on the California coast where California sealions (figure 1-3) are breeding and raising young in summer. Here again a little teamwork, but much less than in the first project, may be necessary. First he must get permission from the property owner to visit the colony, but he needs also at least one other person to work with him because of the dangers involved. There is danger going down the cliffs, and ladders or ropes have to be used so that equipment can be carried safely below and men can climb down safely. There is some danger also from the California sealion bulls, which may weigh as much as 700 pounds, who have been known to try to attack men who bother their breeding areas. Their speed, however, is not as great as that of a running man, and they will not chase a man very far.

For the success of the project it is necessary to observe the behavior of the animals with as little disturbance as possible. Fortunately sealions have rather poor eyesight and are not able to differentiate nonmoving objects from their surroundings. Our naturalist takes several precautions so he can watch them unnoticed.

Figure 1–3. California sealions. (Judith Hennessey)

He dresses in rather baggy-looking clothes so his shape appears not too man-like; he selects clothes of the same dark brown colors of the female sealion, and, when he moves on the beach, he does so in the crawling position of a sealion instead of the upright position of a man. He finds that by doing this and by moving slowly and carefully with his photographic equipment and sound-recording equipment, and often holding still, he is little noticed by the sealions and gradually they begin to consider him as just another sealion female. This is important because it is vital not to antagonize the big males into thinking he is a rival male. By making his movements and noises similar to those of the sealions, he actually merges with their society, and, in effect, becomes one with them.

He also finds that at night it is even possible to crawl among the sealions with a flashlight and observe their activities with no disturbance at all, partly because by crawling over the sand and rocks where they have been he picks up their smell so that the man scent is largely disguised, unless a sealion actually pushes its nose very close to his face, which, by being careful, he can avoid.

With binoculars by day, a flashlight by night, and a handy notebook and camera plus sound-recording equipment both times, he can record the intimate story of their lives during the breeding season. He notes things such as the females extreme jealousy of other females during the first few weeks after they have pups and how they drive the other females away. Later this guardianship relaxes until the young are playing both on shore and in the water largely on their own. He observes the change in the mood of the bull towards other bulls, depending on whether the other bull retreats and acts submissive, or comes forward aggressively. Day by day, patiently and carefully and accurately he records and watches the life of these animals until he has a good picture of their lives during the breeding season.

It is obvious that each project in behavior study will be different, using different techniques, based on the nature of each species of animal, bird, reptile, insect, and so forth. Foxes, for example, with their very sharp noses and eyes and their great fear of man, can only be observed in the wild with the greatest possible care and precautions, so they do not smell or see you. A carefully concealed blind might be put near the den of a fox to watch the vixen and her pups, but if the fox becomes suspicious that she is being watched, all your work is lost.

DISCIPLINES IN NATURAL SCIENCE

Each branch of science is often called a *discipline* because any field in science calls for the development of a disciplined mind and disciplined work. Involved are high ideals in honesty with all the people you deal with; loyalty to your scientific team if you belong to one; extraordinary patience, alertness, and steadfastness, as well as vigilance in all your work to make sure it is accurate and complete; the bigness to admit you can be wrong or when you are wrong; and the intelligence and carefulness to learn from mistakes and not repeat them. In all these things we can grow, but it takes constant day-by-day building of good habits to create the fine scientist, either amateur or professional.

Highly necessary is the desire, aim, and ability to be open-minded in your search for truth and to be very careful not to let your natural prejudices or biases towards other people or their ideas interfere with this. *The scientific method has been defined as the method of multiple working hypotheses.* This means that, as you approach any problem or project in a scientific field and try to find the truth about it, you must write down in detail, analyze and test every idea or hypothesis you or others have about this subject, and allow each hypothesis equal weight in your testing and examining of it. A true scientist should be big enough even to take the hypothesis of another scientist who has violently attacked his work and deal with this hypothesis with the same open-mindedness and honest search for truth about it that he would use with any hypothesis or idea of his own.

As the multiple working hypotheses are examined in the field and in the laboratory, they are tested over and over again until those that obviously do not answer the problem can be eliminated and those that begin to show promise and finally help explain a problem or enlighten the meaning of a project can be combined in a theory that is based on proven facts. Such a theory, if it proves itself correct over time, may be honored by being called a *natural law*. But even at this point all scientists should not only have open minds, but a willingness to investigate any new developments or ideas that may modify or even completely change a theory or natural law.

Thus, for example, the theory of evolution on the basis of the inheritance of acquired characteristics, which was advanced in the early nineteenth century by the French scientist, Jean Lamarck, was later proved largely wrong by new scientific discoveries and was replaced by the theory of evolution through natural selection of Charles Darwin and Alfred Wallace of the mid-nineteenth century. This theory in turn has been modified by discoveries, such as those about genes and mutations in inheritance on the part of scientists such as Mendel, Morgan, and DeVries, and still later insights may be turning this theory back to some admission of parts of the earlier Lamarckian ideas.

Another interesting turnabout in general biological outlook, if not theory, is the way scientists have reacted to what are called "anthropomorphic ideas" about animal life. Earlier naturalists had often described animal behavior as being very much like that of humans, as for example when a walrus mother (figure 1-4) hugged her young in her flippers and leaped into the sea with it to save the infant from attack by men. Later naturalists felt such actions were

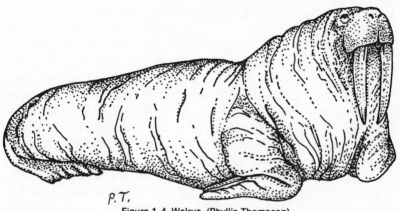

P.T.

Figure 1–4. Walrus. (Phyllis Thompson)

instinctive in animals and not to be put in the same class as similar human actions. They did indeed sometimes prove that such actions in certain animals, particularly those of mammals and birds with smaller brains or among the invertebrates, were indeed instinctive, or what scientists nowadays call "stereotyped behavior." This is something animals and birds do without having to learn how from parents or other animals. However, some more recent scientists have begun to suggest that, since our cellular, muscular, and nervous systems are different only in degree, not in type, from those of the higher animals and birds, their reactions, moods, feelings, and even thoughts must often be similar to ours. They received considerable ammunition to back their ideas with recent proofs by researchers that creatures such as crows, geese, otters, wolves, dolphins, and many others of the whale species actually demonstrate extreme solicitude not only for their own kind, but sometimes, as in the case of dolphins and porpoises, for human beings as well.

This has been making more and more untenable the argument of those men, who make a profit out of killing large numbers of seals, whales, and other higher animals and birds, that these creatures do not have feelings like ours. The shame of man, now that the facts are coming out, is probably that the most really humane living creature on this earth in the best sense of the word is not man at all, but the dolphin.

Divisions of Natural Science and Their Heroes

Let us see how some natural scientists have at least proved they are dedicated to seeking the truth in honorable ways, and how they have used ingenuity, vigilance, and careful testing of their hypotheses or ideas until the facts prove, or at least begin to prove, new theories. In doing so we will see that there are two major kinds of naturalists: those who gather facts until every piece fits in place and they can prove their theories, and those who leap forward because of intuitive genius, and go beyond the present facts to concepts and ideas that later men find to be true. In the past the strictly factual natural scientists have been often jealous or scornful of those who leap ahead, criticizing and attacking them. Today, perhaps, we can be big enough to see that both fulfill vital functions and are needed to balance each other.

Here are some of the major fields of natural history. Following this are some brief but dramatic accounts of scientists in action, stories that emphasize the qualities that make a fine scientist, either professional or amateur. May you learn to follow in their footsteps, but also scale your own mountains of research and discovery.

Anatomy—the science of the morphology or structure of animals and plants. This is a vital study for those who want to paint or draw things in nature. The anatomy of many living things is yet to be described.

Animal and Plant Geography—this science covers the mapping of the distribution of different animal and plant species all over the earth and their effect on the areas to which they have spread.

Biochemistry—the science of the chemical nature and reactions of life. This is an enormously growing field, but the chemical and mathematical training needed to do research in this area is arduous.

Climatology—the study of climates and the phenomena caused by climates. This science ties in very closely with ecology, and the effects of climate on life.

Cytology—the science of the study of plant and animal cells, their nature and functions. It involves a great deal of work with microscopes, but there are so many kinds of cells and so many different kinds of plants and animals still untouched by this study that there are practically inexhaustible openings here for dedicated amateurs.

Ecology—the study of the relations of animals and plants with each other and with their environments. This vast field is as yet so little touched that the amateur scientist can find a myriad of niches within it to use his talents to explore.

Ethology—the scientific study of the characteristic behavior patterns of animals. This includes the study of the social organization of animals, both primitive and complex. This is such a brand new science, like a plant that has just raised its first leaf above the ground, that infinite adventures and explorations lie ahead.

Genetics—the science of plant and animals inheritance involves many fascinating experiments in breeding and crossbreeding to get better strains of living things, for application in agriculture, sports, etc. Amateurs can do well in this field if they work carefully.

Paleontology—the science of ancient life forms. The ancestory of modern creatures and of plants, and many interesting facts about their inheritance, can be learned from a study of fossils.

Physiology—the science that deals with the functions and vital processes of living organisms and their parts and organs. This science spreads its arms into many other branches of biology, and is one of the oldest of the natural sciences, but even it is still in its infancy, and vast fields lie unexplored.

Taxonomy—in biology this is the system of classifying animals and plants into a natural order or relationships, with each species put in its proper place. There are tens of thousands of species yet to be placed properly.

Porpoises and their sonar: To show how specialized the study of animal behavior (*ethology*) can be, and yet how productive of quite spectacular results, let us look at the fascinating research of Dr. Winthrop N. Kellogg into the sonar system of porpoises. Here is a capsule view of his work.

Dr. Kellogg and his assistants were able to isolate some bottle-nosed porpoises in large tanks on the Florida coast, flushed daily with sea water that was so milky in texture that the porpoises could not see through it more than about two feet. The water was thus perfect for testing the porpoises' ability to locate objects and know their structure and nature by the aid of hearing alone, since sight was of no value.

Hundreds of careful experiments with the animals, testing again and again to make sure the full facts were being observed and recorded, proved beyond doubt that the porpoises had an underwater sonar system of astounding ability, probably better even than that which bats use to locate insects and other objects in the air, and much more refined than the sonar of man used by the U.S. Navy for antisubmarine work. The porpoises, like the bats, were found to use many high ultrasonic sounds, repeated rapidly and bounced off objects underwater, but the porpoises had the advantage over the bats of large brains, which were able to interpret their sonar with greater sophistication.

For example, Dr. Kellogg tested the porpoises with two kinds of fish: one 12 inches long, which the porpoises did not like to eat; and the other 6 inches long, which they did like. One of these fish would be lowered on a line into one end of the tank when the porpoises were at the other end. This fish was completely invisible to the porpoise, but if it was the 6-inch fish, the porpoise would come dashing up immediately to grab it. If it was the 12-inch fish, he would pay no attention to it. (One attendant, by sleight of hand, substituted a 12-inch fish for a 6-inch fish just when the porpoise struck at it. The porpoise knew instantly what had happened, gave the attendant a dirty look, and used his tail to splash him violently in the face.)

During some of the tests two tunnels between the two pools were used, both of which could be closed quickly by a transparent plastic window. Using one of the 6-inch fish, which the porpoise liked, as a lure, a scientist would hold it behind the window, but the porpoise would not respond because the sonar was bouncing off the window. But the instant the window was lifted through its slots to clear the tunnel, the porpoise would sense the fish by sonar and dash to catch and eat it.

The results of these and many other clever tests showed that porpoises were able to understand the shape and size and even the nature of most objects simply by sound alone; it was understood that in the porpoise world, hearing was the main sense used, just as with humans, sight is the main sense, while with bears, smell is by far the most important sense.

Darwin's breakthrough to evolution: It is astonishing how many famous naturalists started out as rank amateurs. For example, Charles Darwin (figure 1-5) was so turned off by poor teachers in both schools and college, who made science sound dull, that he came within aces of never being a naturalist at all. Even his father said he probably had no future because all he wanted to do was "hunt" birds, not study them. Yet, Darwin had the potential to be one of the greatest intuitive scientists of all time.

Fortunately, though little trained for it, he was offered a job as naturalist on the *Beagle*, a British ship making a round-the-world survey of continental coasts and islands, a job he got only because

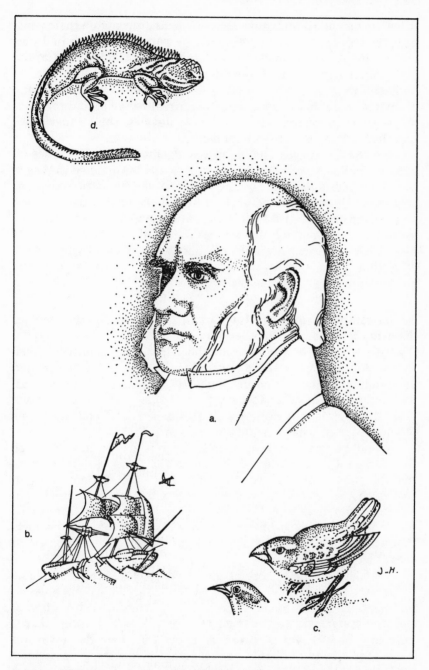

Figure 1—5. *a.* Charles Darwin; *b.* his ship, the *Beagle; c.* Darwin's finches; and *d.* an iguana lizard from the Galápagos Islands. (Judith Hennessey)

it had no pay at all and other naturalists had turned up their noses at it. The opening of horizons of strange and amazing life in different continents and islands acted like a flash of blazing light to the young man and his mind became alive and seeking. Very shortly he began to realize that "hunting for sport" was tame and boring compared to the fascinating study of animal behavior and relationships, their protective and aggressive devices, their inheritance and their adaptations to environments.

On the Galápagos Islands in the Pacific Ocean, 500 miles off Ecuador in South America, his keen eyes and brain noted that each island had a different kind of finch and tortoise, but close enough in structure to show they had evolved from a common ancestral finch and a common ancestral tortoise. From these and many related observations came not only the famous theory of evolution by natural selection but several natural laws about life, some of which were projections of his genius and insight into the future, later proved right by the purely fact-gathering naturalists.

Lost and found: the laws of inheritance: Another famous discovery was made by another amateur naturalist, Gregor Mendel (figure 1-6), a monk and later an abbot in a quiet country monastery in Austria in the 1860s and 1870s. But Mendel demonstrated outstandingly that you do not have to travel to far jungles, seas, and mountains in order to have remarkable adventures or make great discoveries, but can have similar experiences and explosions of knowledge in what amounts to one's own backyard.

Mendel took a small corner of the monastery gardens, 20 by 80 feet, fenced it in, and worked there over the years, carefully studying the inheritance of 22 varieties of peas. It is important to realize, however, that he did this only after carefully stating in writing, after carefully thinking things through, the conditions under which his experiments would work to bring out the facts that would enable him to elaborate a conclusion or theory based on those facts.

Considering the history of the breeding of animals and plants up to that time, Mendel understood that, although numerous experiments had been made, none had been done in such an organized and systematic way as to show us any laws governing inheritance and how it works. Breeders knew that hybrids of various kinds of plants and animals were constantly appearing, sometimes producing entirely new varieties, but they did not know how these were caused. First, he needed to know the number of different

Figure 1–6. Gregor Mendel studying pea plants in his garden. (Judith Hennessey)

forms under which the hybrids appeared; second, evidence of which generations produced such hybrids; and third, the proportions of hybrids that appeared in each generation, that is, their statistical relation (a modern idea that no one had thought about up to that time).

As he started to work in his garden of 22 varieties of peas, he knew also that it was vital to have all his experiments controlled, so that he alone would be responsible for the crossbreeding that was done. He did this by keeping the flowers covered when they came into maturity, and by using a brush to transfer pollen from one flower to another, always carefully recording the date, time, and flowers he used in his recording notebook. In this work he had chosen by careful selection seven characteristics of his peas that he would specially watch for in all future generations.

It is not important here to detail for you these varieties or his experiments with them. Full information can be obtained from books on genetics or inheritance. What is important to realize is that Mendel, without fully understanding what he had discovered, was using the theory of multiple working hypotheses, which means testing every idea about the inheritance of his plants under carefully controlled conditions and with a great number of experiments, until he had overwhelming evidence on which to base his final conclusions, called today Mendel's laws of inheritance. By his numerous experiments he demonstrated that these laws governed how most living things came into their inheritances, although he did not show what was only learned much later by scientists investigating chromosomes under the most high-powered microscopes, the actual mechanisms (the genes) by which such inherited characteristics appeared.

Mendel realized he had made a tremendous discovery, and he presented it in writing to the local Brunn Society for the Study of Natural History. Unfortunately, although this society published his paper, not one of them or anyone who at that time read the article, realized the significance of what he had written. In desperation Mendel sent information about his experiments and even packets of his seeds to the learned Professor Karl von Nageli of Zurich and Munich, who condescendingly looked the information over, may even have experimented a bit with the seeds, but was so overwhelmed by egotistic ideas of his superiority as a scientist that he neglected to really test out what Mendel had done. How foolish and how sad. If he had worked to help Mendel gain recognition, his own name as a co-worker would have remained in history with honor, but today he is completely forgotten while the name of the humble monk, Gregor Mendel, is written large and shall remain so down the ages.

Mendel, unfortunately, was not aggressive enough to push his ideas further and he died in 1884, neglected and forgotten. However, in early 1900 Mendel's laws were on the way to being rediscovered by several scientists, when, with astonishing exactness in timing, these men themselves found Mendel's writings, and, with true scientific generosity, humbleness, and honor, acknowledged Gregor Mendel as the first discoverer. The whole story should make clear to any naturalist of today, amateur or professional, that if he really discovers something in nature that he is convinced is important, he should first get it into print, and then keep trying to find recognition for it even when he is rebuffed or ignored, for he too could be another Mendel.

The exact opposite of Mendel is the naturalist or scientist who has tended to domineer over his science as a result of his tremendous prestige, a prestige that is a result of his own brilliant work as a scientist, but who unfortunately uses this prestige to belittle and ridicule the ideas of others without really understanding them and so hiding and obscuring concepts that may be of benefit to mankind. Such men were Cuvier, great French anatomist, biologist, and paleontologist, who ridiculed the early evolutionary theories of Lamarck; Hrdlicka, the great American physical anthropologist, who discouraged other scientists from investigating carefully the evidences of ancient men in the Americas by what amounted to a dogma that the earliest Americans could not have possibly come to America earlier than 6000 B.C.; and Agassiz, the famous Swiss-American biologist, whose prestige for a long time discouraged American scientists from investigating or accepting Darwin's ideas on evolution.

Lessons to be Learned

It is wise to read many such stories of the great naturalists of the past to find inspiration and warnings for the present. (Books that tell such accounts of different scientists and their work are listed in Appendix C, Suggested References.) From such examples we can take warning, first, not to let ourselves ever become so dogmatic in our ideas that we hinder our own or anyone else's progress in the search for truth, and second, not to let the prestige of any scientist so dominate our thinking that it hinders or stops our own independent investigation of truth. Down through history one of the most serious barriers to our progress in knowledge has been the ego of powerful and famous men who thought they *knew* the truth and that this gave them the right to control the minds of others. How often those who *knew* they were right have been wrong.

Seek then the gifts of character demonstrated to us in the lives of the truly great scientists, their humbleness, their enthusiasm, their perseverance, their careful checking over and over of facts, their determination to deal honorably with their fellow men even when this may mean financial loss or a lessening of their prestige, their eternal alertness and vigilance in the search for new knowledge, and their careful recording of all that they discover. Character can be made by day-to-day building of new and good habits; by minds looking upward in spirit, hope, and dedication; and by scorning all that is petty and mean and self-indulgent. Men and women of good character can, without force and without prejudice, remake the world in beauty and in harmony by the power of their deeds and spirits.

2

TOOLS AND METHODS OF THE NATURALIST

The title of this book, *The Explorer Naturalist*, implies that one who begins to use and read it already has some background in natural science: probably has taken a course in biology in high school, preferably has some knowledge of geology and climatology, and has read one or preferably more beginning books on general natural history. Otherwise too much of this book would be taken up with beginning subjects such as the nature of the cell, the meaning of rock strata and fossils, and the basic structure of plants and animals. If you have not done this, I suggest you get one or more fairly complete beginning books on natural history and carefully study them as a preparation for this book. One of my books will prepare you for the more advanced work here—*The Amateur Naturalist's Handbook*.[1] A few things from it are repeated here because of their special use or for the sake of emphasis.

YOUR NOTEBOOK AND/OR JOURNAL

Two notebooks are best: one for field use, which you do not mind getting dirty and for use of shorthand or abbreviated words to get your information down in a hurry, and the other more of a journal that you keep neatly at home when you have leisure time. Another good reason for the second notebook is that the first is too

---

[1]Vinson Brown, *The Amateur Naturalist's Handbook* (Boston, Mass.: Little, Brown and Co., 1948).

easily lost and thus valuable information would be lost that might have been saved had you rewritten it in the journal as a more permanent record. It is a good habit to transfer notes on a daily basis.

To help you with field notes there is an easy shorthand that anyone can learn in one or two day's practice—*A.B.C. Shorthand.*[2] I suggest using this shorthand, which about doubles your speed of writing, in your field notebook, but translate it into regular English for your journal.

In *The Amateur Naturalist's Handbook* I discussed the use of a notebook in some detail, but my emphasis was mainly on accurate descriptions of animals, birds, etc. that you saw in the field. These you could take home and compare with the descriptions found in natural history books in order to identify what you saw. In this book the emphasis is more on taking field notes of animal and plant behavior and ecology, which lead to new discoveries in natural science or the solving of problems. The other type of note taking you will still do whenever you encounter a species you do not know, but continued careful study of various field guides (such as those listed in Appendix C, Suggested References) will enable you to identify most species you encounter, and, in time, to be able to concentrate on more fruitful note taking from the standpoint of science.

Insects, and related spiders, mites, etc. represent a special problem, because there are so many kinds that few books can describe more than a portion of them. Some, like butterflies and larger moths, because they are generally so colorful, you can learn to recognize from books with color plates, but most of these small creatures, including a large percentage of the moths, need to be taken home as specimens and identified under a powerful magnifying glass or binocular microscope with the use of keys. These keys vary from some that are quite easy to use, such as those on reptiles and amphibians, to those of medium difficulty covering the plants, to those of great difficulty covering the bulk of the insects and their relatives. It is wise to practice on the easier keys first, and then move to the more difficult ones. On the difficult ones your work in identification should always be checked afterward by experts, if at all possible, as it is so easy to make mistakes, and from knowing these mistakes you learn how to be more careful next time. If experts are not available where you live, it is usually possible to send samples of your specimens, by prearrangement, to some biologist at

[2]William A. Brooks, *A.B.C. Shorthand* (Brooklyn, N.Y.: Max Padell, 1973).

a university, college, or museum who will be willing to identify them for you in exchange for keeping some sample specimens.

Gradually, as an explorer naturalist, your note taking will develop with more ability and sophistication and you will learn to write down small but important details that most people would miss. The field you will be exploring often determines the type of notes you take, and it is wise to consult a specialist in that field and get his suggestions on how to make and arrange your notes to the best advantage. In Appendixes A and B you will find glossaries that describe in plain language many scientific words and concepts that will become highly useful for you to use and understand in note taking. Study these glossaries carefully. Similar glossaries covering other fields of natural science are available in books that deal with those sciences. The following are some general points about note taking that may prove helpful to you:

1. Give the exact time of day, date, and place where the notes are taken.

2. Use U.S. Geodetic Survey maps or other maps of large scale to locate the place where you are at the time of note taking, and describe your location properly in reference to these maps; also mark elevations as shown by such maps for your locality.

3. Make your own map or maps on the locality if this is needed to show the nature of the habitat(s) that surround you. To get a still larger scale map it is easy to have a geodetic survey map enlarged photographically to whatever size you need. Some books in the suggested references, Appendix C, explain how to do your own rough surveying, if needed.

4. Emphasize in your notes those things that apply to your particular line of research. Thus, if you are collecting fossils as part of a paleontological project, you need to determine the nature and meaning of the fossiliferous strata in the area, making detailed maps of the strata and marking exact locations where each fossil specimen is found and photographed or modeled. If you are studying the behavior of one particular species of animal, maps showing habitats and all localities where the animal is active, along with notes keyed to the maps that detail movements, feeding behavior, courting, and so on in great detail, should be shown in your notes. If you are studying the reactions of a plant species to different microclimates and different extremes of its range, then your notes would emphasize details of temperature, rainfall, humidity, altitude, amount of shade for rocks or trees or slopes during the day, and so on.

5. If photographs, X rays, samples of soils or rocks, pH of soils, measurement of tracks, or any other similar extensions of your note taking are made on a field trip, these should each be noted under a number in your notes that allows you to synchronize all your observations and techniques in your final journal notes that you make at home, and so be able to locate quickly in your files these extra records.

6. The secret of notes that eventually lead to new scientific discovering is a meticulous attention to detail and the greatest possible accuracy. Do not make guesses, but find facts whenever possible. If you do make a guess, label it as a guess, and try to pin it down as soon as possible so it becomes a fact. For example, you may see an animal leaping through the woods that you guess is a snowshoe hare, but you are not quite sure. Try, by carefully stalking in the direction you saw it going, or finding and carefully studying its tracks, to make sure it is actually of this species of animal.

7. Make frequent drawings. Even though you may have no ability as an artist, rough drawings can still be a big help in recalling what you saw. In drawings, emphasize those things that make a species of animal or plant distinctive, such as the design of a compound leaf, or the way a blacktailed jackrabbit makes a high spy leap to watch for enemies.

8. In your field notes, using shorthand, be sure to write at least legibly enough so you can later translate accurately what you have written. In your final journal notes make sure you write legibly enough for others to understand you, or, if you can, type your notes.

9. Keep your journal or journals in a systematic way so you can refer to them and find what you want quickly. Some naturalists keep their final notes on large filing cards, with the cards arranged by subject in a filing cabinet. This might be the best way when you are doing ecologic work and keeping track of many different kinds of animals and plants, as you would want to have a separate card or card file for each species. Card files have the added advantage of allowing you to file photographs with them.

PHOTOGRAPHY

Photography is a great help in scientific investigations as notes alone too often fail to give an accurate picture of what you have seen. These photographs are extremely important, for example, in the study of a single plant or animal species when you are trying to show its appearance at different extremes of its range or under different habitat conditions, or when it is taking part in different patterns of behavior. Photographs are absolutely essential when you are doing studies of microscopic life or the actions of cells in plant or animal bodies. Photography, in fact, can be used effectively in almost any scientific investigation.

There are excellent books on the subject of natural history photography as well as photography in general, and some of these are listed in Appendix C, Suggested References. These books cover this subject in much greater detail than I can here; however, I do have a few suggestions that may be helpful in scientific photography:

1. Inexpensive box cameras can be used even in scientific photography if the objects being photographed are fairly large, still, or very slow moving, and are shot in good light that is not too bright or too dull. As is usual with camera work, you may need to take a number of pictures from different angles and in different lights to get what you want.

2. The advantage of the more expensive cameras with finer lenses is that your chances of getting good, sharp pictures are increased, and any picture that is sharply focused by such cameras can be blown up in an enlarger to show fine details that are often of value as scientific proofs of your observations. It used to be that you had to buy a camera that took fairly large pictures, 4" by 4" or up, to get the quality needed, but now the finer makes of 35 millimeter cameras, such as Leica or Nikon, do such excellent work, if properly used, that even considerable enlargements with photos from these cameras will maintain the details perfectly. Thus, the smaller, more easily handled camera of high quality can do practically all your camera work.

3. Most of these cameras have magnifying attachments for both close-up work and for enlarging distant views (telephoto lenses), but if you have to change lenses too often in the field this is a handicap when you want to get a picture of a wild creature in a hurry. You can, however, obtain special zoom lenses that with a twist of a lever or even automatically can change from taking a picture of an insect at 3 ½ inches to taking a close-up picture of a running antelope at 400 yards. Discuss these different lenses with a reliable camera dealer.

4. To get the feel of your camera take many pictures of objects in nature at different exposure times and different time settings so

you can learn from practice just what your camera can do. Of course, an exposure meter will help you do this more accurately, but even with it you should try different exposures because different exposures may strengthen certain features of your picture. Even after you have gained such experience remember that very important photos may need several different exposures and angles simply to be sure you get one exactly right.

5. When you are taking pictures in the wild, particularly of fast-moving or very shy creatures, tremendous patience plus ingenuity and an understanding of your subject and its behavior are needed. Thus, if you know of a favorite perch of a particular bird or lookout of an animal, you can set up your camera near this place, using a long extension wire to trip the camera, focusing it just right, and then taking the picture from a distance when your subject comes to the proper place. Ingenuity is further used by camouflaging the camera with brush or in some other way so that the creature you want to photograph is not disturbed by it.

6. Blinds can be made of brown- or green-colored cloth, or cloth blotched with both colors to give an effect that fits the environment, and in these blinds you can hide to take pictures, or you can fasten brush around a blind. Learn to place your blinds in those places near a well-used trail or place where birds often perch in order to be sure to get good pictures. You may need to disguise the man scent by rubbing your body and clothes with some strong-smelling plant such as sage, honeysuckle, or wild mint.

7. Animals, birds, and other creatures that come out at night can be photographed by a flash attached to a camera, also using a blind, and by being very quiet and patient for long periods. Or you can set up a trip wire along a game trail that will cause a camera to take a flash picture (figure 2–1) when an animal passes that way. The trip wire has to be placed at the right height for the animal you want to photo. Thus, a cacomistle or ring-tailed cat is quite small and would have to have the wire only about 6 inches above the ground, while a deer or mountain lion would need it about 3 feet high. Use a fine wire that pulls good but also breaks easily so the camera is not hurt.

8. In life history studies you will need many pictures of the different stages in each animal's life. The key to success is making sure you get pictures of the most critical and important moments or stages in the life of the animal and those that show both typical and unusual behavior patterns. Sometimes two or three persons working together, or even a team, can do this better, as a 24-hour

Figure 2–1. How to arrange a trip wire on a game trail to photograph an animal passing at night. Weight in plastic tube drops on top of shutter trigger and causes picture to be taken. At night flash cubes or electronic flashes can be synchronized with tripping of bulb. (Judith Hennessey)

vigil can be maintained to watch for all things that might happen. Thus, you could catch the exact moment when a moth was bursting out of its pupa, or the moment when a mother deer chases and strikes at a coyote that is getting too close to her baby.

9. A scientific team, having greater finances than an individual and probably more connections with museums and universities, can often obtain or have rented or have other access to equipment far too expensive for the individual. Thus, they may be able to use such highly sophisticated photographic equipment as high-quality enlargers, X rays, infrared cameras and film, three-dimensional film, movie cameras of high quality, and so on, all helping in more effective and exact scientific work.

10. In scientific work each photograph used in any scientific project should be marked with the name (usually abbreviated) of the project plus a number, kept in a file devoted to that project, and filed in such a way as to be found quickly when needed. Perhaps the project is arranged in divisions, in which case each division should have a letter attached to the number of the photograph so the photo can be located in regard to its particular division. Thus, it may be that the project covers the life history of a particular plant, in which there would be four series of pictures, one series for each season of the year: spring, summer, fall, and winter. So a photograph would be marked something like AA-LH (*Arctostaphylos*

arizonae—life history), 1976, F-4, indicating that it was the fourth photograph of a series on the life of the plant taken during the fall of 1976. The photo might be further marked for a particular part of the plant taken in the photo as "leaf" or "flower," or "fruit," as needed.

11. Ecologic photos, showing habitats or other features of the environment, should be clearly labeled as to exactly where taken, at what time of the year, and what the climatic or weather conditions were at the time of the photo. Also, any plants or animals in the photo should be identified if possible, as the more accurately this is done, the more valuable the photo will be.

12. Be sure to keep negatives of all your good photographs as you may lose the originals; also, you may need to make duplicates for other scientists. When you are doing any comparative studies of animals or plants in far different or distant localities, it may prove vital to be able to trade such duplicates for photos taken by other naturalists. Then the more information you can give on the photos you send, the more valuable they will be to others.

13. Photographs taken and used as part of an organized plan of attack in any scientific project or problem are generally more valuable than photos taken randomly without such a plan. The best way to see such a plan in action and to learn from it is to go through scientific magazines along the line that you are planning to research and study articles that have a good number of photos to illustrate the facts given, and the conclusions reached. Notice how each scientist has organized his photos for maximum effect, and learn from what you see, especially from the really outstanding articles in which such photos are used.

OPTICAL, AUDIO, AND MEASURING TOOLS AND THEIR USES

You can always begin your scientific work with very simple and inexpensive tools simply by being sure to select as your first project one that does not require anything expensive. However, even a project so simple as the life history of a plant, or the geographic range of an animal species can be helped by some of the more expensive tools of the scientist's trade. Eventually you may obtain some of these tools through your own efforts, the loan of a friend, the help of a university or college where your work has become recognized, or through the greater financial resources of a scientific team. In any case you should be aware of the major tools that can be used and something about how they are used. Here are listed some of the most common and useful kinds. You can learn about others from reading scientific papers that describe their use, or from talking to experienced scientists in the fields in which you are interested.

Audio Tools

The first tool we use to listen to sounds, of course, is our own ear. If it has not been too deadened by loud noises in our great cities, particularly in our dance halls, the human ear can be a very useful tool indeed for a naturalist to use. But most people do not use their ears with nearly the capacity they are capable of being used. Their ears are too much turned inward to their thoughts, and many sounds never reach their brains because they have not trained themselves to stay aware. A naturalist, however, must constantly be training his ears to listen to all possible sounds and to try to understand what they mean. He can do this particularly when he walks in the woods or fields and keeps turning his head from side to side, listening. He should also write in his notebook the different sounds he hears and try to classify them for their sources and their meanings. By this training he becomes alert and begins to hear and finally understand many sounds he was unaware of before.

Tape recorders and metal ears: The manufacture of reasonably priced, battery-operated tape recorders that are light and easily carried in the field has greatly increased the ability of the naturalist to record sounds he hears in the wild, and thus be able not only to listen to them once, but many times, and to study and memorize them. Also tapes and records of bird calls and songs and other animal noises can now be purchased (see Appendix D, Natural History Suppliers). If a photograph of a bird, mammal, or other creature making a sound you record can be taken at the same time, the proof of who the sound maker was can accompany the recording of the sound.

You need to have a good tape recorder to get good sounds, and a good microphone to catch them. You can catch faint sounds and sounds from far away if you can place your microphone in the middle of a large metal ear or concave metal disk. (figure 2–2). Stores that sell audio-visual equipment usually have these ears for sale along with tripods to hold them at the required height. You can

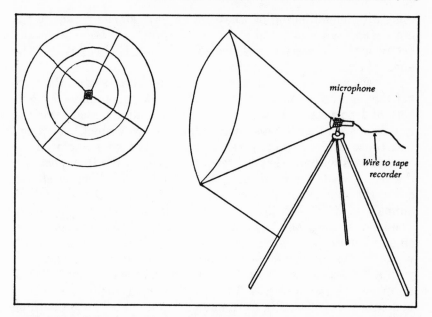

Figure 2–2. Simple metal ear or disc, made out of wire frame covered with tin foil, with hole in center for microphone, and tripod attachment. Depth of cone or disc should be experimented with to determine best shape for catching sounds. (From Vinson Brown, *Knowing the Outdoors in the Dark*, Harrisburg, Pennsylvania: Stackpole Books, 1972, p. 171.)

make your own tripod, crude of course, out of three sticks screwed together at the top or to a round board, and you can build your own metal disk by first making a framework of wire and then gluing to this some smooth metal foil, shaped to form a concave disk, making a hole in the middle through which the microphone can be placed and held by the wire and some adhesive tape. This will not, of course, be as efficient as a metal disk sold in a store, but will be helpful. The tripod and metal ear can be turned with the microphone in whatever direction you wish to catch sounds on your tape recorder.

All such tapes need to be filed and labeled carefully so they can be easily found again whenever you need them as evidence of your work on a scientific project involving sound. For example, you might keep a file of tapes of all the sounds of sparrows heard within a kilometer of your home, each tape labeled with the names of the sparrows heard on it, and the exact locality and habitat where each sound was heard. Notes in your journal or on file cards would tie in with the tapes by number, each describing the actions of each bird at the time it sang or called. Out of such a study would come an understanding of what the various sounds meant to the birds who used them, and you could determine if there were any behavior patterns especially tied to each sound, plus possibly the effect of a given habitat on the sounds.

There are now still more expensive tape recorders on the market that can record high-frequency sounds. Many animals, such as bats and porpoises, as well as many birds and insects, produce sounds of such high frequency that human ears cannot hear them. But these high-frequency recordings cannot be translated for human ears without slowing down the speed of the frequencies to the point where they are in range of our ears. When so slowed down, the sounds can be studied and compared to the actions the animals made at the time, so that some meaning for the high-frequency sounds may be determined. Such sounds can also be put on an oscilloscope, available at most universities, which makes the wave motions of the sounds visible so they can be photographed with a high-speed camera to give records that can be published in an article on the subject. All of this, of course, includes expenses and training not usually available to the amateur, but something he may later find affordable as a member of a scientific team.

Optical Tools

Our eyes are marvelous instruments for observing when we use them logically, alertly, inquisitively, and to the utmost of our ability. Most people walking in the midst of nature are not inquisitive or alert. Their minds are often far away from their surroundings and they miss a hundred happenings that occur before their eyes. The glory of the naturalist and one of his major joys in living is to watch and observe things with his eyes that perhaps no man has seen closely before, or even a vision of something that everyone else has believed was lost. Can you imagine the extraordinary joy, exhilaration, and the feeling of marvelous adventure that Alec Chisholm, the Australian naturalist, experienced when, after years of searching, he saw what were probably the last of the paradise parrots, birds of such extraordinary beauty of feather and loveliness of voice that they had been hunted to the verge of extinction by foolish men. When he saw these delightful creatures, a pair, in the woods of northeastern Queensland, he knew he was seeing a sight both rare and sad, for his view of their exciting courtship, and the exquisite trilling of their voices was perhaps never to be heard or seen again by man. Indeed, a last pair of such a species has little chance of bringing its kind back. His writing of this event poignantly should emphasize to all men and women of good will that we should never again allow destruction of such a wonderful creation.

Field glasses and telescopes: A good pair of field glasses of 7X power or greater and a good field telescope with tripod and 15X power and up are both highly useful to any naturalist who wishes to watch birds or mammals or other creatures from afar without disturbing them. The binoculars have the advantage over the telescope in that they are easily carried, give better vision because of the two eye pieces, and can be quickly directed in different directions to catch new scenes. The telescope, on the other hand, with magnifications from 15 to 50 power or even more, if used with a good tripod to hold it steady, can have much higher magnification and thus can bring very close to the observer some scene involving creatures in the far distance, too far to be made out clearly with the binoculars.

Either 7X or 8X magnification with a wide field of vision have usually been found to be best in binoculars, and of course a quality pair give the best service. Zoom lenses are also available in binoculars, which means you can change the amount of magnification from say 4X to 12X with either manual or automatic turning of a lever. A magnification of 10X or more requires a more steady hand than most people have. This is why a new invention called "steady state binoculars" may prove a big step forward. Such binoculars have their lenses held steady resting on floats within the instrument so that even if your hands shake the image stays steady. Thus, magnifications up to 12X or even more can be used with such field glasses, giving you a much closer look at distant animals than in any other field glasses. The cost, however, is around twice as much.

In using binoculars intelligently and carefully practice will teach you to scan back and forth over an area with a steady slow sweep that helps locate anything of interest in the area observed. The sweeps must be close enough to overlap slightly, and should be repeated for the whole area if you glimpse something move. Once you locate what you are looking for, hold the field glasses on it steadily, following all movements, and concentrate your mind on recording everything of interest you see. As soon as the bird or other creature disappears write down quickly in your notebook all that you have observed. Also, at all times keep the lenses of your binoculars clean, the best way being to use special lense paper for the cleaning, and keep your binoculars in a safe, dry place when not in use. In the field keep the strap around your neck to prevent these valuable instruments from falling onto a rock.

Telescopes used for field observations are always refracting telescopes and generally not of very high magnification, rarely beyond 50X power and more often in the 15 to 40 range, as these ranges bring most objects as close as needed. Different eye pieces can be used on the more expensive telescopes for different magnifications. A tripod is always best to have, although it is possible to be without one by lying down and resting your telescope on a pile of dirt or other steady object to keep the scope from shaking. The higher the magnification the more likely your telescope will blur your vision from the tiny movements of your hands. But with a solid tripod and the ability to hold your eye to the eyepiece without actually touching it, a telescope can be highly useful, particularly when you are dealing with very shy animals like foxes and wolves, or are separated from wildlife by the sea or by a deep canyon.

Magnifying glasses and microscopes: A good magnifying glass is highly useful in the field, especially when you are examining the parts of plants or investigating insects or other small creatures. Many plants can best be identified by the use of the magnifying glass on their smaller parts where the best keys to their identity lie hidden. A magnification of 10X is about right, but there is a kind that has two or more folding lenses that can give you two or three different magnifications in one instrument. Try to get a quality instrument that has good lenses. I usually carry my magnifying glass on a string or chain tied to my belt so it will always be handy and never be lost. Often it may be helpful to draw what you see through your magnifying glass and have it as part of your record, though close-up photography enlarged, if well done, is better still.

Microscopes are extremely useful instruments for any natural scientist who enters fields like cytology or microbiology where everything is invisible without the microscope. Choose a quality scope, if possible, and one with several lenses for different magnifications if you are going to do very fine work and need high magnifications. The average naturalist, however, who is not involved with such tiny things as cells, bacteria, and so forth, can usually do all the work he needs with a binocular microscope of comparatively low power. The binocular vision gives you better control and sharper images over what you see, and is very useful in examining plant parts or the parts of insects you need to study closely for identification. Under the binocular microscope it is possible to hold a fine forceps or dissecting needle and adjust or pull apart or turn over what you are looking at in any way necessary for your particular needs. When you get a view that is exactly what you are looking for to help solve a scientific problem or that explains a part of your research, it would pay you to attach a camera to the microscope and take pictures that can be used as dramatic evidence. There are immense worlds of nature yet to be explored by microscopes, and thousands of species of animals and plants as yet untouched by the world-opening view of these powerful instruments.

Very expensive but also giving immensely higher magnifications than other microscopes is the electron microscope. It is highly useful in studying such infinitely tiny things as viruses or molecules, but only a person doing highly specialized work in such fields of extremely high magnification will have need to use such a scope. But it is well to learn something about the electron microscope and its uses, for one can never be sure when it might come in handy to have access to one, particularly when you are part of a scientific team.

Mirrors are another but far less expensive optical tool some naturalists find considerable use for. Taken along on a field trip, a mirror in cooperation with a flashlight, can be used to look into such a hard-to-see place as a bird's nest in a hollow tree or to peer down at an animal in a deep cranny in a rock. If a clamp is attached to the mirror, it can be used to clamp the mirror to a twig or other projection when you are trying to peer into some hollow.

Chemical Sensing Tools

The nose and tongue are both chemical sensing tools that often prove useful in scientific work, although care must be taken not to bring them into contact with poisonous or otherwise harmful smells or tastes. It is not at all wise, for example, to test mushrooms by taste, as some tasty ones are poisonous, and some, like the deadly amanita, can kill. Once my wife cooked a delicious mushroom sauce that she thought was safely made from *Boletus edulis*, but she made it by mistake from the similar-looking *Boletus satanus*, which made our whole family violently sick.

Some people have a delicate and finely developed sense of smell or taste, as, for example, is known among wine tasters, and this power can be used to analyze and describe different tastes and smells in the wild. One rule in tasting is wise and that is to spit out immediately anything that tastes bitter or rotten, and wash out your mouth. These tastes are warning tastes of something wrong. One scientific test in which the nose can be used is to test the smell of flowers that attract beetles, finding out which smells do this attracting, and seeing if the flower that uses such smells is doing so to get the beetles to come and pollinize them. There is much we can learn about such things.

Oftentimes in life history studies of plants we want to know all about their surroundings and the effect these surroundings have upon their growth and development. One such thing to test for is the pH of the soil, or the amount of acidity or alkalinity that can be found in it. You can obtain a reasonably priced pH indicator at some plant nurseries and, by following the instructions in the box, find out the acidity value from 0 (high) to 7 (low), or an alkali value from 8 (low) to 14 (high). This knowledge of soil pH helps us understand why certain kinds of plants grow in one kind of soil that is acid, while others like a soil that is alkaline, or any of the variations in strength of either alkali or acid.

Various chemical reagents are used to detect or measure the amount present of another substance that is mixed with water or other liquid, determining amounts that are harmful or beneficial. Such reagents are also used to convert one substance into another by means of the reaction caused when the reagent is added to the other chemical. Since enzymes and hormones may act as such reagents in the body, the study of how reagents work comes in handy in studying how the physiology of an animal or plant works during its life, and what effect such changes have on its ability to live and function successfully. The subject is too deep to be taken up here, but can be studied in books on biochemistry. In some scientific experiments and projects a knowledge of physiology, including the actions of reagents, may be vital, and it is wise to know something about it.

Many insects, especially ants and bees, appear to communicate with each other through scents, tastes, and chemical reactions. For example, an ant may exude a particular substance, which combines with something in the environment to produce a special smell, or it may even produce a chemical reaction that tells another ant a message of importance. How this is done and the meaning of each of these actions and reactions is still largely a mystery and worthy of much scientific investigation. (See "Pheromones" in the glossary, Appendix B.)

Measuring Tools and Their Uses

A great deal of measuring is done in scientific work and more of this measuring is done using the metric system because it is much more logical and easier to keep track of than feet, inches, pounds, and ounces. So it is wise for the amateur scientist, just as for the professional, to learn how to use the metric system. You can often buy at a hardware store, or at least at a scientific supply house, a metric convertor, to convert English measurements into metric and vice versa. You should also obtain metric measuring cups, rules, and weighing machines in time so you can change all your scientific work into this more scientific system.

Your own body and its parts can be used in measuring. Spread your hand so that the tip of the little finger and the tip of the thumb are as far away from each other as possible and then measure the metric distance across this space. This can be used as a measuring tool for small distances. Measure the distance across your right thumb and the length of your right index finger as two other measured distances, and do the same for the distance on your right arm from finger tip to elbow when bent. Put all these measuring distances on a small card that you carry with you until you can memorize them. They will often be useful in the field.

Now measure accurately with a tape measure a distance of exactly 100 meters on a comparatively flat surface. Walk at an average stride for you over this measured distance and count how many strides it takes. Do this about five or six times and then figure out the average number of strides you took to cover the distance. This you can use thereafter as a rough guide in measuring distances between objects when doing rough mapping in the field, something the naturalist often needs to do. Of course, there are many other tools that will help you do measurings of many things more accurately than this. Some of these are discussed below.

Rain, wind, and other weather gauges: Rain and wind affect life and soil in several ways. If too much rain falls, and too hard, good soil is washed away, trees and other plants may be uprooted, creeks and rivers rise to flood stage, many animals are drowned or driven out of their burrows or other shelters, and much in nature is drastically changed. If there is too little rain, then there is drouth and this affects life in different ways, killing some, and driving other life underground or to retreat to better areas. Wind is also both helpful and harmful to life. It spreads smells through woods and fields, telling animals of the approach of enemies or friends or mates. Gentle winds clean the air of bad smells and other pollutions, or may carry the pollen of certain trees and other plants from one to the other, fertilizing them and bringing new life. But fierce winds rip away soil, or produce blizzards in which much life is killed, or create terrible dust storms that smother life and carry away precious soil.

Thus, the scientist often finds good reason to measure wind and rain, and the humidity that is associated with both, and measure also their effects on life. With the wind it is necessary to measure not only its force, but its direction, in order to see how differently directed winds affect the land and its life.

A very simple rain gauge is shown in figure 2–3 and can often be bought at a nursery or hardware store or made out of a narrow jar with straight walls. The jar is marked and numbered on its side with centimeters. These are not true centimeters, but the same distance multiplied by four, as the funnel above is of a size that catches four times as much rain as the top of the jar would catch alone. This more accurately measures the fall of rain in small amounts as the change is easier to see.

Wind gauges can be purchased that have cupped arms that go around and around with the blowing wind, indicating speed by a

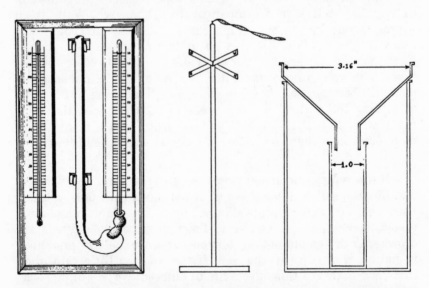

Figure 2–3. *From right to left:* simple, easily made rain gauge, wind-direction indicator, and wet and dry bulb thermometer for measuring daily humidity—three useful weather instruments for a home weather station. (Judith Hennessey)

needle on a gauge below. The needle pushes a little gauge marker to the highest speed each day and it stays there until moved lower again for the next day's marking. A light, cloth sleeve cone, attached by strings to a high pole by a turnaround sleeve or ring, blows in the wind and indicates the wind direction in regard to markers for compass directions set at the bottom of the pole.

If you are living in snow country, you could measure the amount of snowfall, by having two or more metric poles set up, marked with centimeters, decimeters, and meters, perhaps with broad red and black painted divisions for the meters. These poles are used to mark the amount of snowfall each day and the highest amount of snow on the ground for each month.

Another often necessary weather gauge is the humidity indicator or gauge. This is an instrument that combines dry and wet bulb thermometers. The difference in temperature between the two thermometers can then be used with a special table, obtained from a weather station, to record the exact humidity recorded during the day and also the dew point, or the point on the thermometer indicated when dew will fall.

A regular thermometer is also used to push upward a marker to the highest temperature of the day and to push down another marker to the lowest temperature of the day. This thermometer can be either Fahrenheit or centigrade, but centigrade is gradually supplanting Fahrenheit over most of the world as standard. Centigrade has its 0 at the freezing point and its 100 at the boiling point. Most of these instruments should be kept on a single stand, protected by a roof, and each should be read at least twice a day and marked in your journal or a special weather journal. If careful records like this are kept over a period of a year, you can obtain recognition as a weather station by the U.S. Weather Service, and your station will then be of scientific interest not only to the weather people, but to any scientists interested in the long-range effect of the weather on life in your particular area.

A barometer is also useful to have, as it measures the air pressure and this is an indicator of the condition of the atmosphere in your area as related to other areas. As you become expert at barometer readings, you will be able to tell whether a high or low pressure system is developing nearby, what direction it is moving, how it is affecting the winds and rain or snow, and what is likely to be happening to your neighborhood in the next day or so or even longer. It will help you to determine which days are best for your natural history explorations.

Tremendous numbers of explorations of life can be made on the basis of the effect of weather upon living things. For example, how does the weather affect the life of a particular ecologic niche, or all the life in a particular habitat, such as an oak woodland near you, or the total relationships of the weather with a single organism?

Land measuring tools and map making: Something about map making has already been described in chapter 1. Study this again and then add the extra information given here.

A scientist may be required to make a fairly accurate map of an area in which he is carrying out a scientific project involving either many species of plants and animals, only a few, or even one. For example, the study of the effect of weather and topography on one species of wasp in a particular area would require a fairly accurate contour map, on which you could show such things as the prevailing wind directions for different times of the year when the wasp was active, and how the contours of the land plus any woods or forests protected certain areas from wind, plus where the north-, south-, east-, and west-facing slopes are. This would give you an idea of the amount of sun found in each locality during the year, a very important factor in its influence on life, particularly in either a very hot climate, such as southwestern Arizona, or a very cold climate, such as northern Montana. Thus, in the one area shade is a very important factor in protecting plants and animals from excessive heat, while in the north a good exposure to every bit of possible sunlight allows plants and animals to exist that would otherwise be wiped out by the cold.

Using a U.S. Geodetic Survey Map of your area and enlarging it photographically to whatever size you need allows you to have almost immediately a map that shows all the major contours without all the work involved in mapping out your own contours. Since you can see on this map the height of every hill and the altitude of every bit of low-lying land, you can determine fairly accurately where the contours are on the intervening hills, slopes and flat areas, and then fill in the details by pacing off compass distances between the different major landmarks, such as large rocks and large trees. How to know the length of your paces has been described earlier in this chapter. Compass readings are put in your notes, but not marked on the map, since the map already has the compass directions marked on it by lines.

Remember that a compass does not point directly north, but instead to the north magnetic pole. Thus, you must know the compass declination (or error) from true north in your particular locality. In my location at Happy Camp, California, for example, true north is about 19 degrees west of the way the compass needle points. When using the compass be sure no metal objects are near it to deflect the needle. Your compass should be a comparatively good one that is not easily broken or deflected.

If you are mapping an area too small to use even a magnified geodetic survey map to help you, or if no geodetic survey map is available for your area, then you will have to do all the mapping yourself. Here again you can choose to do either a rough map or an accurate one. If you do a rough map, all you need is your compass and your pacing. You can then pace off the area of your map, try-ing to walk in as straight a line as possible, following the compass direction. Say the map is to cover an area 220 meters wide by 300 meters long. If you want to get your map onto an ordinary sheet of typing paper, 11 by 8½ inches, or about 28 centimeters by 21.6 centimeters, then you could make your map scale at 1 centimeter equals 0.8 meter on the land, or 1 decimeter equals 8 meters. Then fill in your landmark objects like large trees and rocks, creek, etc., by pacing off the distances between each and two other objects al-ready marked correctly on the map. If such a map covers a flat area, showing the contours is not necessary.

If necessary to show contours, they can be crudely figured by using a pole that comes in height just an inch below your eye level. Measure this pole accurately as to its metric length, then mark all your contours on the map to units of this height as follows: (1) Find the lowest elevation in your map area. Mark this on your map in relation to your landmarks. (2) Stand at this low point, holding the stick or staff in front of you with an inch-thick level on top. Point the level at one of your landmarks up a hillside and make sure the level is held level. Peer along the top of the level and have a friend stand on the hillside so his feet are just visible over the top of the level. Have him put a stake there. (3) Pace the distance to the stake and mark this place on your map with a line to indicate the first contour line. (4) Mark this line in several other places on the map by turning in a complete circle and measuring to and marking several other places where the contour goes. On the basis of what you see roughly fill in this contour line on the map. Repeat for each new contour as far as the hills rise. Remember this is a rough map, but it may be accurate enough for your purpose, which should be to show the general lay of the land, the places of light and shade, the contours, and the prominent land marks by which you can orient the different species of animals and plants you discover in the area.

If a more accurate map is desired, you will have to survey it with some of the methods of the true surveyor, though you may not need the expensive equipment to do the total accuracy his work demands. How to do more accurate surveying is described in books on surveying listed in Appendix C, Suggested References.

USEFUL TECHNIQUES FOR OBSERVING LIFE

Constant self-training produces the top-notch scientist, either professional or amateur. You should carefully watch naturalists of good reputations whom you meet and learn from them how to avoid mistakes and do a quality job. *Quality* is one of the key words. Simply never be satisfied with a slipshod job. True quality is manifested in you or anyone else by learning to work with enthusiasm and dedication, which shows itself by taking infinite pains to make sure you have done a thorough job.

A nonscientific thinker may get what he thinks is a wonderful idea. He finds other people that agree with him and may publish his idea as a great breakthrough into truth. The true scientist, however, will probably go through the first two steps and even be very pleased with his idea when he finds many people agreeing with him, *but* he will immediately begin to put the idea to a series of careful tests and experiments, never being satisfied until he has checked out the whole idea thoroughly. If it proves faulty, he freely admits he has been wrong, and works hard to find an idea that does fit the facts, and is never satisfied till it does. Even then he keeps an open mind.

Patience and Silence

With patience and silence the naturalist merges into the wilderness. He becomes one with the wild things, especially if he comes to watch and not to kill. In time, if he is patient enough, they may come to know him as a harmless companion of their environment, and go about their business almost as naturally as if he were not there. That is the time they open their secrets to him.

As a young naturalist in the high mountain jungles of Panama, several times I heard the singing of the bell bird, and spent hours trying to see it. The name bell bird conveys hardly more than a hint of the beauty of its song, like a bell indeed, but a bell so liquid and lovely in tone, so ethereal as it tinkles through the forest stillness of midday, that it seems to come from the gardens of paradise far beyond the ken of man. When I finally did see it, I expected to see a gloriously colored creature, but it was a plain olive-brown bird. I would have been disappointed had it not opened its beak there in the treetops among the hanging lianas, and dropped its silver and golden notes on my enthralled ears. Be patient and silent, and one day you too may see or hear something of equal magic.

Dr. James Paul Chapin had to use greater patience than I used, in fact many years of searching and watching in the jungles of Africa, until he saw his magic bird and heard it sing. He called it "the invisible bird of Africa" because it eluded him and other scientists so long. It was so hard to find that even the natives of the jungles had never seen it. It was in 1910 when he first heard its thrilling cry from the tops of the great Itrui Forest in Central Africa. Again in 1913 he heard the strange "peme-peme" call, but still no bird could be seen although he searched and searched. Finally, in mid-April 1914, while exploring the jungle with a keen-eyed native named Nekuma, he chanced to hear the thrilling call above him and turned his binoculars upward to see in amazement that the bird he expected to be a huge creature was only as big as a starling, olive-gray in color, although with a fancy tail with three brightly colored plumes, two curved and one like a wide spearhead. Today it is known as the lyre-tailed honey guide, but rare indeed is the naturalist who has ever seen it.

Sharpening Your Senses

To your hearing, seeing, smelling, tasting, touching, try to add the sixth sense, a *feeling* that may cause you to turn your head and see something that otherwise you would have missed, or may bring you into rapport with a bird or animal you have been watching for a long time so that it responds by coming towards you. Sharpen your sight by watching one place in a field or forest or marsh until you can separate the different plants you are seeing, or until suddenly what seemed to be only a green leaf becomes a tree frog poised for a leap, or a stick that moved ever so slightly becomes a snake, or a little black jumping object becomes the tail tip of a wildcat. Sharpen your ears by listening until you hear the scurrying of a mouse over the leaf mold, until you hear the soft feathery sound that may be the wings of an owl, only a whisper that most ears never hear.

Most people do not know that they can develop their sense of smell and be more aware of tiny differences in the smells that come to them. You can practice this by sniffing different flowers, taking a deep breath from each and savoring the smell until each takes on a different meaning for you. Often flowers of the same genus smell very much alike, but gradually your nose will be able to pick up the differences between them. Of course, a nose that has become fouled by the corrupt smells of a great city, the smoke and smog and exhaust fumes, finds it hard to do these things, but fortunately some cities are being cleansed of such smells and it is possible to go into their larger parks and find the smells of nature. Lick your finger and then rub it around your nose. The moisture often helps your nose become more sharply aware of different smells. Sometimes, also, putting your nose near the ground helps you detect new scents on the warm, near-earth breeze. In the woods or fields when you become aware of the smells that are coming to you down wind, you can follow them upwind and discover what the wind is sending to you.

Tasting is a field of which we still know very little. Of course, there are professional tasters of foods and wines, and these men and women become very expert after a while in detecting variations of quality in what they taste, some being able to tell you the exact ingredients of what they are tasting. This is proof that tasting can be of value in some scientific work if properly applied.

To a blind person, sensing by touch becomes of tremendous importance. His fingers indeed may become very sensitive in their ability to tell by feel not only the nature of objects by their surface touch, but sometimes what lives under the surface, as when he can touch your hand and tell whether you are frightened or angry, calm or upset. The naturalist should develop the use of the sense of touch in the dark to know the names of plants he is touching or the nature of other objects in his environment that may be of importance in his research. Much can be learned in this field and there are realms of scientific research connected with it that remain to be explored.

Camouflage

In nature all kinds of creatures use camouflage to disguise themselves from either their enemies or the animals that they prey upon. The bark butterfly of Mexico and Central America appears bright and beautiful when it is flying and easy to see, but the instant it lands on the bark of certain trees, as I have often witnessed, it disappears. This is its way to suddenly escape an attacking bird. Crabs on the seashore disguise themselves by allowing seaweeds to grow on their carapaces so that they are mistaken for plant growth by the shrimps and other small creatures they prey upon.

The naturalist can learn from these arts of camouflage to make himself look like something entirely different from a man. One way is to take some old clothes and paint them with a combination of brown, gray, and greenish splotches that cause you to look like a part of the woods when you stand still. If such clothes look lumpy on you this is also good, as it breaks up the sharp silhouette that means "man," the deadly enemy of so many wild creatures. If you are also relaxed when you are watching in the wild, filled with interest and love towards all living things, this may be another form of camouflage because animals can sense in man his usually exploitative feelings toward them, his desire to kill, and this is what they have grown to expect when they see a "two-legged one." But the other feelings, if accompanied by very slow and careful movements and much standing still to watch, in time may disarm their fears.

One of the best ways to camouflage yourself and at the same time be comfortable when you are watching for wild creatures is to build a blind. There are many ways to do this (figure 2–4). One is simply to make a shelter that surrounds you made out of leafy branches, allowing a couple of small open places to look through. Another is to put up a rectangular box-like structure, covered with canvas and painted in blotches of green, gray, and brown. Leaving

Figure 2–4. Three kinds of inexpensive blinds. *Top:* tepee made out of several long sticks bound together at the top and covered with green- and brown-splotched tarp or c .th. Can be used in tree on platform. *Bottom left:* large cardboard box with view slot, the hole covered with brush. *Bottom right:* long marsh grass or reeds tied together at top. (From Brown, *Knowing the Outdoors in the Dark*, p. 19.)

it out to get weathered soon makes it look like part of the woods. Slits cut in the sides at the proper height give you a view through which you can watch with your binoculars. You can also put inside the blind a comfortable camp chair and a narrow table on which you can keep your notes. If watching for wild animals in severe weather, a blind made of waterproofed plyboard and strong enough to stop the wind would be useful, especially on a cold, windy day.

Sometimes it is wise to have a low blind so you can watch for creatures at a low level and also so the blind has a low silhouette, and is little noticed. A low pup tent may be useful for this purpose, so you can lie down in it and pear out through a partly lifted flap. But, since sitting up is more comfortable for both watching and taking notes, it would be better still first to dig a trench about 2 feet, or 0.6 meter, deep and wide enough for your feet, and place the little tent over this trench. Then you can sit on the ground with your feet in the trench, while looking out through a hole or break in the flap, being quite comfortable and able to take notes.

An old beach umbrella can be used to make a good blind. You have to sew a circular piece of canvas together to hang down from the umbrella to which it is sewn or clipped, and provide an entrance slit as well as slits for watching.

There are many other ways of camouflaging that can be developed. Watch how animals do it, think, use your own ingenuity. Rocks and piles of brush can be used. I have even hidden behind a waterfall and watched wild creatures come to the pool below it. Remember to get rid of the man scent by rubbing clothes and body with a strong-smelling plant.

Tracks and Other Animal Signs

There are excellent books on tracks and other signs left by wild animals (see Suggested References, Appendix C). Besides tracks (figure 2–5) animals and birds leave signs such as holes in trees; claw marks on the bark that usually tell of a male animal, such as bear or mountain lion, leaving a territorial sign and a sign of its power and strength; holes in the ground; nests in trees; droppings; and the regurgitated pellets of owls. Owl pellets, and also the dried droppings of carnivorous mammals, often tell us fairly exactly what these birds and animals have been eating by the hair and bones that are found inside them. Barn owl pellets prove beyond doubt the tremendous value these owls have to the farmer by their destruction of myriads of rats and mice that would otherwise

TRACKS

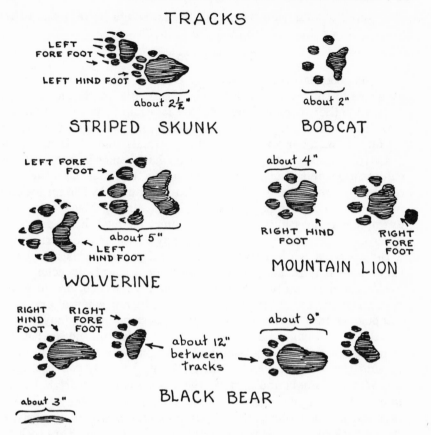

Figure 2–5. Examples of animal tracks. (From Vinson Brown and Robert Livezy, *The Sierra Nevadan Wildlife Region,* 1962, with permission of Naturegraph Publishers, Healdsburg, California.)

destroy the farmer's crops. In the same way, the droppings of coyotes and foxes also show us how these carnivores are helpful to man by their eating of harmful rodents and rabbits, making up for those coyotes who kill sheep—the latter alone need to be destroyed to protect the sheep, not all. The droppings tell us which are the sheep killers and which are not.

Snow, sand, mud, and fine soil are places in which animal tracks are best observed. Also, you can make your own sandy or dusty places to catch tracks. Simply sprinkle enough sand or fine soil over an area large enough to catch the tracks of animals coming along a trail or out of holes or dens. You can often determine some of the actions when they cross over your track-catching place.

It is important for you, when doing this, not to leave around the man smell, as this will frighten the animals away.

Sensitivity to Life

The good naturalist eventually trains himself to become very sensitive to the feelings and moods of animals and birds, even insects and other invertebrates and possibly plants, so he can anticipate and understand how these moods and feelings affect their actions. Remember that the higher animals and birds are very sensitive creatures, capable of sad or happy moods, moments of exhilaration and of depression, and so on. Here on our ranch we constantly are aware of and enjoy or are amused by the antics and moods of our domestic animals. Epomo, our big black mare, for example, can look sulky, eager and alert for food, hurt, angry or annoyed at her pesky son Nomad, happy to see us and anxious for a rub, relaxed while eating, and several other moods all in the same hour. It is amusing to watch an octopus change its color as its moods change, pale pink or whitish when frightened, brown when relaxed or hiding in brown seaweed, bright red when angry. One octopus Captain Cousteau wrote about became very annoyed at a small fish that popped in and out of holes so fast on the sea bottom that the octopus could not catch it. The fish seemed actually to be teasing the octopus, which finally turned furiously red in anger.

Watch animals and birds to see the signs they give that indicate their inner feelings. Often these signs are hidden to all but very sharp eyes. Other times they are obvious as when hairs bristle on the back of a dog or pig to indicate sudden anger. Ears cock to indicate alertness and awareness of the approach of danger. Watch carefully for these and many other signs. Record them in your notes. Try to feel with the animal as it feels. As you become more expert at this, animals and birds may sense your feelings toward them and become less afraid and more friendly. By gradual stages I have taught spotted skunks to feed out of my hands as they came to know that I was not dangerous but a friend.

Uniqueness of life: Each living thing is unique. They may all look alike, one kind of animal or bird, but they are not. Even the famous Dione quintuplets, who all came from exactly the same egg and sperm, and so should have been exactly alike, grew up to be unique and different human beings. One was stronger, one proved more intelligent, another shyer, another more interested in people than the others, and so on.

It is this uniqueness of all life that makes the work of the naturalist particularly interesting. He is always finding new things never known before. He may find an animal(s) doing things totally unexpected. You may read in natural history books, for example, that a certain kind of shark never attacks human beings. This may be true of this shark for all previous human experiences with it, but one day one of this kind will attack a man and prove there are exceptions to any such rule. For some time naturalists believed that the chimpanzee could never be taught a true language that expressed ideas and so it would always remain an animal, forever incapable of anything like human speech. But recently a naturalist taught a chimpanzee how to use sign language and actually create ideas in a way similar to humans. All such experiences prove that it is not wise to become too dogmatic about what any form of life can or cannot do, but to keep an open mind and be watchful for the unique qualities and abilities you can discover in living creatures. We are, for example, just beginning to have some kind of inkling that plants may have what could be called feelings, probably on a very different level than ours, but possibly present. New worlds of insight are opening up. We must, as naturalists, be ready for them.

Being at the Right Place at the Right Time

A southern general in the Civil War once said that battles are likely to be won "by being there fustest with the mostest men!" In the history of the great naturalists, time and again they have had either the luck or the wisdom to be at the right place at the right time. Such wisdom comes from having the intelligence to look ahead and make plans to take advantage of the right conditions, which may rise at only one time.

Thus, Charles Darwin arrived in the Galápagos Islands in August 1835, at a time when the islands were still unspoiled by too many humans, and he was able to see evolution in operation among the animals and birds of these isolated islands. He came by luck at the right time to the right place.

But other scientists have planned to be at the right place at the right time. Thus, Dr. David Lack and his wife, on October 15, 1950, came to the Gavernie Pass in the high Pyrenées Mountains of southern France to prove what many other naturalists of that time did not believe: that many small birds used these high mountain passes to migrate through on their way south. Before this most naturalists believed that such birds were forced to use the lower altitudes along the seacoast of southwestern France and northeastern Spain to reach the southlands. The Lacks climbed to the top of the pass, and as they neared it they watched hundreds upon hundreds of chaffinches, goldfinches, wood pigeons, linnets, and other birds streaming over the pass southward that cool, fall day. They also made a discovery that entomologists, students of insect behavior, should have made, but did not because of lack of foresight and effort. They watched thousands upon thousands of dragonflies, butterflies, moths, and tens of thousands of tiny hover flies also flying over the pass the same day, all migrating to the south. It is interesting that down in the lower parts of the pass and even up to 500 feet below the summit, there was no sign whatsoever of these insects and birds. All had come over the pass flying high. So only by going up to the top of the pass itself during just a few days of this particular time of the year could such a magnificent discovery have been made.

Every naturalist should be alert to seize the opportunity to be at the right place at the right time, on a high pass when a migration happens, at the right place in the right ocean when the humpback whales gather for their great sings, at the place in the jungle where Indian elephants dance (told in Kipling's story of *Toomei of the Elephants*, but believed by some naturalists to be quite possibly true), or by a pond at the time when the dragonfly larvae come up the steps of the water plants and burst from their last molts as fully winged hunters of the air, or the time when the kit fox mother lets her new pups come out of their den for their first day of playing under the blue desert sky.

There is magic indeed in being at the right place at the right time, and many new discoveries to be made.

Hazards and Perils: How to Avoid Them or Overcome Them

I remember vividly one day many years ago when I was climbing with two other young men, members of the Sierra Club Rockclimbing Section, up the southern Sphinx Rock on the coast of San Mateo County in California. I was hoping to study the animal, bird, insect, and plant life on the top of this great rock, which rises about 150 feet out of the edge of the sea and where no man had climbed before. The other two men were much more experienced climbers, but even they found the rock treacherous and crumbly to climb. This was emphasized when I seized an outjutting part of the rock wall to pull myself higher and the whole thing came away with me. Fortunately I only dropped about 6 feet before the rope by which I was attached to the two other climbers brought me to a jolting stop, as they braced themselves and quickly took up the slack. But the experience was unnerving, and, coming down the rock later on the other side, we found a place even more dangerous, not only mostly straight up and down, but with one section where the rock actually curved inward. When I reached this place I was in a blue funk, completely scared to death, clinging to a couple of small ledges and frozen to my hold. At this time the two more experienced climbers, one above and one below me, could not get me to move any farther down the rock surface, even though they had ropes on me. No wonder, for the sea was below me about 30 feet straight down and full of sharp rocks like cruel teeth.

Gradually the two calmed me by talking kindly and explaining exactly how I had to go to get down, and how I must not look down as I climbed. I knew I had to get hold of myself. I took several deep breaths and finally felt calm enough to try the steep descent, knowing that it curved inward below me. But courage came back and I made it with greater ease than I would have thought possible.

This story emphasizes the need for self-control in a dangerous situation. When I did not have it, I was in great danger; when I gained it back, the danger became much less.

Dr. Olaus Murie, famous author of the *Field Guide to Animal Tracks*,[1] tells how he was trapped in a storm in an almost capsized boat among Three Arches Rocks off the Oregon coast while studying sea birds. He became frantic with fear and despair and would surely have drowned in the raging sea if he had not forced himself to become calm and think things through. Then he realized the three arches signified that the sea waves went through these rocks. He remembered that the cave through the middle rock was quite large and knew that the waves would be comparatively calm inside. Working furiously he just managed to reach this cave and, in the calmer waters, was able to slip the rope from his boat over a rock to hold it. When the sea dropped, the boat was held vertically against the rock and all the water ran out. With the boat free of water and floating lightly on the surface, he was then able to escape from the raging sea. Once more self-control was the answer, for with it came confidence that he really could escape his danger, and he found the right way to do it.

Many accidents happen because of carelessness. The true explorer naturalist should be always alert to avoid dangers and plan his trips ahead so these do not happen. The following are some suggestions:

1. Whenever you plan a hike or camping trip into strange country take a map and show friends or relatives exactly where

---

[1] Olaus J. Murie, *Field Guide to Animal Tracks* (Boston, Mass.: Houghton Mifflin Co., 1954).

you are planning to go and for how long so that if you do not return at the correct time they will know where to look for you. One time in my early twenties I was very foolish and took a group of boys to explore an old mine. We climbed down almost rotting ladders into the heart of the mine to hunt for beautiful minerals, which we indeed found there, and fortunately all of us got out alive. I say fortunately, for a few days later that mine caved in. If we had been there when the mine collapsed probably none of us would have escaped since no one would have known we were there.

2. On such trips take along things of vital necessity in emergencies, such as a box or bottle full of waterproof matches, an axe for cutting wood for fires (vital to save yourself from cold if a storm comes or to send smoke signals for help if injured), a snakebite kit for a possible bite by a poisonous snake, a compass to give you directions and keep you from becoming lost by going in circles (I was twice lost this way in the Panama jungles because I had no compass), and an illustrated book on the edible plants of your area if you are to be gone long and may need emergency food. Other items that may be important are extra warm clothing to spare in case of a severe drop in temperature due to a sudden storm, a 30- to 40-foot length of light nylon rope for use in case you have to climb up on down cliffs, an extra light tarpaulin to give some protection against storms, a good, sharp pocket knife, and a dependable flashlight.

Avoid poisonous snakes by always looking carefully where you are about to step, particularly in brushy, rocky, or swampy areas. All these snakes want to avoid you, but if you step near or on one suddenly he is likely to strike. If you are struck use a sharp knife, sterilized by running the blade through a flame, to cut a number of quarter-inch deep cuts near the bite to let out poison and blood, but be sure to cut parallel to veins and arteries and not across them. If struck on the arm or leg, put a tourniquet between the bite and the heart to slow the blood flow heartward, keeping it tight for no more than 10 minutes. If struck on the hand or arm, you can wave the arm around in a circle while walking for help, creating centrifugal force to pull the blood away from the heart. Walk for help, but do not run as exercise causes the heart to drive blood through the body too rapidly carrying the poison with it. Get to a doctor as soon as you can without running. Good high hiking shoes will protect against such bites.

3. There is little likelihood of meeting another dangerous animal in the woods as almost all bears and mountain lions run from man except the exceedingly rare grizzlies. A moose or wild

boar might attack if startled suddenly or wounded. If a tree is handy, climb it. Grizzlies do not climb trees except when young. Usually staying calm and not showing fear helps prevent attack as does speaking in a calm, friendly tone of voice. If you are actually charged in the open by a grizzly or bull moose where there is no apparent escape, there are two alternatives: One is to yell in a loud commanding voice, putting all your force into it. The other is to throw yourself flat on the ground, belly down, and lie perfectly still, with your hands shielding the back of your head. At night a flashlight is a big help against attack if you can sound fierce enough and flash the light repeatedly into the animal's eyes. I did this successfully against a number of bears in Yellowstone, including a grizzly, when we were the only campers in camp and they were all after the food in our trailer. (Perhaps you had better not try this on a grizzly!)

4. If trapped in quicksand when wading a river and you feel it grabbing at you to pull you under, get your body out flat as quickly as you can and swim up out of it.

5. Avoid trying to cross swamps unless you are with an expert swamp man who can show you how to travel.

6. Avoid insect bites in the summer by carrying a good mosquito repellent.

7. Insect bites can be relieved by plastering them with mud. Vinegar is another common reliever of bites, also soap allowed to dry over the bite.

8. When in danger from poison oak or ivy due to touching the leaves, wash all over with cold or lukewarm water, never hot, using a strong soap.

9. If you are using guns for collecting specimens, be sure you have been properly trained in their use, and have a gun or hunting permit if necessary. Allow no untrained individual to handle your gun. Never carry a gun loaded unless you are about to use it and have it on safety.

SPECIAL SUGGESTIONS

Use of Libraries and Museums

Libraries and museums are both of tremendous value to naturalists. Use them with the utmost courtesy and reliability, returning your books on time to the libraries and thanking the librarians or curators for any services they give you. The reference librarian in particular will often be of aid to you in looking up literature on a particular subject, including scientific papers in scientific journals, or master's and doctor's theses, if the library has files of them. A museum, college, or university library is more likely to have past volumes of scientific journals as well as copies of theses. Whatever the subject of your scientific project, you will need to look up every possible bit of literature that refers to it in these scientific journals (see the names of such journals listed in Appendix E).

By being friendly and courteous to the librarians in these institutions and grateful and thoughtful of their time, you establish a feeling of harmony with them that they will deeply appreciate and will encourage them to give you more and better service when you come again.

Museums have large collections of all kinds of specimens and when you are doing research you may at times need to study these museum specimens if they will help you in your study of species in the field. Then, when you climb a mountain, for example, to find the range and habitats lived in of particular species and how different habitats and climates affect their appearance, you will be comparing what you see in the wild with what you saw in the museum and from both observations increase your knowledge. But show the utmost courtesy to the museum curators and their assistants and thank them for their help. Be extremely careful of any specimens you handle and put them back exactly where they came from, as a museum's value lies in having everything in its proper place for immediate reference. If you injure or displace anything at all, let the curator know right away. This is the only courteous and honest thing to do. Your friendship and cooperation with the curators of such museums and their helpers will bring you many rewards in increased knowledge and they will often help you find exactly what you need for your research.

It often happens when you are doing research that you will need help in identifying specimens. With invertebrates and many plants it is often very difficult to be sure of your identification. My own early experiences as a student in insect and plant taxonomy or identification taught me how easy it was to make mistakes in identification, for the experts such as Dr. Van Dyke at the Entomology Department at the University of California, and Dr. Abrams of the Botany Department at Stanford University often pointed out with kindness, but sometimes with laughter, how wrong I was. From mistakes, of course, we learn, but it is wise to remember that until you have gained professional competence in such identification, you can make mistakes that can throw your whole research off the track unless corrected.

Fortunately the experts you need to help you can be found in most university, college, and other museums across this continent. These experts, however, are generally quite busy and are not willing to help you unless you show the proper respect for their time and, wherever possible, return their courtesy and help by giving them sample specimens for their collections. Such specimens should be correctly mounted and labeled so they have true scientific value. If it is not possible to give them specimens because of it being against the law to collect certain species or because of rarity, then you should present them with good photographs or models made with rubber or plaster of paris, also properly labeled scientifically.

Collecting and Preserving Specimens

While the collecting and preserving of specimens is necessary in certain scientific work, the modern naturalist is now reluctant to do such collecting except where it is absolutely vital. The reason is plainly because modern man has destroyed or partly destroyed so many living species and their habitats all over this world that naturalists everywhere are keenly aware that the tide must be turned now in the other direction or we will destroy too much of our beautiful world and its life. Thus, even the taking of specimens for research comes close to being a sacrilege of nature and should be done with the greatest care possible not to destroy the balance of life. So the true naturalist when he does take specimens for scientific research tries to make sure there are plenty left to reproduce and replace them.

Suggestions on how to collect are kept to a minimum here as this book is not meant to be a collector's manual but a guide to more advanced work. For those who need more instructions on collecting, such books as my own *Amateur Naturalist's Handbook*,[2] and William Hillcourt's *Field Book of Nature Activities and Conservation*,[3] as well as the various special books on birds, mammals, reptiles, amphibians, insects, and so on, listed in Appendix C, Suggested References, will all be of aid and can be obtained at most libraries. Remember that most birds and many mammals as well as reptiles cannot be collected at all in certain countries without special permits.

In this chapter I am only going to explain briefly how to make

---

[2]Vinson Brown, *The Amateur Naturalist's Handbook* (Boston, Mass.: Little, Brown and Co., 1948).

[3]William Hillcourt, *Field Book of Nature Activities and Conservation*, rev. ed. (New York, N.Y.: G. P. Putnam's Sons. 1951).

scientific collections of plants and of insects, as these are the two fields of nature in which most collecting is done today. You can, also, of course, collect and trade photographs, tapes, models, and other similar items of use in your scientific work.

How to collect plants: Plant collecting may be vital when you are doing ecologic work in plant and animal communities, or when you are making special studies on plant behavior, distribution, and so on of certain species or genera. Often in such cases you may need to send properly mounted and labeled plant specimens to botany departments or herbariums at a nearby university, college, or museum in order to make sure of your identifications. Be sure to get permission first, and promise to allow them to keep extra specimens of those you send for their own collections. Once you are sure of your identification of a particular species, you may be able to do the rest of your scientific work on distribution, ecology, behavior, and so on with the aid of good photographs, in order to preserve the species from too much collecting, particularly if it is at all rare. If you are working under the direction of a professional scientist on any scientific project, he can tell you when you will need to collect, or you can ask for advice at a museum or at a university or college biology department.

The three main instruments needed for plant collecting are a trowel, a vasculum for carrying plants, and a plant press (figure 2–6). Sometimes you will need a sharp knife or a clipping tool to cut branches of shrubs or trees. The trowel is used for digging the plant out by its roots when it is necessary to show in your collection as complete a plant as possible. Dig with such care that you get most of the roots. Roots of a bush or tree will ordinarily not be necessary, as a good branch and samples of leaves, flowers, fruit, and seed will usually be enough. With many species you may want to get specimens at different times of the year, as when they are budding and flowering and later when they are fruiting and seeding.

The vasculum is for carrying plants back to your laboratory or camp headquarters where you can dry and mount the plants. Keep the plants a little damp, if possible, in your vasculum so they will not wilt. If there is too much danger of wilting, you may want to bring your plant press with you on a hike and do your plant pressing in the field. However, remember that a pressed plant is harder to identify than one that is still fresh, and you may want to take a

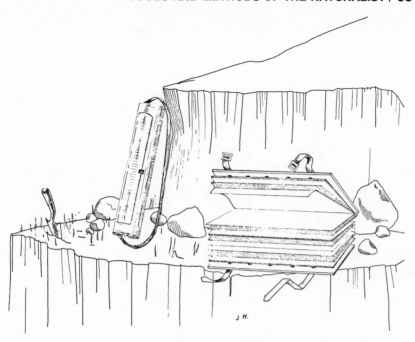

Figure 2–6. Plant collecting tools. *From left to right:* trowel, vasculum, and plant press. (Judith Hennessey)

book with a plant key with you into the field to identify the plant if possible before it is put into a press.

You can make either of two kinds of plant presses very easily: The most simple method is simply to cut two pieces of plyboard ⅜ or ½ inch thick into boards 12 by 16 inches, the same size as a folded newspaper. Drill these boards with holes about ¾ to 1 inch, spread around 4 inches apart. This is to let air into your press to help the drying process. Now find two canvas straps with buckled fasteners, long enough to go around the middle of the two boards and allow space for about 10 inches between the boards when you strap them together. Next collect a goodly number of newspapers that can be used to blot moisture from your specimens. These newspapers are folded to fit inside the plant press between the boards, allowing about 10 sheets between plant specimens, and one single or double fold to hold each specimen.

A plant specimen is first cleaned of all dirt and then laid on this open sheet. (See figure 2–7.) With the specimen is placed a label giving the following information: (1) exact date of collection, (2) exact location, (4) altitude and habitat, (5) names of main

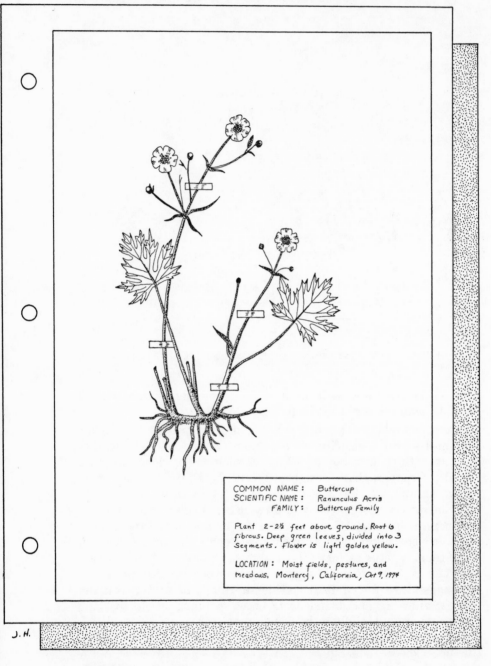

COMMON NAME: Buttercup
SCIENTIFIC NAME: Ranunculus Acris
FAMILY: Buttercup Family

Plant 2-2½ feet above ground. Root is
fibrous. Deep green leaves, divided into 3
segments. Flower is light golden yellow.

LOCATION: Moist fields, pastures, and
meadows, Monterey, California, Oct 9, 1974

J. H.

Figure 2–7. Plant properly mounted and labeled on sheet of botany paper for preservation after pressing and drying. (Judith Hennessey)

plants found associated with it, and (6) common and scientific names of the plant you are pressing, if you can identify it. If you have any doubt about the name put a question mark after it, and have it checked later by an expert.

The paper is then folded over the plant and it is placed on top of a thickness of 10 newspaper sheets, and between these sheets and another 10 thicknesses of newspaper placed on top of the plant, at which point another plant specimen can be placed in position, and so on until your plant press is full of plants to a depth of about 10 inches. Now bind the whole press tightly with the straps, place in a dry place, and leave it for 24 hours. Change the papers surrounding your plants (putting them out to dry), replacing them with fresh newspaper sheets, once a day for five to eight days, depending on whether the weather is dry or moist. At the end of this period each plant that has been dried in the press should be ready for mounting.

To mount the plant lay it on a flat sheet of fairly heavy art paper or botany paper 12 by 16 inches, and fasten it with glue and with strips of tape that experience has shown will hold the plant tightly and permanently in place. The label, now typed neatly, should be glued onto the same page with it. These mounted specimens should be stored in boxes, or preferably drawers in a cabinet, with those of the same genus and family put together, or if your scientific project deals with a specific habitat, then in a single habitat box or drawer of a filing cabinet. It is best to arrange all specimens in the drawer alphabetically by genus and family, or alphabetically by ecologic niches, if this is your approach. You will find from experience the best way to file your plant specimens for maximum effectiveness, and you can also learn about different methods by visiting herbariums at universities and colleges. Remember to keep your specimens in a dry part of a building and never in a damp area where they can become moldy. Mold can be prevented by putting dry carbolic acid crystals about the specimens.

Collecting and mounting insects and related invertebrates: The large numbers of insects in the world make their collecting and mounting for specimens much less likely to upset the balance of nature or endanger a species than is the case with vertebrates. However, we should be careful not to collect the rarer species of insects, such as the rare swallowtail butterflies like *Papilio pergamus* and *Papilio indra*, which have been overcollected

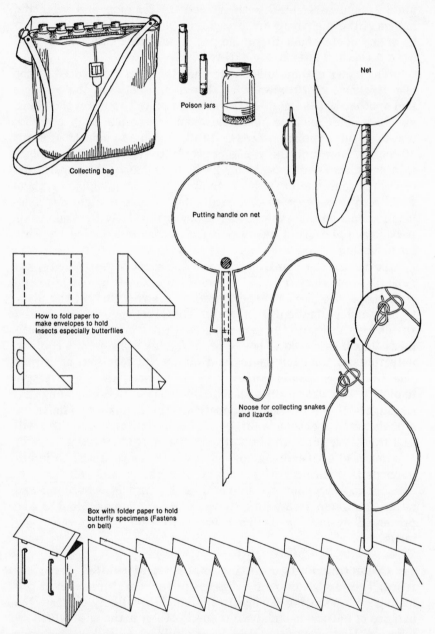

Net

Poison jars

Collecting bag

Putting handle on net

How to fold paper to
make envelopes to hold
insects especially butterflies

Noose for collecting snakes
and lizards

Box with folder paper to hold
butterfly specimens (Fastens
on belt)

Figure 2–8. Equipment used in collecting insects, plus detail of a running bowline noose for collecting lizards by slipping it over the head. (Judith Hennessey, after drawings by Don Greame Kelley, in Vinson Brown, *The Amateur Naturalist's Handbook,* Boston, Massachusetts: Little, Brown and Co., 1948.)

by too enthusiastic butterfly collectors. These beautiful creatures have a right to live and there is something ugly and selfish about boasting of having rare species in your collection when such collecting endangers the species, just as there is when a big game hunter boasts about his mounted polar bear head and skin when that species is in extreme danger, as it is today.

To collect insects, a good general-type insect net is needed made of bobinette, green voile, nylon, or other soft netting that will not spoil the insects' wings. Figure 2–8 shows one that can be made by sewing the net into a long U-shape, although somewhat more pointed, and using an old broom handle with the broom head cut off. You drill two holes at the head end of the handle and twist the two ends of the net wire to fit into the holes at right angles, then shape your wire to form a circle over which the net can be sewn (as shown). A cloth strengthener around the rim will make the net last longer. Other types of nets are described in the books already mentioned.

If this net is made with strong enough wire and cloth, the net can be used both for general collecting and for light beating. Light beating means you use it to sweep through the leaves of bushes and tree branches that are not too rigid and heavy, collecting the insects that are hiding there, or sweep through grasses and herbs. These insects can be dropped carefully into a wide-mouthed killing jar, with the lid off but put back on quickly once you have the insects inside. Use cotton soaked with ether, chloroform, or formaldehyde as a poison in the bottom of the jar, covering the cotton with a couple of stiff cardboard discs that fit fairly closely the walls of the jar.

The only trouble with this kind of killing jar is that it loses its power rather soon and the poison for killing must be renewed frequently. You can have a more permanent-type killing jar by finding a druggist who will agree to make a killing jar for you by putting some cyanide into a wet plaster of paris mix he has put into the bottom of a wide-mouth jar, and allowing this to dry and harden. You can then cut two or three blotting paper discs to cover the plaster of paris, and this poison jar will last for a long time. However, you must remember that cyanide is a very deadly poison so that the jar must always be kept out of the reach of children, and, whenever broken, all parts must be buried deeply in a hole in the ground. All of these kinds of jars should be plainly marked with the word POISON in large letters on the outside.

Insects captured in a net can be dropped into the jar, or, better

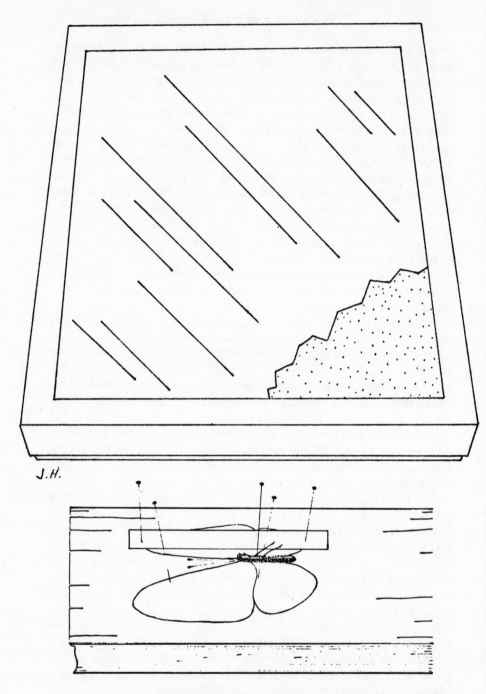

Figure 2–9. Riker Mount used to display insect collections, with insect spread correctly on composition board. (Judith Hennessey)

yet, the jar can be inserted into the net, which is folded over to keep the insects captured, and then pushed up under them to catch them. In using the net for catching a swift-flying insect, it is brought up quickly behind the insect as it is flying and then swished forward at high speed to catch the insect from behind in flight, as otherwise it can often dodge the net. If the insect is dangerous, as is a wasp or bee or an assassin bug, you need to be very careful how you insert the jar into the net and bring it up under the wasp as it clings to the netting. Or you can use a forceps to hold it from the outside, using the jar to put over the wasp until you can get the cover on quickly.

The Riker Mount, shown in figure 2–9, is easily made from a handkerchief box, whose top has been cut out carefully in four straight lines with a razor, leaving a rim. The inside is packed with smooth cotton on top and rough (packing goods) cotton underneath, to hold the insects firmly against the glass that is cut out to fit and then glued tightly inside the cardboard top. The cotton should be sprinkled underneath with para-di-chloride of benzine crystals, or something equivalent, to guard against pests. Freshly killed insects can be placed on top of the cotton with their legs and wings spread in a natural manner and a hand-printed label under each, giving its name, place collected, date, and any other important information needed. The box is then sealed with tape to help further in keeping out pests. Though this type of mount is not scientific in the strict sense, it is particularly useful for special displays, for example, the insects found in one ecologic niche, such as under a log or inside rotting wood.

Mounting and spreading insects for the Riker Mount is easily done by putting the insects on some smooth corrugated cardboard or better still on a soft composition type board into which pins can be firmly stuck. Each specimen to be spread on the board should be recently caught and killed so it is relaxed and not hard or stiff. If you are too late for this, insects can be relaxed by putting them in a tight box in which there is some damp sand under a layer of blotting paper, the sand being first sprinkled with some carbolic acid to kill any fungus growths or mold. Usually insects become relaxed in about 24 hours.

The insects are spread by pinning strips of stiff paper across their wings to hold them in a natural-appearing manner and the legs teased out with a pin so they appear natural too. If put in a dry place while spread, they usually harden in about 24 hours and can then be placed face down in the Riker Mount, each with its

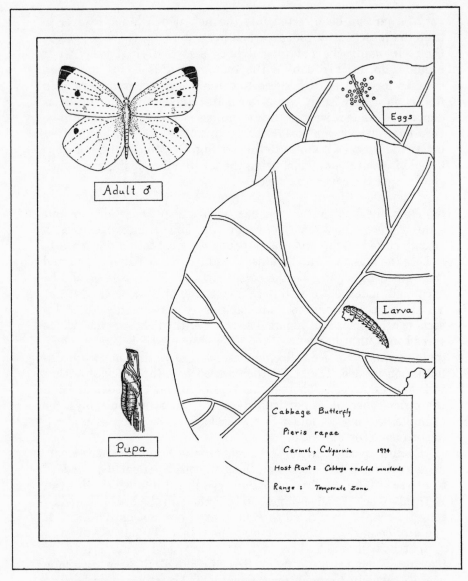

Figure 2–10. Riker Mount showing life history of butterfly. (Judith Hennessey)

own label. How they are arranged in the mount will depend on your particular project and what you want to display in order to tell the story of your research. The whole mount, if neatly done and arranged, can be photographed as a part of your scientific paper on your research. (See figure 2–10.)

The usual scientific collection of insects is generally kept in air and pest-tight specimen boxes or in tight, glass-covered drawers in specimen cabinets. These can be made if you are fairly good at carpentry, or purchased from biological supply houses such as those mentioned in Appendix D. These boxes or drawers usually have bottoms lined with cork or other material into which pins can be pushed firmly and held.

You also need special insect mounting boards (figure 2–11), which you can make or obtain from the same supply houses. They are made of soft wood into which pins can stick easily, and the insects are mounted in them on pins (as shown) at just the right height. Pins can be bought from the supply houses, and range from size 0 (very tiny) up to size 5 (very large). Numbers 2 and 3 are the ones most commonly used, with 2's for medium-sized insects, and 3's for most of the larger ones. The insect should be about ¾ inch above the board to which it is pinned in the box or drawer, allowing the space below to be used for labels, as shown. The proper places to push the pins through the bodies of different kinds of insects are also illustrated here. The insect must be relaxed when the pin is pushed through it, and the pin is then pushed down into the cork or cellotex on the bottom of the mounting board, and the wings spread out on the side boards (as shown).

If the insect has no wings, or wings are not important enough to show spread, as in the true bugs and beetles, then you need a different type of mounting board, but much simpler. You simply take a piece of cellotex, or similar type composition board, about 14 by 14 inches, nail ¾-inch deep strips of wood around the four sides and stretch tightly across the top of this a piece of stiff bristol board or equivalent, and tack this down tightly to the side boards. You can then pin insects on top of the bristol board, spreading the legs in a natural way with a needle or pin and leave them to dry. Labels should be placed with each specimen, and later placed on the bottom of the pin as shown in the illustration.

Inside the box or drawer the insects are pinned in rows according to genus, family, and order. The species and genus label is pinned to the bottom board. The upper label gives the name of the collector (placed about ½ inch above the pinpoint), while the middle label gives the place collected, the date, and the food plant on which the insect most often feeds if this is known, or it may be marked as carnivorous on flies, grasshoppers, etc., or parasitic on certain insects. The labeling of the letters should be done with black India ink, making them appear as neatly as possible, or as if

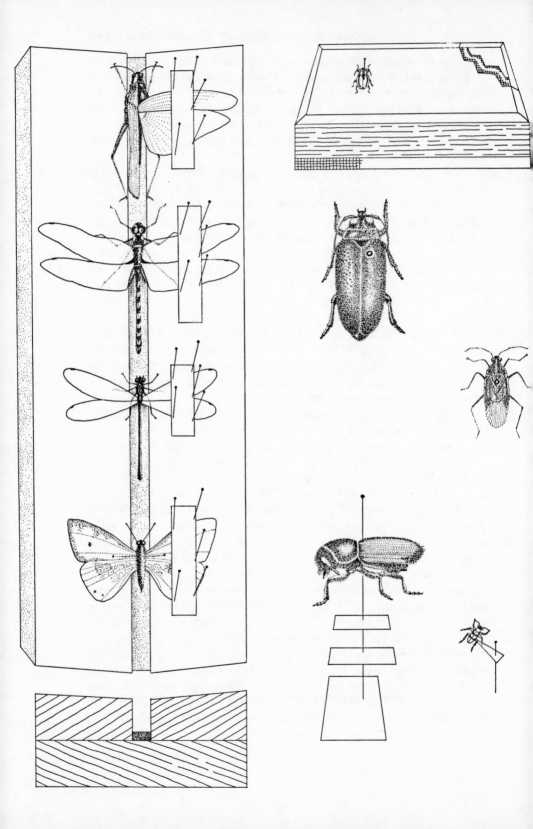

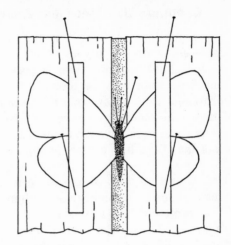

Figure 2–11. How to mount insects scientifically. (Judith Hennessey)

actually printed. If your collection gets large at all, you may want to have some of the commonly used labels printed with very small type.

Very tiny insects, too small to be mounted in the usual ways, are usually put on triangular pieces of white bristol board or pieces cut out of filing cards (as shown), which are pinned through the widest part by a standard pin. The tiny insect is then glued to the end of the point of the paper and teased with a needle to appear natural, with the legs spread.

The information given here is only sufficient to get you started with collecting, as needed. Refer to other books mentioned in Appendix C, Suggested References, for more complete information on collecting and mounting of biological specimens.

Capturing Live Specimens and Keeping Them in Captivity

Sometimes in doing research into plant and animal behavior it is necessary to watch your plant or animal close at hand, although under as natural conditions as possible, in order to observe it more carefully than may be possible in the wild. The suggestions and drawings that follow in this section are only meant to get you started, as books have been written on this subject alone, and there is no room here for such details. Further information can be found in some of the books listed in Appendix C, Suggested References.

Bringing wild plants to your home garden: Whenever wishing to study these plants close at hand, you may want to transplant a few specimens from the wild where you find them and get them going again near home. Remember, however, that if your home conditions are too different from their natural habitat, this may not be successful. In any case, you should do this transplanting only when absolutely necessary, digging up the whole plant (as shown), and bringing enough of its native soil to fill up a hole you dug for it in your garden. Try, as much as possible, to reproduce the conditions of light and shade in which it was found, and give it water in amounts close to what it would have had in its home location, as much as you can determine this. Draw or photograph the plant, or both, at different times in its growth, and compare these if possible with similar drawings and photographs of the same species in the wild, so you can determine differences in its behavior at the two localities. Any further things you need to do will depend on your special project. Advice from a botanist or horticulturist may prove vital.

Keeping microscopic life: Any jar full of water brought from a normal wild pond will be full if microscopic life, such as the three types of protozoans illustrated in figure 2–12: the euglena, amoeba, and paramecium. Bits of this water put in a little hollow built up with clear balsam resin on a microscope slide and covered with a cover glass can be viewed for several minutes without harming the animals and plants under a good microscope. Be sure you have a microscope with a substage light that throws a beam up through the water so that everything can be seen clearly. Just what you do with these tiny creatures depends on the nature of your scientific project, but you will need to organize your use of water and slides in the form of a definite plan so your research can answer questions and evolve towards definite hypotheses. Study similar scientific projects as described in scientific journals to get ideas as to

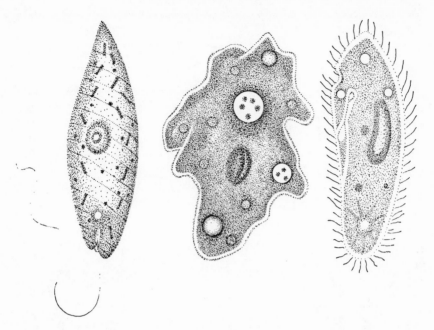

Figure 2–12. Typical one-celled animals. *From left to right:* euglena, amoeba, and paramecium.
(Judith Hennessey)

how to organize your own project. Many fascinating paths of research can be followed, as there are many of these microscopic
creatures about which a great deal is yet to be learned, and each is
different and unique in its growth, feeding, reproduction, and other
behavior. You can also bring water from many different kinds of
sources, to see how varying species act under differing habitat conditions.

Keeping general aquatic life: A bucket or net dipped into
any developed pond will bring you many kinds of aquatic life, but
you need to try to bring the environment with you so as to produce
similar conditions in your home. Try to get samples of most of the
plant and animal life in the wild pond and get them to live and
grow in similar type ponds in your backyard or home. Figures 2–13
and 2–14 show both an aquarium that can be kept in the house,
and a plastic base pond, made with a wide piece of strong plastic in
your backyard. Mud from the original pond, with the roots of water
plants still on the plants, can be brought to your backyard pond
and to your aquarium.

The home aquarium can be bought, or you can build your own

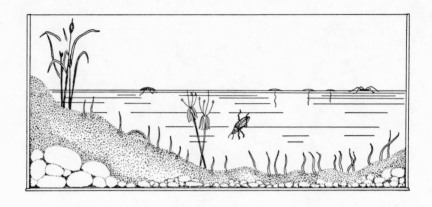

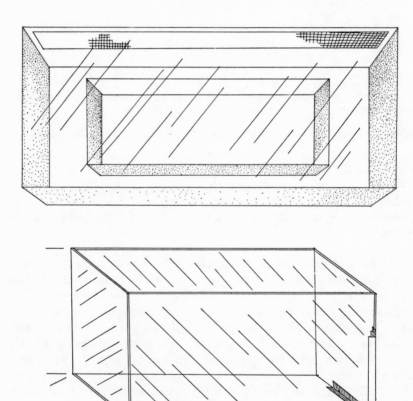

Figure 2–13. Aquarium fitted with shallow pond habitat to suit water insects (*top*). Cage with box in center that can be made into a maze by using doors and partitions (*middle*). Making either an aquarium or terrarium out of glass sheets glued together with waterproof plastic strips or tape (*bottom*). Wooden frame can be added, built to fit tightly and give added strength. (Judith Hennessey)

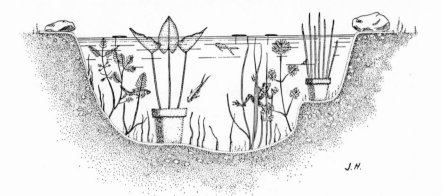

Figure 2–14. Backyard pool with plastic bottom to hold water. Plastic is molded to bottom of dug hole and held down by weighted pots. (Judith Hennessey)

with sheets of plate glass (for strength), and waterproof plastic strips to hold the sheets together, then building a wooden frame to fit that. Remember that both your aquarium and your backyard pool need to have a balance between animal and plant life so that your "ponds" maintain themselves with little work on your part. Snails and other scavengers and plant eaters keep down the dead plant debris and prevent algae from taking over a pond. You also need to decide whether you are going to allow predation by predators in your pond and how much. Thus, if you are studying the lives of small fishes as a scientific project and put too powerful predators in with them, such as giant water bugs, you may soon see your fish population wiped out. Of course, if you are studying the life history of such a ferocious predator, then you will have to keep it supplied with various prey animals in order to watch how it preys upon them. For special studies of the behavior of different fish to each other in an aquarium maze, build the maze as shown in the picture.

Collecting insects live and keeping them in display cages: Besides collecting live insects in nets and transferring them to large wide-mouth jars, or large glass cages (built like aquariums but with fine mesh on top to allow air in but to keep the insects from getting out), you can also collect them with forceps from off the ground, digging up ant nests (being sure to capture the queen ant), or burying jars in the ground (figure 2–15), with large rocks or small boards placed above them on small rocks, to collect many ground-dwelling insects, or placing leaf mold in a large funnel

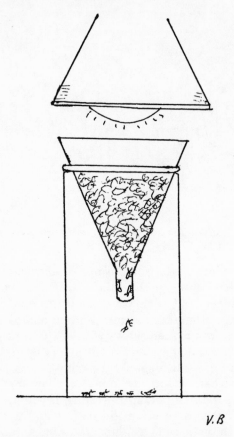

V. B

Figure 2–15. Collecting small insects to feed amphibians or small reptiles, using light and heat to drive insects out of leaf mold in funnel. (Vinson Brown)

whose end is in a jar and placing a bright light over the top of the funnel. This latter method drives the insects in the leaf mold down into the jar where you should have some damp blotting paper and some leaves. These tiny insects can often be used as food for larger insects in your cages.

Display cages for insects should duplicate their own natural surroundings as much as possible if you want to see their behavior under conditions resembling those they make in real life. This is why such cages should be fairly large.

Artificial ant nests are fairly easy to make (figure 2–16), but different ants vary in their requirements for amounts of humidity or dryness, so it is vital to try to duplicate the conditions they have in their own natural surroundings. Usually a sponge soaking up

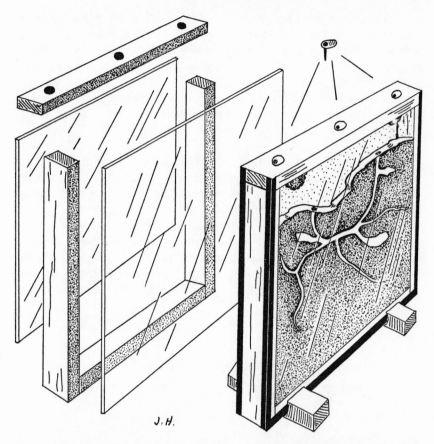

Figure 2–16. Artificial ant nest. Strips of waterproof plastic tape are used to hold the glass plates to the wooden frame. The interior is filled with sandy loam or other soil that is best adapted to the ant species being housed in the artificial nest. The two sheets of glass are close enough together to allow viewing of the tunnels and rooms the ants build underground, but are covered with black plastic or paper when not being viewed. (Judith Hennessey)

some water in a small dish or jar lid will give them enough mois-ture as well as liquid to drink. Openings covered with fine wire mesh may be necessary to let enough air into the nest. The dirt put into the nest for them to dig their passages in should be similar to that in their natural nests. The sides of the artificial nest are made of glass so you can watch their activities underground, but these sides should be constantly covered with black paper or cloth to keep the light out except for the few minutes you may desire to observe them, as too much light will inhibit their actions. At night you can watch them using a red plastic-covered flashlight, as this light will bother them much less than white light.

You can expand the way of watching their behavior by running tubes or a tube for passageways out of the artificial nest and into a flat box with a glass cover where you can put some of their natural habitat, or even put a maze to test their intelligence, and give them their food, including insects for them to catch if they are carnivorous. Such secondary boxes can be increased and enlarged in several ways, and even attached to other ant nests to see what the different kinds do when they come together.

Collecting and raising larger animals: Amphibians and reptiles can be noosed with a slip noose connected to the end of a long stick or fishing pole, or trapped in larger under-rock traps such as that shown for insects (figure 2–17). Small mammals can be live trapped in the two kinds of traps illustrated in figure 2–18.

Use bait of the kind of special interest to each kind of animal you want to live trap. Keeping any kinds of animals or birds in cages should not be done unless you make them as comfortable as possible, keep their cages regularly clean, make the cages as much

J H.

Figure 2–17. Hole in ground with buried jar, for collecting live insects or small reptiles and amphibians. (Judith Hennessey)

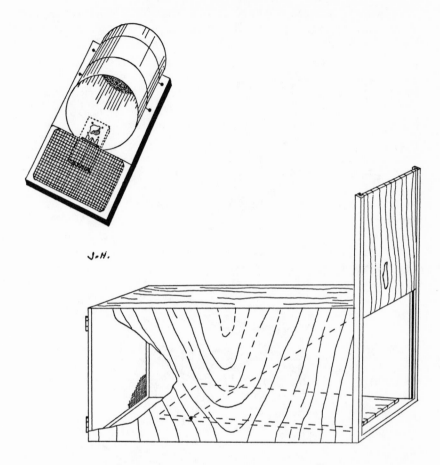

J.H.

Figure 2–18. Tin can trap (*above*) with regular mouse or rat trap attached to the can so that wire mesh snaps shut over opening when trap is sprung. Box trap (*below*) with thin board inside slightly slanted above floor so that string to nail in door is pulled out and door drops when animal steps on board to get bait; opposite end of trap is covered with wire mesh. (Judith Hennessey)

like their actual habitat in life as you can, feed them regularly the food they like, give them exercise if possible (figure 2–19), and let them go the minute you no longer find use for them in your research.

How to cage and care for them properly can be learned best from books on the subject. I have written one called *How to Make a Miniature Zoo*,[4] which goes into this subject with considerable detail.

---

[4]Vinson Brown, *How to Make a Miniature Zoo* (Boston, Mass.: Little, Brown and Co., 1957).

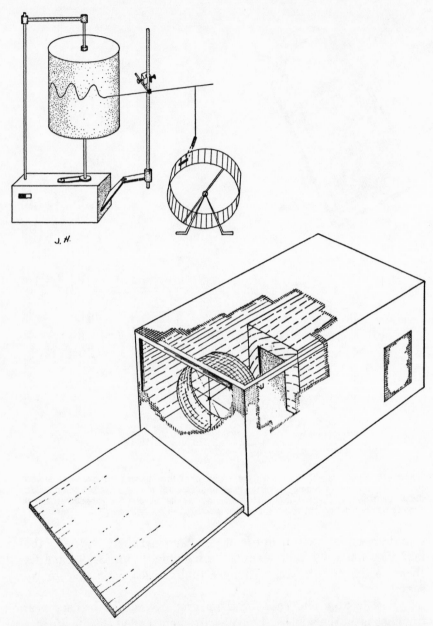

Figure 2–19. Wire exercise wheel inside cage with small mammal has magnet on one part of rim, which activates the other magnet connected by stiff wires to pencil that marks paper on revolving drum so that number of revolutions of the wheel per minute can be recorded. Drum is run by small electric motor. Total length of time wheel turns can be checked with stop watch, to determine total number of revolutions and total energy used. (Judith Hennessey)

Wild birds should not be caged at all unless you have very strong research needs to have them in cages, and it usually requires a permit. Phone your local Fish and Wildlife Service for information about this.

OBSERVATIONS ON CLIMATE AND WEATHER

It is wise to know the natural laws of weather and how they operate in your area. This is best done by going to a local weather station and asking questions and perhaps getting booklets they have on local weather, or going to a college or university where one or more scientists has special knowledge on the local weather. Weather and climate vary so much for different localities that it would take a big book indeed to cover just the climate and weather of North America alone. (See Appendix C.)

One of the great common phenomena of weather is the rising of hot air over continents, particularly in summer and early fall, and the coming in of cold air, especially from the oceans, at night or in the early dawn to replace it (figures 2–20/21). This rising hot air and sucking under of cold air do a lot of things of interest to the

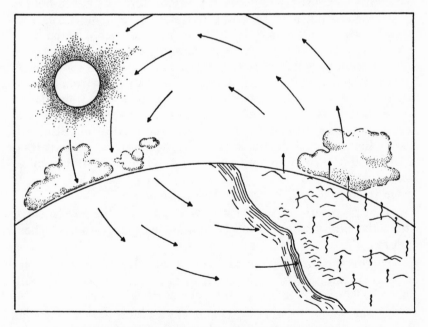

Figure 2–20. Air circulation over ocean and shore during day.

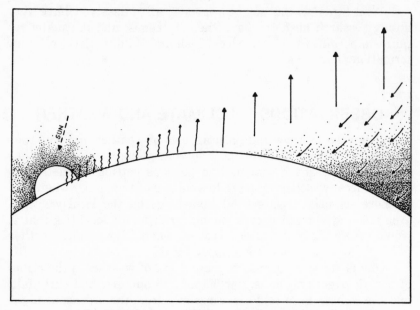

Figure 2–21. Movement of cold air under warm air, creating wind.

naturalist in his study of plant and animal life. The rising hot air is of tremendous help to birds, particularly soaring birds like eagles, hawks, and many of the large sea birds, for it helps them stay aloft with much greater ease, actually floating on the rising air. It produces clouds in thunderstorms and other kinds of clouds if there is enough moisture in the air. It sucks in fogs from the sea, which make such great natural fog forests as the redwood forest along the Pacific Coast, and it produces many varieties of winds, which do both good and damage to the land and to life. Study all these effects in your particular neighborhood, so you have at least a basic knowledge of how weather and climate affect living things where you are doing any research. Many fine books to help you are listed in Appendix C, Suggested References.

Clouds are useful in studying weather and climate. To start, study the different kinds of clouds and learn to recognize them (figure 2–22).

Cirrus: (or horse-tail clouds), the far out-flung scouts of a coming storm system if they thicken. They are high in the sky, usually above 30,000 feet, and are partly made of ice crystals

Cirrostratus: almost as high as cirrus; thin sheets of clouds that appear as nearly invisible, but make themselves known by

Cirrus

Cirrostratus

Cirrocumulus

Altocumulus

Altostratus

Stratocumulus

Nimbostratus

Stratus

Scuds

Fractostratus

Cumulus

Cumulonimbus

Fractocumulus

J. H.

Figure 2–22. Chart of cloud types. (Judith Hennessey)

rings around the sun or the moon, which usually indicate a storm coming still closer.

Cirrocumulus: groups of small flakes or balls arranged in long, glistening ripples or lines are found at 15,000 to 22,000 feet. They can turn either way, towards either fair or wet weather.

Altocumulus: appear like large, white, cotton streamers or balls, in waves, lines, or groups. They usually appear in good weather, above 13,000 feet.

Altostratus: thick, dark sheets, blue-gray or ashy in color. They usually mean bad weather is near, and are found above 13,000 feet.

Stratocumulus: large rolls or balls of gray cloud masses. These clouds could go either way, into rain, or clear weather. They are found under 10,000 feet.

Nimbostratus: masses or torn sheets of gray clouds from which rain usually soon falls. They are found below 10,000 feet.

Stratus: usually sheets of gray fog that rarely rise more than 3,000 feet above ground level.

Scuds: small, ragged fragments of clouds usually travelling fast in a storm wind.

Fractostratus: stratus clouds or fog being shredded by the wind, particularly seen on mountaintops. They are a sign of high wind.

Cumulus: clouds looking like large, woolly, white sheep or masses of snow usually drifting slowly through the sky. They usually mean fair weather unless they begin to thicken and darken. These and the next two are clouds of the rising currents of air between 5,000 and 25,000 feet.

Cumulonimbus: tremendous dark and white piles of clouds getting bigger until they bring thunder, lightning, and often heavy rain.

Fractocumulus: tattered pieces of cloud torn by the wind from the bottom or top of large cumulus clouds. They may be a sign of a coming storm.

3

ECOLOGY, CLIMATE, AND MAN

Ecology is the study of the relations of plants and animals with each other and with their environment. It is vast and all-encompassing in its uses of the many variations of human knowledge, and it is critically important in efforts to bring to man a true picture of himself in relation to this small planet Earth and its future. Combined with man's choice between spiritual maturity or immaturity, ecology is probably the major factor on which hinges the future life or destruction of our world. Many major scientific disciplines, from physics and astronomy to mathematics and economics, to biology and even anthropology, have some part to play in the study and understanding of ecology. The naturalist who starts with ecology as his major field can find his way to new interests of incredible diversity, promise, and fascination simply through the awareness that comes to him in the ecological study of the complexity of life and all that influences it. Presented to him are innumerable worlds to explore that no man has yet penetrated or at most has touched only their shallow beginnings.

Ecology has as yet only begun its task to unravel the complex relationships of life. When we realize that the complete knowledge of even one comparatively small ecosystem, such as a sagebrush desert or a pond, is a hardly reached-for dream, we see that ecology is yet in its childhood. It is nibbling at the beginning surface of the living world.

However, the need for vastly increasing this knowledge and

spreading as much as possible to the rest of mankind is desperate. Man's dream of conquest of the earth by what he calls "progress" is in danger of burning out in bitter ashes within one short century. We are enamored of the complex machines we have created, the luxuries, the push-button contrivances, but of what use was the touch of King Midas that turned everything to gold when in the end he found he could not eat the gold? Of what use is our seemingly vast and powerful material civilization if it drowns us in the end in swamps of pollution, overpopulation, destroyed resources, and war?

Consider what happened to one small oak forest on the slopes of the Alps in Switzerland. In the seventeenth century men went into half of this forest and strip-mined its wood, which means to clear-cut that half of the forest. They apparently did this at least twice in their lust for the money such quick cutting would bring. The other half of the forest, however, was cultivated with understanding and affection. The men who worked there trimmed out the right trees at the right time. They understood the forest and the forest repaid them by giving high-quality oak wood for furniture down through the centuries. Their children and their children's children reaped the benefit of foresight and wisdom by being paid from their forest many times over what the other men, foolish and in a hurry for money, ever received.

Today, after 200 years of attempts to rebuild the old forest that was destroyed and to cultivate it instead of killing it, the formerly stripped area is still far behind the other half of the forest. One half seems able to grow only poor quality pines, the other beautiful oaks. One half finds that dead trees do not decay fast enough to really renew the soil, the other has a tree die and sink into the ground to decay almost overnight and produce good soil. It is all because one has comparatively few of the fungi, bacteria, and other agents of change working in its soil to produce quality wood, while the good forest is overflowing with these organisms that make life so rich. One forest was destroyed by men who knew nothing about ecology, the other was saved by men who, while not trained ecologists, somehow had gained the wisdom of the earth and its life that makes for balance and growth instead of the shallowness, frustration, and final failure of a frantic search for gold.

All over America, all over the world, human beings are making these kinds of choices today. The study of ecology can show them how to choose wisely, to save the land, to save life, to understand it, and to come into harmony with it. The ecologist shows us what is lost and how it was lost, but also how it may be regained.

Today there are few nobler or more direly needed pursuits in the world than that of the ecologist.

To be a well-grounded ecologist is next to impossible because of the enormous extent of the job. You would need a good background in a dozen sciences, plus a working knowledge of several languages, including English, German, French, Spanish, and Russian, to be able to read all the important papers on your subject. Of course a worldwide international language would solve all this language nonsense in short order, but we have not reached that point of maturity as yet.

Most ecologists become specialists in some phase of ecology, for example, plant ecologists, animal ecologists, or even forest ecologists or desert ecologists, and so on. As an amateur scientist you can, of course, choose such a speciality in time, and then do what most ecologists have to do in their work these days—work as a scientific team. Right now it is best to get some general idea of the meaning of ecology, and a good beginning is to understand at least the commoner ecologic terms, for in ecologic work you will be constantly using them. These terms have been arranged in alphabetical order in Appendix A for ease of use as a glossary. The definitions are easy to understand so your first step into this field will not be too difficult. After studying these terms, I suggest you ask a friend to read the names to you and see if you can remember their meanings. Then have him read back to you the meanings and see if you can remember the terms. By this means you will be able to talk to a scientist about ecological problems and use and understand the correct words to define your meanings. It will also give you a good basic knowledge of the subject and suggest many possible paths to research.

SCIENTIFIC PROJECTS IN ECOLOGY

The glossary of terms that appears in Appendix A is by no means complete, but it is sufficient to unlock most of the major subjects of interest to ecologists. It also gives you an almost unlimited number of projects for possible exploration scientifically. Here I describe a few suggested projects to give you ideas on how you could use some of the subjects described in the glossary. One is taken up in special detail to show you some of the steps in research.

Before reading this list of suggested projects or studying the one project that is described in more detail, you should go back to chapter 1 and review the steps to be taken by a scientist in tackling a scientific problem. Remember the questions asked here are only a few of those that could be asked. As you study your project,. you will ask others. For every question try to find good answers.

1. Take one species of animal, such as the rice rat, *Oryzomys palustris*, of the southeastern states, which makes nests under piles of debris above the high-water level in marshy areas, and study its territorial habits in a square kilometer area of marshland, particularly in relation to its environment. The shape of your survey area can be a long rectangle, if necessary to fit a marsh. *Questions:* What are the shapes and sizes of the home ranges of this rat, and how are these shapes related to the plant growth and the water? What differences in territorial preferences do you find between rats and what can you find that influences this? What is the influence of man on the rats' territory and environment and do you find any ways the rat counters the activity of man?

2. Take one species of animal, such as the California ground squirrel, *Citellus beecheyi* (figure 3–1), find another amateur scientist by correspondence with a college or university, who lives near a natural habitat of this squirrel that is very different from the area where you live, and plan with him or her a comparative study of the thresholds of activity and reproduction of this species in the two different habitats. Thus, if you lived in the foothills of the Siskiyou Mountains in northwestern California and found California ground squirrels in the meadows of a coniferous forest there, you would probably want to compare this habitat with one such as the dry foothills of the Coast Range in the southern San Joaquin Valley of California. *Questions:* How are the major climatic factors in the two areas liable to limit foraging activity or reproduction? How do these factors change during a year's period? At what points during the year do any of these factors stop either food foraging activity or reproduc-

Figure 3–1. California ground squirrel. (Jerry Buzzell)

tion? What combination of factors have the most effect? What times during the year do these squirrels go into long periods of quiescence, either aestivation or hibernation? What comparisons can you make between these two widely separate habitats of this squirrel that help define its limits of toleration in regard to activity and reproduction in these two very different areas?

3. Take an example of beneficial disjunctive and conjunctive symbiosis in plants, such as the relations between the large tree called the southern magnolia, *Magnolia grandiflora* (figure 3–2), which is found in southern river-bottom forests and accompanying low-angled slopes, and the plants that grow in its shade and on its bark, all in an area of one square kilometer. *Questions:* Which plants make the most successful use of the shade of this tree and what causes can you find for their flourishing? Which plants make the most successful use of the bark of this tree or its limbs and what causes them to flourish there? Does the magnolia itself derive any benefit from these other plants, and, if so, which ones and how? Is there any plant that has a harmful effect on the tree, and if so, which one (or ones) and how? What is the general symbiotic relationship of this tree with all these plants?

4. Suppose you live in southern Ohio and find a female of the black- and white-tipped velvet ant, *Dasymuttila nigripes*, wandering about on some sandy soil near a small stream. If so, you are seeing a parasitic creature that lays its eggs on the larvae of burrowing insects so that when the eggs hatch the velvet ant larvae parasitize their hosts. The whole story of this parasitism is as yet little known because the velvet ants are very secretive and are little studied as yet by entomologists mainly because of their lack of economic importance. However, their importance may be greater than we realize, and they are surely one of the most interesting and mysterious of all insects. So if you run into this or another kind of velvet ant (not an ant at all, but a kind of wingless female wasp), why not observe it closely enough over a long period to find out how it parasitizes other insects and then describe accurately all the steps of this parasitism? *Questions:* What kind of holes in the ground do you find it going into? Dig out such holes with great care not to disturb (if possible) their occupants and find out just what kinds of insects use these holes for nests. Are they flies or bees or wasps or other? You may have to sift out the material dug out from a hole to find the insects and their eggs and larvae as well as cocoons, if any. Do you find two different kinds of eggs (as observed under a good magnifying glass)? If so, one kind may be the eggs of the host insect and the others eggs or larvae of the velvet ant. Put

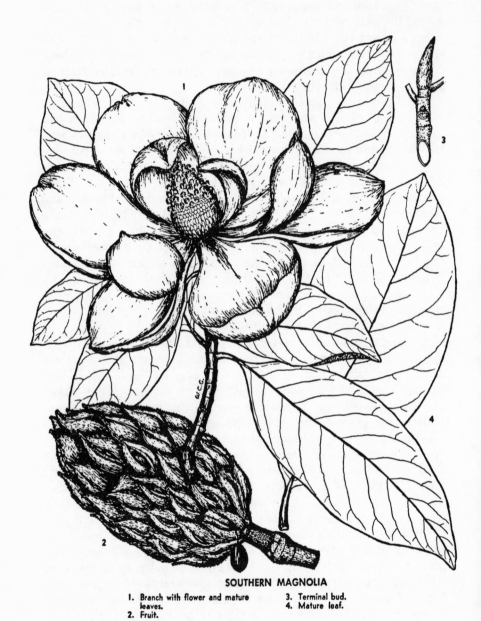

SOUTHERN MAGNOLIA

1. Branch with flower and mature leaves.
2. Fruit.
3. Terminal bud.
4. Mature leaf.

Figure 3–2. Southern magnolia. (From William Carey Grimm, *The Book of Trees*, 2nd ed., Harrisburg, Pennsylvania: Stackpole Books, 1962, p. 238.)

them together into a hollow you make between sandy soil placed between walls of glass, as in the ant nest illustrated in chapter 2. Observe them day and night, but cover up the glass sides with black paper or cloth when not observing them. Keep the top of the sandy soil slightly damp. What happens over a period of many days? Does one larva eat the eggs or another larva? Try to find out exactly what happens and if your insects die, try again with greater care the next time. Probably much trial and error will be necessary till you find the answers to this puzzle.

5. Succession of communities in a forest or woods is a highly interesting ecologic phenomena to study. Why not try a fairly simple one the first time, like succession in a pinyon–juniper community in eastern Colorado on the edge of the Great Plains. Take an area of about 10 square meters and cut out all plants and their roots so far as possible down to the bare rocky soil; then fence it in so no animals or men can get on it to bother it. Keep a day-by-day record of the weather so you can study its effect on the plants that will begin to grow in this bare area. Over a period of a few years you should be able to watch the complete sere of succession of communities in your experimental area until it reaches the climax. If carefully done, such a steady record of a sere in that particular community, showing exactly the order in which different plants came to grow there, will have scientific value regardless of whether the same succession of communities has been studied before or not. *Questions:* What is the name of each plant community that develops during the sere? What grasses are most successful first? What insects appear during the different successions and what relations do you observe between them and the plants that grow at different times? What birds appear during the different successions? Are they always the same or do they differ, and if so, how and why? What overall hypotheses about the development of this sere and its plant and animal life can you make? Test them carefully by the facts you observe and see which seems to be most correct.

CARRYING OUT AN ECOLOGIC PROJECT IN DETAIL

Here we can consider in detail number 2 of the above projects, the study of the thresholds of foraging activity and reproduction in the California ground squirrel, in one area four miles north of Happy Camp, California, in the foothills of the Siskiyou Mountains, and the other at the southern end of the San Joaquin Valley, at Maricopa, California. Table 3–1 shows the weather records for precipitation and temperature for one year, given monthly. The graphs that show the food foraging activity and the reproductive activity of the squirrels for the same year in the two localities (figure 3–3) can be compared to this table so you can see how the research determined when the two activities of the squirrels reached their highest and lowest points and how this compared to the weather patterns.

To get the full picture of the comparison between the squirrels at the two different localities, we have to do the following:

TABLE 3–1

Weather Records for Precipitation and Temperature for One Year, Happy Camp and Maricopa, California

Month	Temperatures in Maricopa			Temperatures in H.C.			Rainfall in H.C.		R. in Maricopa
	L	H	M	L	H	M		Snow	
January	19	78	47	20	39	33	10	4 days	1.11
February	22	83	52	22	41	38	9	2 days	0.88
March	29	90	58	27	66	52	9	2 days	0.88
April	31	98	64	27	82	54	4	—	0.64
May	41	107	72	35	95	61	3	—	0.25
June	48	114	69	41	103	67	1	—	0.10
July	54	116	86	45	110	74	0.36	—	0.00
August	54	115	84	39	109	72	0.15	—	0.00
September	47	113	78	34	102	66	0.50	—	0.11
October	33	105	68	30	90	56	3	—	0.28
November	28	91	56	25	63	46	7	—	0.52
December	22	86	49	22	56	43	10	6 days	0.92
Totals of rainfall							56.51		6.09

Note: L = lowest temperature; H = highest temperature; M = mean temperature.

1. We will need to keep accurate records of the high and low temperatures for each day for the year at the actual places where the ground squirrels are being covered, and the mean temperature

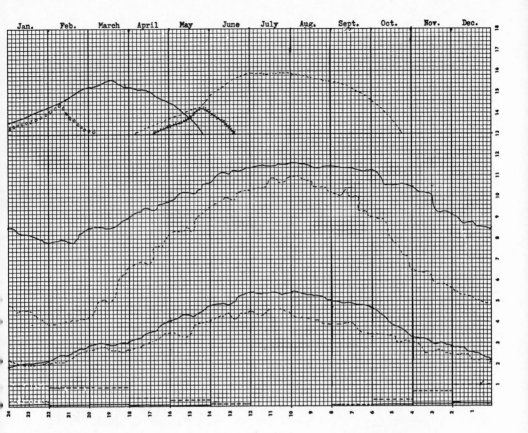

Figure 3–3. Graphs to show effects of climate on the same species, the California ground squirrel (*Citellus beecheyi*), in two widely different localities: Happy Camp in the cool, wet Siskiyou Mountains of northern California, and Maricopa, at the south end of the dry, hot San Joaquin Valley. The graphs are divided into comparable sections for each month of the year, but the upper graph shows the percentage of time spent by the squirrels in food foraging and reproductive activity during different times of the year, while the lower graph, separated from the upper by a solid straight line, shows the differences in the temperature and rainfall of the two localities at different times of the year.

In the lower graph the solid black lines indicate temperature and rainfall for the Maricopa area, while the dashed lines show temperature and rainfall for Happy Camp. The highest solid and dashed lines represent the average daily highest temperatures in degrees Fahrenheit in the respective localities, the middle lines the lowest average daily temperatures, and the lowest lines the monthly rainfall or precipitation in inches. From this it can be seen that the Maricopa area has much higher temperatures on the average, while the Happy Camp area has a good deal more rainfall.

The reaction of the squirrels to the differing climates is reflected in the top graph. The solid line indicates that the ground squirrels at Maricopa are most active in February, March, and April, when there is less heat and more plant growth, while the line made of little circles shows that reproductive activity among Maricopa squirrels is strongest in February at the beginning of this period, allowing the young to be born when plant food is most plentiful. The dashed line indicates that the Happy Camp squirrels are most active in the months from June to September, when the Maricopa squirrels are asleep in their dens during the hot weather, but water and food are plentiful in Happy Camp. The line with crossmarks shows that most of the reproductive activity of the Happy Camp squirrels takes place in May and June so that their babies are born in midsummer, when food is most plentiful. See text for further information.

for each day, plus records of the daily rainfall or snowfall (counting snowfall as melted down into water). These are the absolute essentials as it is moisture plus temperature that determine both the optimum times of activity for the squirrel and the times when they need to stop all activity and hide deep in their burrows to avoid either the cold or too much heat and dryness. We know these ground squirrels store some food for these times of food scarcity, but they also sleep for long periods to avoid expending energy that would require more food than is available. Because of these features of their lives, there is not much need to keep records of wind velocities and directions, as it is obviously either the cold and wetness or the heat and dryness that drive them underground, the former acting mainly in Happy Camp, whereas the hot dry days in Maricopa are the danger to the squirrels there.

2. Next it is important to keep records daily throughout the year of all activity, including reproduction activity (matings and first appearances of new young squirrels from the dens, from whose sizes we can gauge approximately the time of birth). To watch activity, both parties in the two localities should be watching the squirrels daily at the times of their greatest activity, which may be different at the two locations. Perhaps one hour of observing in the morning at the time of usual strong activity, and one hour in the afternoon or evening would be sufficient if done regularly. Actual sightings of movements should all be recorded, and any signs of courtship, male rivalry, and matings should be put into the notes with full details. Binoculars should be used and blinds set up so the squirrels can be watched with the least danger of disturbing them.

3. Possible improvements on observations can be made if we use our ingenuity. For example, if we could find a way to dig a human tunnel alongside a ground squirrel tunnel and put a window between the two for a few feet, which we would cover with a black cloth when not in use, and use a red plastic covered flashlight when it was in use, we might get some rare glimpses of underground activity. Another possibility would be to build a platform 3 by 7 feet, about 6 to 8 feet off the ground, so that a person lying on it can look into some of the ground squirrel holes to see deeper inside them. After a while the ground squirrels would get used to this platform, and, if you would lie on top of it perfectly still with binoculars, you could observe activity part way down the holes. Other ideas will develop as you continue watching the ground squirrels.

4. As the observations continue at the two localities, it should soon be noticed that there is a very great difference in activity of the squirrels in the two areas. At Maricopa the optimum time for both food and reproduction activity is during the winter and early spring when there is enough moisture and coolness for plants to grow and for the squirrels to be active without discomfort, but during the hot summer and early fall they will spend the time completely out of sight, apparently aestivating (in deep sleep) for long periods. The reverse will appear at Happy Camp, for there the squirrels will be most active in late spring, summer, and early fall when plants are growing and bearing fruits, nuts, and seeds and the temperature is warm but not too hot. Winter will be for long sleep.

5. At the end of the year of double observations complete graphs should be made of all activity in relation to the changes of the weather. These graphs should answer the questions about where the thresholds of activity and reproduction can be charted in conjunction with actual changes in temperature and rainfall or dryness and heat that cause these thresholds to appear.

ECOLOGY AND MAN

I have already touched on the subject of ecology and man, and consider it again in the final chapter. As you do projects and problems in ecology, let it train you to be constantly alert to man's effect on nature and how we may counter by explanation and the clear presentation of facts those things that human beings do out of ignorance that harm the earth and its life. We live on a shrinking planet and our time is short to convince others that there is no future for mankind unless we can learn to come into harmony with ourselves and our surroundings.

4

ANIMAL BEHAVIOR

Animal behavior or *ethology*, as it is also called, is a field of exploration of particular interest to the amateur scientist because it is possible to start in it with less technical training and usually with less expensive technical equipment. However, behavioral study, although often highly interesting, should not be entered into with any thought that it is going to be easy. Instead, it is often a gripping challenge, calling on all your ingenuity and physical and mental energy. Jane Van Lawick-Goodall, the famous investigator of the intimate life of the chimpanzee in Africa, had to spend months alone in the African wilderness, oftentimes in storms and with danger from leopards, poisonous snakes, and other creatures, before she finally won the friendship of the apes and found the secrets of their lives. Read her book *In the Shadow of Man*[1] to see how she overcame this challenge.

Of course, less difficult and dangerous work can be done with such creatures as insects or frogs, even in your own backyard, but there is always a challenge and there is always hard work and close observation involved. Read Karl von Fritch's *Bees, Their Vision, Chemical Senses and Language*[2] to see what great work can be done even with very small creatures.

There have been two main approaches to animal behavior on

---

[1]Jane Van Lawick-Goodall, *In the Shadow of Man* (Boston, Mass.: Houghton Mifflin Co., 1971).

[2]Karl von Fritch, *Bees, Their Vision, Chemical Senses and Language* (Ithaca, N.Y.: Cornell University Press, 1971).

the part of scientists: *ethology*, which has been primarily field work with wild animals, and *comparative animal psychology*, which has been conducted by psychologists rather than biologists, and done mainly in the laboratory with such animals as dogs, rats, and cats. There has been some jealousy and misunderstanding between these two scientific disciplines, but gradually they are coming together as more scientists are combining field work with laboratory experiments with animals when possible. With the smaller creatures, particularly insects, it is often possible to reproduce in cages in the laboratory or in the backyard habitat backgrounds very similar to those in the wild so that such creatures can be watched close at hand under close-to-natural conditions.

THE PHYSIOLOGY BEHIND ANIMAL BEHAVIOR

How animals react depends a great deal on how their nervous and glandular system as well as their whole bodies handle stimuli from outside, and moods, drives, and thoughts from inside. Some knowledge of the physiology of animals that deals with behavior is necessary. The following, however, is only a beginning, and there are good books listed in Suggested References, Appendix C, that will take you farther along this interesting trail.

Today both ethologists and animal psychologists are deeply involved in the physiological basis of animal behavior, including the use of very technical machines such as the kinds that register electric impulses from the brain, the electron microscope, and instruments that register the chemical reactions of the body to outside stimuli. But the beginning explorer naturalist need not worry about this expensive equipment at this time.

Figure 4–1 shows the nervous system of a rat plus the organs and other parts of the body that have a particular association with behavior. It also has enlargements of the eye, the ear, the nose, the tongue, and the nerve endings and receptors in the skin that deal with touch. Included are the locations of the major glands that give off hormones and enzymes to the blood and also influence behavior in various ways.

The Nervous System in an Animal

The nervous system is made up of two major parts: the peripheral or outside nervous system, and the central or inside

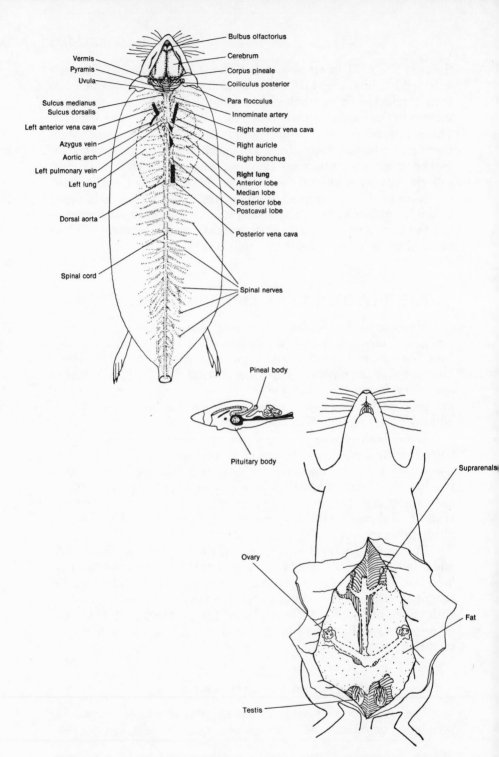

Figure 4–1. Physiology of a rat. *Top:* nervous system, with some associated organs. *Bottom:* endocrine gland system. Brain and body are sectioned in a median sagittal plane. (Judith Hennessey)

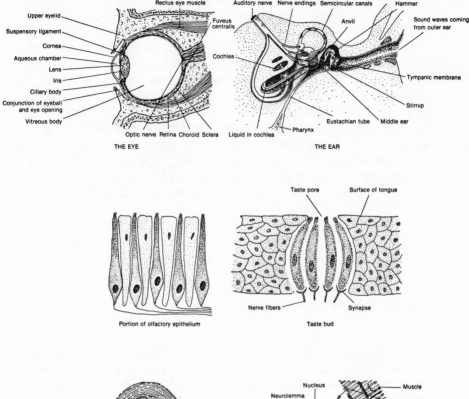

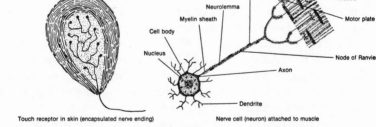

Figure 4–1. Physiology of a rat (*cont.*). Sense organs and nerve cell. (Judith Hennessey)

nervous system. The *central nervous system* includes the brain and the spinal cord, while the *peripheral nervous system* consists of all the nerves of the body outside of the brain and the spinal cord. You can actually feel one of these nerve cords by bending your elbow and pressing with your finger at the point of the elbow where the "funny bone" is.

The nerves themselves are of two kinds: the *afferent nerves* that take messages from different parts of the body in to the central nervous system, and the *efferent nerves* that carry responding messages from the central nervous system back to the necessary part or parts of the body where a reaction can be made. A very simple reflex response, for example, happens when you put your finger on a hot stove. There is no need for this kind of message to go by afferent nerve to the brain. It flashes to the spinal cord by electrochemical impulse and comes back immediately by an efferent nerve to the finger that causes the finger to be jerked away from the stove. A much more complicated response happens when, for example, you see a person in danger for his life by fire, and you have to make a decision how to save him and then act. This is taken by afferent nerves to the brain, where the decision is made and flashes back to several parts of the body that go into action, perhaps to roll a person with burning clothes on the ground and put out the flames, or to throw water on him if it is immediately available.

The ordinary nerve cell itself is usually quite long, with a cell body and nucleus in the middle, from which comes the main part of the nerve fibers, called collectively the *axon*, extending to the dendrites at both ends of the nerve, which are made up of branching fibers. Between two nerves there is a narrow gap called the *synapse* over which the nervous impulse has to leap, very much as an electric spark will jump between two closely placed wires. This gap is important in being one part of a pattern in the nervous system that prevents unimportant impulses from going too far and bothering the higher parts of the nervous system. For example, when I am writing a book or thinking about something important, I often concentrate so hard that my brain protects me automatically, without my knowing it, by command to one or more synapses, from hearing noises that would bother me, such as the sounds of my wife cooking, or a barking dog. Animals are the same.

As animals rise in the scale of life from the comparatively simple single-celled animal such as the amoeba, to the highly complicated mammal, such as the whale or man, the nervous system becomes more complicated and the variations and adaptations of the animal's behavior become more numerous.

The entire nerve in a higher animal, enclosed in a membrane, has its most important parts made up of salts and fluid. The electrolyzed salt solution forms the perfect passageway for the flow of negative and positive ions (particles) along the nerve fibers, much as an electric current moves along a wire from positive to negative centers. Thus, in an afferent nerve fiber the dendrites or nerve endings in the skin are caused to change their electric potential by a touch, shooting an impulse inward to the spinal cord.

If you could cut the spinal cord of an animal in two, you would find that the outer part of the cord is white and the inner part is gray. This white part is largely made up of nerve fibers, while the inner gray matter is made up mostly of nerve cell nuclei. In the brain this is reversed, as the outer part of the brain, which is called the *cortex*, is gray and is made up of nerve nuclei, while the inner part of the brain is white and is made up mainly of nerve fibers.

The large bundles of nerves that come to and from the spinal cord are called *posterior*, or sensory, and *anterior*, or motor, nerve roots. Branches from the afferent nerves eventually reach intermediate neurons in the central (gray) part of the spinal cord, and these pass simple impulses in response back to more neurons (efferent nerves) that control the actions of the muscles. This is all at what is called the *reflex level* where the animal body does things automatically without having to think about it.

Nerve tracts that lead up and down the spinal cord from the brain are called *ascending* and *descending*, the ascending tracts taking up to the brain the more important messages that cannot be answered by reflexes in the spinal cord, and the descending tracts taking the responses or commands sent back by the brain to the muscles. In very simple animals, such as flatworms or coelenterates, the brain is no more than a pair of enlarged ganglia, and most reactions are *instinctive*, though even these simple animals, and the still simpler one-celled protozoans, are capable of a certain amount of simple learning. Instinctive and learned reactions are considered in more detail a little later.

In more complex animals the part of the brain that joins immediately to the spinal column is called the *medulla oblongata* (see Fig. 4–1, rat's brain). In this part of the brain are neurons that carry out the organization of vital bodily functions such as breathing, swallowing, the beat of the heart, digestion, and so on— things we regularly do without thinking. Above this the main part of the brain is divided into two large cerebral hemispheres in the most advanced animals, where thought processes take place.

There is another division of the nervous system that really does not belong to either the central or peripheral nervous systems. This is the *autonomic nervous system*, which might be called an "alerting system" as it prepares the body for events soon to happen.

Thus, it alerts the digestive system to get ready for digestion when the animal first sees food it is about to eat, or it alerts the muscles and the inner organs to prepare for violent action if the animal is about to flee from or to attack an enemy. It also prepares the body for excreting fluids or solids, relaxes the body at night to prepare for sleep, and other similar activities.

Closely associated with the nervous system and sometimes actually incorporated into parts of the nerve cells is the glandular system of the body. Thus, some neurons or nerve cells become neurosecretory cells that secrete from their endings chemical compounds such as hormones that activate things such as the reproductive processes or the growth of fat for food storage. In the case of the reproductive system the hormones secreted by the sex glands, such as the gonads and the ovaries, would directly affect the sexual behavior of the animal. The various glands that are associated with such glandular secretions are shown in the illustration of the rat. For further information on the glands and their secretions see books on this subject mentioned in Suggested References, Appendix C.

Receptors for the Five Senses and Others

The animal's five major receptors, eyes, ears, nose, skin, and tongue, all have specialized nerve cells and sometimes organ shapes associated with them to bring to the animal knowledge of its surroundings. This knowledge is then carried to different parts of the brain, associated with each receptor, which works with associated neuron groups to make decisions about what to do in response. Remember that different animals vary greatly in the location and use of their receptors. Thus, some fish have receptors for taste in both the mouth and scattered over the skin of the body. In a cricket the eye alone is not enough with which to make decisions, as it is with many animals. If a female cricket sees a male in a bell jar where she cannot hear him, she is not stimulated to move toward him until the bell jar is removed and she can hear his strident call.

The *eye* was slow in developing in the evolution of animals, but long before the eye appeared some kind of sensation to light was found even in the lowly protozoa or single-celled animals, since many of these creatures respond to light by moving away from it or toward it. More specialized animals, such as the earthworm, have areas near the head end in which the nerve endings respond to light, but no definite eyes appear. The same is true among the starfish and sea urchins and their relatives, but in the mollusca (sea shells), and arthropods (crustaceans, insects, etc.), the first true eyes begin to make their appearance. At first they were very simple, as with the simple eyes carried on stalks by snails, the row of simple eyes found under the mantle of a scallop, or the single eyes of primitive spiders and insects. These eyes probably see only enough to distinguish between light and dark and detect movements of a predator towards the animal or movements of prey animals away from the animal.

The most complicated eyes among the invertebrates developed among the insects and the cephalopods (squid, cuttlefish, and octopods). The eye of a dragonfly, for example, is very large and complicated. It consists of a mass of hundreds of single eyes or lenses formed into a large sphere or oval compound eye. Early scientists thought that each of these single eyes looked straight ahead, so that the curve of the compound eye shape produced a mosaic of cell-like views of the surroundings, not overlapping, but more recent research has shown that each simple eye in the compound eye has a view that overlaps that of the other simple eyes surrounding it. This makes the total view from the compound eye much more uniform and precise, and explains the ability of the dragonfly or butterfly to dodge a butterfly net or an attacking bird with great skill, as I learned well when I was a professional insect collector in Central America. So the dragonfly can capture in flight tiny midges, flies, and mosquitoes with great accuracy. However, it is doubtful if such an insect can see with much precision for long distances.

The most highly developed of invertebrate eyes, however, is that of the squid or octopus. The eye of the octopus is very similar to that of a mammal. It has an iris, lids, crystalline lenses, and a retina. It has a feature that the eye of the mammal does not have: the eyes are partially stalked and can turn in almost any direction. Another difference is that the pupil appears as a black rectangle. Inside, though, the eye has less receptor cells and these are less differentiated than those of a mammal, so that the picture it sees is probably less precise. Nevertheless, its reactions to what it sees show very considerable knowledge of exactly what is happening and its movements are quick in either escaping or opposing an enemy and in seizing its own prey.

Most mammals are to some extent color-blind, but the eyes of the order of primates, including man, the great apes, and monkeys, are capable of detecting color. This is because they have photo-receptors called *cone cells* as well as rod cells in the back of the retina. The cone cells are of three kinds, one for each of the primary colors, and so can combine in various ways to detect all the other colors of the spectrum except infrared and ultraviolet. *Rod cells* detect movements and light and shadow. At night we use only our rod cells because then we cannot see color anyway. Other creatures that can see color include the birds, many reptiles, certain insects, such as the butterflies, moths, and bees, and most of the fish. Color is vital to the bees in finding the flowers, but bees cannot see red, although they can see ultraviolet, a color we do not see. Thus, most red flowers in America are fertilized by hummingbirds, while red European and Asiatic flowers are pollinated by butterflies, and African red flowers are pollinated by sunbirds.

Some mammals can see much better in the dark than others, particularly cats who do much hunting by night and flying squirrels who have very large eyes. The irises of both of these creatures can open far wider than those of a man, allowing in more of the faint light. Birds, on the other hand, particularly hawks and eagles, can see much better than man or other mammals by day, and their eyes are definitely of a higher order than ours. Watch, for example, a sparrow hawk a hundred feet in the air as it sights an inch-long grasshopper and dives for it with great precision. Owls, of course, have eyes particularly adapted for night hunting and can see much fainter objects in the dark than we can.

Ears, like eyes, probably started their evolution as tiny nerve endings that became receptive to the vibrations that produce sounds. Many animals without visible ears, such as earthworms and octopods, probably catch vibrations through their skin and can respond to them. Thus, earthworms try to go deeper underground when they hear heavy footsteps coming.

The ear in the usual mammal is made up of an outer ear, a middle ear, and an inner ear. The *outer ear* is generally of a trumpet shape to funnel sound into the middle ear, which lies on the other side of the membrane called the *tympanum*. From here the vibrations of sound are translated to the inner ear by three little bones called the *hammer*, the *anvil*, and the *stirrup*, which lead to another membrane behind which is a circular, curled chamber called the *cochlea* in which are the sensitive nerve endings that convey the meaning of each sound to the brain. Also in the inner ear is a set of tubes called the *semicircular canals*, which have nothing to do with hearing, but help through the circulation of fluids

Figure 4–2. Two mule deer, showing their long ears cocked in different directions at the same time. (Jerry Buzzell)

within them to determine whether the body is in proper balance or not. If these tubes are not working correctly in a man, he finds it hard to stand upright and may get dizzy and fall down.

Many mammals have the ability, as does the deer (figure 4–2), to turn the ears in different directions at the same time, so catching the different sounds from opposite directions at the same time. Also some have much larger ears than we do and so can catch more sounds. One of the most unusual types of hearing is found in owls, particularly the barn owl (figure 4–3). The faces of owls are concave, and evidently act to catch sounds they hear while hunting at night. Thus, barn owls have been put into a room that was pitch dark, but were able to catch mice in such a room by sound alone.

Many birds, and especially sea birds, can detect small differences in the qualities of sound better than we can. When cormorants, gulls, and other sea birds crowd together on rocks in the ocean they create a tremendous noise, but an individual mother can detect immediately the cry of her own youngster and know exactly where he is in all that mass of screaming birds. A fur seal mother can do the same in the midst of all the roaring and barking of a fur seal rookery.

Another difference lies in the range of hearing. Sound waves come to us in so many cycles per second, 500 to 2,500 in man, although some people with sensitive ears can hear as low as 20 cycles

Figure 4–3. Barn owl, showing concave face (James Gordon Irving), and striking at a gopher on the ground in a dark night, using sound to locate its prey. (Jerry Buzzell)

per second and as high as 20,000. Compare this, however, with cats who can hear up to 50,000 cycles, rats up to 90,000, and some bats up to 120,000. Bats use very high-pitched sounds as a form of sonar, bouncing the echoes off the insects they catch while flying through the air of dusk, and telling from the echoes exactly where each insect is. Interestingly, some insects, particularly moths, are capable of hearing these high-pitched bat cries, and, when they hear them, immediately make fast evasive motions or quick dives towards trees or brush where they can hide. Over many centuries these moths that could hear these sounds best and take escaping motions fastest are those who lived longest to produce offspring. So does natural selection in evolution work. An interesting development with bats is that they were forced to make their high-pitched calls very short so that the echo would not bounce back while the note was still being made, which would create a confusion of sounds. Mice and shrews also use such echo location, as do some cave-dwelling birds in Peru and swifts in the South Seas.

Another mammal capable of using this kind of sonar, but this time in water instead of in air and with incredible efficiency, is the porpoise or dolphin, including also some of the other toothed whales. The porpoise may make vibrations of sound in the water at about 80,000 cycles per second, much higher than man can hear (see also chapter 1). Whales and dolphins, by the way, do not have any outer ears at all, but just a small hole leading to the middle and inner ear. However, their ears are especially adapted to water sounds, which travel farther and faster than sounds in air.

Olfactory (smell) and gustatory (taste) receptors in most animals are so closely connected that they need to be discussed together. If you catch a bad cold, you will often notice that this affects your sense of taste and some things cannot be tasted at all. This is because some foods affect both the smell and taste receptors and if one is cut off, the taste is different or even vanishes. Much is yet to be discovered about these two senses, and just how they operate is less well known than it is for the ears and eyes.

The olfactory receptors in an animal's nose are cells whose outer tips have delicate hair-like cilia that are constantly moving in contact with a mucuous membrane that always stays damp. These cells are held in place by supporting cells that surround them, and each olfactor receptor cell is activated by molecules coming through the air that have the requisite characteristics to rouse the sensation of smell. One theory of olfaction states that the odor particles must be changed from the air to become part of the moist membrane over the cilia. Here they are smelled if they are volatile, soluble in water and liquid (fats or oil), and have molecules of the proper shapes and sizes to activate the olfactory receptors. Another theory is that the molecule must have the proper vibrations to set up equal vibrations in the olfactory receptors. Some scientists combine these two theories into one, which assumes the molecule carried to the receptors through the air must have a special low vibration rate and also be of the proper size and shape to conform with the olfactory receptor. There are also supposed to be different receptors for different smells, which would explain why some people cannot smell certain odors. Generally speaking this combined stereochemical theory of smell helps scientists predict whether some unknown substance will have an odor, and what kind of smell it will be. There is much research yet to be done into how the extraordinarily keen sense of smell of a good hound, or of a wolf, bear, or fox, operates in the wild.

The *taste receptors* within a taste bud in the tongue are very similar to the olfactory receptors, as they too have tiny cilia at their tips, which come up to the moist surface of the tongue and react to various water soluble molecules that touch them. The molecules probably have to be below a certain range of size and be solluble in lipids (liquid fats). In both taste and smell reception man is below most mammals in ability, but probably as good or better than most birds, as birds sense their world mostly through sight and hearing.

On the other hand, whales, dolphins, and their relatives are mammals who have completely lost their sense of smell, but may have a weak sense of taste.

Many insects and other invertebrates have good senses of smell and taste, but we know less about them than about mammals. Termites, ants, and bees all use smell to be sure of their own city or nest mates and to detect the smells of strangers whom they may attack. Scout ants leave smell trails to guide parties of foragers from their own community to new food or a new home. Many female insects give off smells that can be detected a long ways off by the males. For instance, when a virgin queen bee or ant rises in the air at the time of mating, males may come from a long distance to find her. Still farther, often for several miles, saturnid (or giant silk moth) males come to find their females. These males have antennae that look like complicated radar antennae, which are loaded with olfactor receptors of great accuracy and delicacy for detecting the tiniest scent in the air from a female. By weaving back and forth like a hound dog on a difficult trail, they follow the scent to its source.

Cutaneous (skin) receptors are used to feel things in the environment. The skin of any animal is filled with thousands of these receptors ready to signal even the lightest touch, and quick to shoot any sensation of pain to the proper center that will send another signal to relieve it. Recording electrodes placed beneath the skin and next to the affector nerve endings catch the number of nerve impulses passing along the nerves and amplify them so they can be shown on an oscilloscope, where they can be seen as jumping lines of light and can be photographed. By this means scientists have been able to show that the light sensations, such as a soft tickling of a fly crawling on the arm, move only along the largest nerve fibers. A stronger stimulus causes somewhat smaller nerve fibers to be stimulated, and the person may feel as if soon it is going to be painful. But it is only when the very smallest nerve fibers begin to be stimulated and carry sensations that true pain appears. The smallest nerves of all are the ones that carry severe pain.

By attaching electrodes to the brain of an animal in different areas, it has been possible to find what certain parts of the brain do in sending signals to different parts of the body. Thus, the septal part of the brain connected to the hypothalamus (in the brain's base) has been found to create feelings of intense pleasure, while stimulation of parts of the hypothalamus itself have created feelings of anger and fear.

Possibly among the most sensitive of all living things to touch is the octopus, and its close relatives the squid and cuttlefish. The touch of the tentacles of an octopus is extremely delicate and it is obvious the creature can feel vibrations of many kinds. The octopus also shows the close relation of its skin surface to its nervous system by the way it turns bright red when angry and white when afraid or exhausted. How touch operates in many different animals is still a mystery, worthy of much serious exploration.

This brings up the subject of moods. Human beings get moods of depression and exhilaration, worry and happiness, excitement and boredom. These moods then manifest themselves in the way we act and certainly influence the ways our glandular and nervous systems behave. For a long time some scientists refused to believe that animals below the stage of man had such moods, but any farmer could have told them about plenty of examples from his barnyard. Now we are beginning to realize that even such creatures as the lowly flatworm, an animal with no apparent brain at all, can show moods. One flatworm, for example, was taught how to choose between two holes in its small aquarium, one of which led to food, but after a while it became bored with seeking food in this way and stubbornly refused to go down the hole. The subject of animal moods is a new world just opening for investigation, and with many possibilities for an alert and ready explorer naturalist.

There are some other senses known to animals of which we are only beginning to be aware, and which can be mentioned only most briefly here. One is the *heat sense* found in the pit vipers, of which our American rattlesnakes and copperheads are good examples. These poisonous snakes have a pair of pits or holes just back of the nose, which are filled with numerous heat-sensing receptor nerves. These receptors tell a rattlesnake when a warm-blooded animal is near it, and it is even able to sense the exact moment when it should strike, even though it may be in pitch darkness. After the strike it also uses the heat sensors to follow down the trail of the stricken animal and finish killing it. This heat sensing is thus a completely separate sense from those already mentioned.

One other different sense of this sort is the *electrical sense* found in electric eels and other fish that generate electricity. These fish form electric fields around their bodies, which give them knowledge of objects and creatures close by even in dark muddy rivers where sight is of no use. They are told by the electric fields whether an enemy or a prey animal is near, and so whether to attack or flee.

There are at least two possible senses that have not yet been explored deeply enough to be sure they really exist: One is based on the fact that salmon come across a thousand miles or more of ocean to find the exact river in which they were originally born and then go up it to spawn in the same small, side stream where their own original spawning happened. The last part of this journey has been shown probably to be made by following tiny taste–smell molecules that come down the river in its current, though this requires extraordinary sensitivity, as the molecules may be only one part in 10 million of the river water or less. But this could not be what led them across the ocean to the main river mouth, and it is here that a *magnetism sense* may have had something to do with it. This would be a sense based on contact with the earth's magnetic fields, which extend from pole to pole. By orienting themselves to this force they could possibly find their way correctly across those miles of ocean. A similar sensing may guide the eels in their great journeys in the Atlantic Ocean, and the sea birds that cross from continent to continent.

The other sense is something that is still more guesswork than anything else but tantalizes our imagination as a possible explanation of things we cannot yet understand. There is a *homing ability* that certain creatures show, including birds, mammals, insects, and sea animals, that leads them directly home often from great distances without any possible way of knowing landmarks. A bird, for example, is moved in a closed box for a thousand miles or more and yet finds its way home, or a cat or dog is also taken a great distance in a closed car or even by airplane, and somehow escapes in that distant place and finds its way home. Maybe it is a sense based on the magnetism spoken of above, but generally this is a sense possessed by only a small percentage of a particular kind of creature, and yet, when had, it leads them home with marvelous exactness. Maybe it is a kinetic sense, based on the movement of the very earth, and maybe it is something more mysterious still—a spiritual sense that once most scientists laughed at, but which strange facts are beginning to shake. It is obvious that a lot of fascinating and also very difficult research lies ahead in this field.

PLANNING RESEARCH INTO ANIMAL BEHAVIOR

Again, as with ecology, Appendix B introduces an alphabetic list or glossary of common terms used in ethology, the science of animal behavior. This, if studied carefully, will enable you to speak with scientists who deal in this field with a beginning understanding of what they are talking about. Explanations are as simple and clear as possible, but some of them are still very complex and it will require further study to truly understand them. However, this glossary should prove useful to refer to at all times when you are doing research in this field, and, by learning many of the terms and their meanings by heart you will be giving yourself some basic background knowledge in this science. Also, throughout the glossary there is a treasure of ideas for different kinds of research.

Study carefully this glossary, first to get an overall view of ethology, second to begin to use the terms with some familiarity when you are talking with scientists, and third to search for possible lines of research in animal behavior that would particularly interest you. Probably as your first project in such research it would be wise to choose an animal or group of animals that would be easy to find and watch. Also, be sure to choose a subject that is fairly simple to do, and not too complicated or technical, as such projects should be left until you are more experienced or are working as part of a scientific team. Even before you start, it would help to review the first chapters in this book so you will have well in mind the scientific method and how to put it into effect.

A Suggested Field Project

Probably only a relatively few species of ants have been researched on their scent trails and how they operate. The species in your neighborhood, or at least some of them, may never have had such research done on them. Find an area that includes mixed woods and fields and map out a plot 30 meters by 30 meters in size where you can find a fair number of ant nests of different species. On the map show all major trees and rocks or other significant landmarks. Your job will be to map all the ant nests in the area and the trails they use in foraging for food, especially checking and mapping the way scent markers or pheromones are used by scout ants to lead other ants to food. You are to find out as much as possible just how these scent markers work for the different species of ants and what behavior the ants show in relation to them. At the end of this preliminary research you would write down every possible hypothesis you can think of to explain this behavior and system of scent signals, and then test them against all the facts you can find by further observation. The following are suggested steps in this project.

1. Go to a library that has a good collection of scientific books and keeps files of scientific magazines. Many of these magazines are listed in Appendix E. Find books and magazines that include chapters or articles on ants and ant behavior. Usually the last issue of a scientific magazine for each year has an index in which it lists the year's articles by subject matter. Study this literature on ants and particularly search for ones that cover information on the chemical and scent signals of ants. Make copies, if possible, of such chapters or articles that cover this matter. Such copies can usually be made on the library copying machine at a low cost. If you cannot do this, then make careful notes of anything in the articles or chapters that apply to your particular project. This information, brought home, can then be kept as references for study while you are working on the project, and will give you good ideas on what is already known on the subject, what techniques have been used in such research, and what still needs to be discovered.

2. Map your 30-square meter area as has already been described in chapter 2, but now add onto the map locations of all ant nests in your area and whatever trails you find them using.

3. Collect a small number of specimens of each kind of ant found at each nest and mount and dry correctly with labels as explained for mounting specimens in chapter 2. Give each ant nest you have found a number, and put this number with each set of specimens for each nest. Compare your specimens under a magnifying glass, and, while keeping each group from a particular nest somewhat separate from the others, put those groups together that obviously belong to the same species.

4. Write or phone your nearest museum or university or college where they have specialists in insect taxonomy (identification), particularly of the ants, and ask a scientist if he or she would be willing to identify your specimens to help you with your project. Be sure to offer the taxonomist several specimens to keep for himself and also offer to pay the postage both ways. If he agrees to help, mark your mounted specimens with labels that tell exactly where they were collected, etc., as described in chapter 2, but also number them by the ant nests they came from. Prepare these specimens carefully mounted on a firm base like cork glued to the bottom of a box (a cigar box will do), reinforcing the box to prevent breakage in the mail, and put this box in a larger box with stuffing around it to prevent too much jarring. Then mail this box to the person who is going to identify the specimens for you. Send at least 10 specimens of each species, so he can keep half the number. If

you can, send samples of eggs, larvae, and pupae, as this would help, too.

5. When you get your named specimens back so you can tell what species each of your ant nests belongs to, be sure to put this information in your notebook and journal, and memorize what each species looks like so you can easily identify it in the field.

6. Now you are ready for the actual work of studying ant communication by scent markers in the area you have mapped. Your first step is to watch carefully the ant scouts as they travel forth from the nests looking for food. You can put some bits of food you know they like to eat in places separate from their main trails. Watch and note everything they do as they search and especially their reactions when they find some food.

7. When they do find a food source, either one you put out or another, mark this on your map with the number of the nest from which the ant came plus a letter for the food. Watch carefully to see if they act excited about their discovery and what they do. Such an ant will usually head back for its nest on a new trail, which may or may not merge with an established trail, but show what it does with a special line in a special color that you identify in your notes. Wherever it puts pheromones or scent or chemical markers, mark these on your map with a special sign. For this part of your work, you may need to draw a new map on a larger scale for just this part of your area so you can show these things in detail. Such map would cover just the area used by the ants of the one nest. As you study different nests and their operations, note carefully any differences in the way their scouts locate new food supplies and also in the ways they use chemical signals on the trails.

8. Observe carefully how the ants at the nest or nests react to any messengers when they come home, and whether and how they follow the trail left by the scouts in the form of chemical pheromones. Every detail of this behavior should be put in your notebook.

9. You can experiment with the way the ants find food, by placing bits of food the ants would like to eat in different places around the nest and timing how long it takes for each food cache to be found, noting also differences in behavior between the different nests and the different species of ants.

10. In time you may want to collect some of the pheromones (scent signals) put down by the ants, taking each up with a razor edge and placing in a small plastic envelope, which is then marked with the nest number and ant letter, date, place found in relation

to the map, and any other information of interest. You can find out from a university or college biology department where to send these for chemical analysis, and also how much it would cost. If too much, perhaps later you can have such tests run when you are part of a scientific team that can afford such things.

After you have completed the research that seems necessary to get a clear, comparative view of what all the ant nests in your area are doing in the way of chemical signalling and trail marking, you can see if you can answer such questions as the following:

1. What behavior in the ant scouts is the same with all the nests?

2. What behavior is different and how is it different?

3. Can you see any advantages of one kind of behavior over another?

4. Is there any behavior of the ants that seems useless or even harmful to them? Explain.

5. Answer the same questions in regard to the behavior of the ants that follow the scent trails of the pheromones to the food sources.

6. If ants act differently in their behavior after touching or smelling some pheromones than others, does your examination of these pheromones under a good microscope show you any differences in color or appearance? If so, possibly describe or color photograph these pheromones under the microscope and be sure you have each description or photograph numbered by nest and attached by number to notes that describe the different kinds of behavior.

7. Can you write any hypotheses that would explain fairly fully the meaning of ant behavior as shown by your observations? If so, test each one carefully by repeated observations and experiments until you can establish, if possible, which hypothesis most fits the facts.

There are many other questions that could be asked. Think of them.

This is the kind of research that eventually could lead to the writing of a scientific paper to explain your discoveries. Your first experiences in carrying out research will probably not warrant this, but keep trying.

A Suggested Laboratory Project

This project, like the one preceding it, is purely a suggestion. By going into it fairly thoroughly I am giving you a framework to use as an outline for how you could do work of this sort in many different fields. You can develop and grow with your own projects. Many similar laboratory projects are explained in other books (see Suggested References, Appendix C).

Often laboratory projects can get rather expensive, so I am giving one here that can be done in your own backyard quite easily. Let us suppose that you live in central Nebraska and are going to study the habitat preferences, habitat influence on behavior, and interaction of behavior of two species of pocket mice: the plains pocket mouse, *Perognathus flavescens*, and the hispid pocket mouse, *Perognathus hispidus*. These two mice are common in the Nebraska plains, the first mainly in short grass plains with sandy soil, the second in several different habitats, including short grass plains but with less sandy soil, also along fence rows and in cultivated areas. The two mice are quite different in appearance, the plains pocket mouse being quite small (2¼ to 2¾ inches), pale yellowish in color with a white belly, while the hispid is much larger (4½ to 5 inches), with speckled, yellowish and brownish rough hair.

In your backyard or other near locality dig an area of about 5 square meters or not less than 4, down to about 2 decimeters below the present surface. Surround the whole area with a wire fence about 6 decimeters high and with mesh across both top and bottom, the openings all too small for the smallest mouse to get out. Fix doors, however, for easy access to the cage on both top and sides. Make a wire fence down the middle of this area, cutting the cage area into two halves. In one half use sandy soil and replant the area with the equivalent of a short grass prairie, bringing in sod from such a prairie and placing it in the depression you have dug to fit. Make it as natural as possible, including a few rocks. In the other half produce a weed patch similar to one that might be found on the border of a cultivated field, by removing the sod of such patch to your cage. Arrange it as naturally as possible. You will keep the weed patch sufficiently well watered to keep it in the condition it would be if near cultivated land that was watered by sprinklers. The other half you would water only enough to make sure the short grass did not die. Be sure the whole cage, top, bottom, and four sides, has no escape holes.

Build two glass-sided and glass-covered observation boxes, about 10 centimeters thick, ⅔ meter high, and 1 meter long, with holes from their two ends leading into both habitat sides of the cage, the entrances just large enough for each species of mouse to crawl through. (See figure 4–4.) Sliding doors should be fixed al-

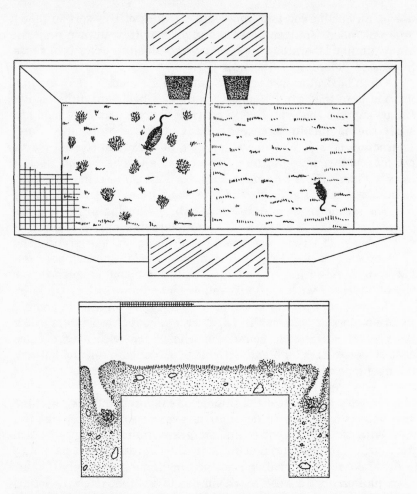

Figure 4-4. The small plains pocket mouse (*Perognathus flavescens*) and the larger, rougher looking hispid pocket mouse (*P. hispidus*) dwell in neighboring habitats in the Great Plains. The experimental cage layout shown is made to research their reactions to different habitats and to each other. *Above:* view from top. *Below:* detail of cross section, showing underground tunnels and nests of the two species in side boxes. Note smaller entranceway for plains pocket mouse to keep hispid pocket mouse from entering. (Judith Hennessey)

lowing you to close and open at will these four entrance ways. In the bottom of each observation box have at least a half meter of dirt so that the mice can dig holes into the dirt to make nests below the ground level, putting sandy loam-type dirt into the box for the plains mouse, and friable, more humus-type dirt into the box for the hispid mouse. Boxes should have hinged wooden covers on top that can be lifted to put in food and water when necessary. The boxes should be weatherproof and covered during the day over the glass on both sides so that all light can be shut off from the nests. This can be taken off at night so the activity of the mice can be observed under red light, which should not disturb them. Now you can start your rather simple experiments, as follows:

1. Capture specimens of both mice, necessarily a male and female of each species, in live traps, and put each pair into the proper observation box, making sure by their actions that they are male and female and are compatible. Keep each pair in its observation box about a week to let them get thoroughly used to it, keeping them supplied with seeds for food and with water. It may take a good deal longer, however, before they will decide to dig a nest in the dirt at the bottom of their box.

2. Open the gate for each pair of mice that leads into the proper habitat, the plains pocket mice going into the short grass habitat, and the hispid pocket mice going into the weed patch habitat. Let them explore each for about a week and get to know each other on opposite halves of the cage, but do not allow them together at all. Observe both species at regular periods day and night, and make careful notes of everything they do, including photographs of their different actions if possible. You can observe them at night in the observations boxes with red light to see if they are digging nest holes.

3. For the next week, keep the hispid mice in their observation box, but allow the plains mice access to both halves of the cage, and carefully observe both pairs of mice, taking careful notes at regular intervals during this time. Did the plains mice show any preferences for habitats? How different did they act in the weed patch than in the short grass habitat?

4. For the fourth week, reverse the situation and let the hispid mice into both halves of the cage. Observe and answer the same questions.

5. For the fifth week, allow the plains mice into the weed patch half of the cage, while the hispid mice are allowed into the short grass habitat only. Observe carefully. Do the mice show dislike in any way for these reverse habitats? What is their reaction to each other through the wire mesh? Do they feed as well?

6. For the sixth week, allow both pairs of mice access to both halves of the cage at the same time. Observe carefully both day and night. Do they avoid each other? Does one kind of mice try to attack the other, and if so, which, and what do the attacked mice

do? Does either pair during this week show any marked preference for one kind of habitat over the other?

7. During the seventh week, allow the hispid mice access to both habitats, but limit the plains mice to just the short grass habitat. Observe carefully, and photograph unusual activity. Do the hispid mice force the plains mice to stay in their observation box? If so, how? If not, why not?

8. During the eighth week, allow the prairie mice access to both habitats, but limit the hispid mice to just the weed patch habitat. What happens now? Describe everything in detail and photograph if useful. Do the hispid mice limit the plains mice to the short grass habitat? If so, how?

9. For the ninth week allow both species in both habitats at once and see what happens.

In spite of the attempt to make the habitats as natural as possible, and this can be done best, of course, by having a larger size cage, it must be admitted that this experiment may be somewhat artificial, as it is hard to duplicate true natural conditions. However, it does have the advantage of easy observation of the animals both day and night, and by night with the use of red light in their nests. It may be that some very interesting things can be learned. By making the holes into the prairie mouse observation box too small for the hispid mouse to enter, we protect the smaller mouse from possible annihilation by the larger mouse, but close observation will show how much this is true. The smaller mouse may be too fast a dodger and runner for the larger mouse anyway. If any mouse is killed or otherwise dies during this experiment, try to replace it immediately with a mouse of the same sex and species, but be sure in any case that the new pair is compatible.

Many questions need to be asked about this experiment. Here are a few samples. See if you can think of several others.

1. What patterns of behavior if any showed that each species had a strong preference for one habitat over the other?

2. How do you account for these patterns in relation to the colors, size, and shape of the two different species?

3. What particular adaptations did you see either or both species making towards a particular habitat?

4. Did either species show any mating or nesting behavior and what conclusions can you come to as to why not if they did not?

5. If there was nesting and mating behavior what did it show about the behavior and adaptability of each species?

6. What were the interactions in behavior of the two species

when they were allowed to come into direct contact with each other?

7. Were their methods and times and places of feeding sufficiently different so that they did not come into direct competition for the available food and water?

8. Or was it obvious that they were able to get along better if each was kept separate in its own favorite habitat?

9. What behavior changes occurred over the entire time of the experiment and what seemed to cause these changes?

At the end of this experiment, which, of course, could be continued longer if the experiment seemed to be answering many questions, you should write down as many hypotheses as possible to explain the behavior you saw over the whole period. To be complete the experiment should then be continued or improved upon in the size and variety of habitats to see if you can find out by further observation which of your hypotheses on the behavior of these creatures most fits the facts.

It would be wise in both the projects outlined in this chapter for you to present to a qualified scientist your typed major observations and the conclusions you have reached in order to get his reactions and criticisms. Be extremely courteous in approaching him and make sure he is willing to do this for you. In time you should be able to conduct and describe a scientific project that would be worthy of publication in a scientific journal.

With this you will have had in this chapter a beginning introduction and hopefully some experimental and observational experience that will prepare you for deeper involvement, if you are interested, in the science of ethology. Many books mentioned in the classified Suggested References, Appendix C, will lead you more deeply into this field. One way to learn such experience quickly is to take into your home some young animals of wild background and rear them like your own children over time. I assure you that you will learn much about wild animal nature from this experience, even though it will be in artificial surroundings. Of course, if you can handle them well enough to take them into the fields and woods, you will deepen your experience even more. But study books on such wild animal care, and handle them with wisdom. Those with sharp teeth and claws can be dangerous, as well as those with horns; however, our family has had some marvelous experiences with such wild creatures.

5

EXPLORING THE PLANT KINGDOM

It is impossible in this short chapter to do justice to such an immense subject, but it is important for the explorer naturalist to realize some of the possibilities for exciting exploration among plants. I have many dear memories of years at both the University of California at Berkeley and at Stanford University, studying the green kingdom at the feet of such fine taxonomic botanists as Dr. Herbert Mason at Berkeley, and Dr. Leroy Abrams and Mrs. G. F. Ferris of Stanford, as well as the wonderful plant geographer, Dr. Carl Sauer at Berkeley. Throughout the years their early encouragement has kept me interested in every plant I have met in North and Central America.

It is vital for every explorer naturalist to have an interest in and a steadily increasing knowledge of the world of plants, as they tie in closely with animals, as is shown in the concluding chapters of this book on the major habitats of North America. Indeed, to understand animals thoroughly it is necessary to know the plants with which they are associated, since these plants not only supply the basis of all animal food, for plants must be translated into meat to supply the meat eaters, but they give protection and shelter in one way or another to nearly every animal. It is to be hoped that at least some of the explorer naturalists who read this book will become especially interested in plants and take up their explorations. By such balance of endeavor is our knowledge of the natural world rounded out, and there is plenty of adventure to be found with plants.

PLANT BEHAVIOR

We usually think of animals behaving in various ways but not plants. However, if we really investigate this we can soon see that plants also have forms of behavior. Most behave simply by growing and then producing flowers, fruits, and seeds, but the kinds of plant parts they have usually show the plants' special relationships with their environment. Plants spread in numbers in an environment they are well adapted to, while they shrink in numbers in an environment that is unfavorable to them. Some plants appear to be much more adaptable then others and spread into several different habitats, whereas certain plants are limited to just one habitat; some are very rare, while others are extremely plentiful. These are all elements of plant behavior and they pose many interesting questions that the plant explorer can help find the answers to. Why indeed are some plants rare and some numerous, some very adaptable and others much less so? There must be reasons and we can search for these reasons.

Plant migration alone is an immense field for exploration. Plants cannot walk or run like animals, but they do have many fascinating ways of spreading their seeds, some to be carried on the wind, others by birds or animals or man, but some plant migrators totally tantalize the botanists by appearing in strange places suddenly hundreds of miles from their usual habitat. Other, more rare plants, may give equal tantalization by being found in only two or three widely separated localities, maybe hundreds of miles apart, and no sign of them in between. Why? There are many such mysterious puzzles, and maybe you can find one of the answers.

Plant population dynamics involves some of the most fantastic plant behavior of all. Plants give off literally billions of seeds every year, but only a tiny fraction of these live to maturity, especially among trees. A newly dropped tree seed faces a most terrifying array of enemies or conditions that wait to destroy it. Cold can bring death, as can too much wetness or too much dryness, fungi and insects are ready to attack it, birds and animals may crush it or eat it, other plants try to crowd it out and overwhelm it with roots or shade, and the number of enemies can go on and on. A fine botanist, Dr. Henry A. Gleason, in his excellent book, *The Natural Geography of Plants*,[1] has estimated that one mature sugar maple

---

[1] Henry A. Gleason and Arthur Cronquist, *The Natural Geography of Plants* (New York, N.Y.: Columbia University Press, 1964).

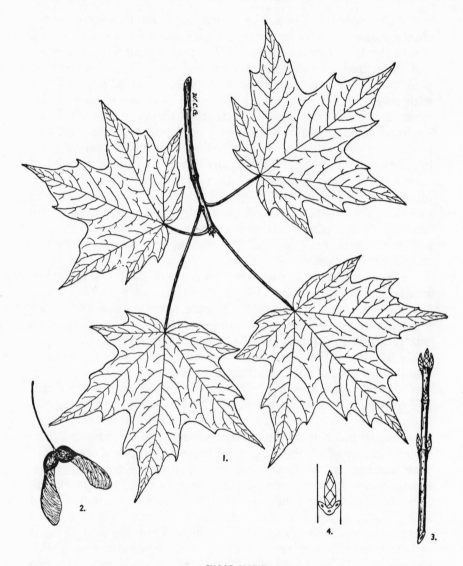

SUGAR MAPLE

1. Branch with mature leaves.
2. Fruit.
3. Winter twig.
4. Detail of bud and leaf scar.

Figure 5–1. Sugar maple (*Acer saccharum*). (From William Carey Grimm, *The Book of Trees*, 2nd ed., Harrisburg, Pennsylvania: Stackpole Books, 1962, p. 340.)

tree (figure 5–1) in an eastern forest occupies about 400 square feet of the forest floor in which about 4,000 young sugar maple trees spring up every year, producing in the total lifetime of the tree around 1,400,000 seeds. Out of these seedlings only about 70,000 probably last into the second year, and maybe 1,400 of these live to around 10 years, but of these only perhaps 35 grow over 20 feet high, fighting for the light up through dense shade. In the long, fierce struggle for life, perhaps 2 reach an age of over 150 years, and 1 of these will be extremely lucky if it lives to full maturity. Think of the waste, but also think of the food that has gone to millions of other organisms.

On the other hand, if an old tree decays and dies or is chopped or sawed down by man, suddenly where it has been hordes of new young plants leap up to take its place in the fresh sunlight. Again a fierce struggle comes to determine who the winners will be, some of them temporary for a few years, but only one or two for the centuries. Yet, under the thickest shade there are some plants especially adapted to that shade and they flourish where other plants would die. Question? There are a myriad questions to be asked and some day to be answered about population dynamics by future explorer botanists.

Plant ecology and climatology is another giant field for exploration. How do plants adapt to different environments and climates? We know there is a line across southern Florida north of which tropical plants are in danger from unusual frosts, while south of it they are generally safe. Always they creep north of that line during comparatively warm years and always they are driven back when the cold years come. We know that climates go through long-range and short-range rhythms or cycles between wet and dry, cold and warm years. What do plants do about these cycles? Botanists are trying to find the answer and plantsmen everywhere are looking for economically valuable plants that will be able to withstand the cycles by adaptation and live when other plants die.

My wife was raised on a cattle ranch in the Great Plains of southern Colorado. She was there as a girl during the great drouth of the 1930s when farmers and ranchers stared with hopeless eyes at their dying crops and pastures, when family after family was forced off the land and back to the cities. She tells a dramatic story of survival that drives home man's eternal need to understand the plants he is dealing with, and the disaster that comes when he does not think things through.

Over wide areas where she lived in those days most grass simply vanished because of the drouth and because of overgrazing by cattle, forced to eat everything down to the roots. However, in many parts the tree cactus increased greatly in numbers because of three reasons of better adaptation to the drouth: (1) It was able to store water in its thick, fleshy leaves and so continue to use this water to stay alive during the dry months; (2) its leaves were covered with thorns so the cattle and other grazing animals could not eat it; and (3) it was generally considered of no use by man and so was let alone.

Human beings of the area reacted to the drouth and to the plants in different ways. Some simply gave up when the drouth came, seeing no way to succeed, and moved to the cities. Others decided to stick it out when they were told by government agricultural experts that they could feed their cattle on the tree cacti by going around with blow torches and burning the thorns off. But this caused the cattle to become addicted to cacti, so they not only ate the cacti with burned-off thorns, but also started eating those with thorns, usually getting sick from the effects of the thorns and often dying. Many of the people who did this were forced to leave the plains when too many of their cattle died.

My wife's mother and father, Mr. & Mrs. William Black, felt desperate. Their ranch supported only a little over 100 head of cattle in the first place, so that only a few would need to die to wipe out their future and drive them from the plains, too. They suddenly realized that the reason the cattle of other ranchers were eating the cacti that had not had thorns burned off was because the unburned and the burned cacti looked so much alike. But there was good food value in the cactus if it could be given to the cattle without their recognizing it as cactus. So they devised a new method of treating it. They cut great bunches of it and pitched it into the back of a pickup. Then they made a huge pile at the ranch headquarters and ran the cactus down a conveyer belt to a grinding machine that ground it into little pieces. They dumped this ground-up mash into a huge pit, covered the cacti with straw and a layer of dirt, and left it to ferment for about two weeks. Then the fermented, ground-up cactus silage, looking no longer the least bit like growing cacti, was shoveled into long troughs to which the cattle were led to feed. They enjoyed this soft feed tremendously and it had a lot of food value. At the same time these cattle did not associate the fermented catcus mash with the original cactus and so did not try to feed on cacti. By using their brains and thinking things through about plants, the family at the ranch was saved from the drouth.

Recently I learned that some years back cacti were imported to Australia and became a pest, covering many thousands of acres of land and driving many Australian ranchers off their lands. It is too bad they, too, did not investigate the nature of this plant and its great food value for stock when put to use properly. Instead, they spent millions trying to fight the cactus and finally imported an insect pest into Australia that killed it. What a terrible waste of effort and money. The whole story shows us that adaptation is the key to survival for human beings as well as for plants. In a way we can think of such adaptation by humans as simply using the scientific method and trying every avenue of research until you find the right one that answers the problem. This is another lesson to you as an explorer naturalist to be determined when you are tackling a problem in science—not to give up until you have found the answer.

Some plants sing to us similar stories of adaptation and courage and stamina. The white-barked pine of the White Mountains in eastern California struggles for life against cold, high winds and stinging ice at the edge of timberline on 14,000-foot peaks, but has somehow found a way to adapt to these rigid conditions even though often its lifeline is a thin, little ribbon of cambium layer on the southeast side of a huge, otherwise-dead trunk. With such tenacity to hang on, it may live to be over 5,000 years old, the oldest living thing on earth. There are many other plants that can tell us similar stories of heroism.

SUGGESTED EXAMPLES OF PLANTS TO EXPLORE

Here I am giving you some interesting examples of the innumerable plants of this world that are worthy of being researched. To prepare for this research, besides reading this book, it would be wise to investigate books on plants, probably a good general book and then another book(s) on the plants of your neighborhood. Several of these are listed in the Suggested References, Appendix C. Remember, if this book were devoted to nothing but the study of plants, it would still give you only a beginning look into this immense field. There is indeed much to learn. Below, the plants are described as they are placed in their major divisions, but remember there are many other plants and parts to these divisions, as you can find out from any good book on botany. Before you start any plant research project it would be a good thing to review once more chapters 1 and 2, where you are given elementary instruction on how to start and carry out scientific research.

DIVISION THALLOPHYTA—Leafless, stemless, and flowerless plants.

Subdivision PHYCOPHYTA—The algae. Plants are green or bluegreen, making food by photosynthesis; generally aquatic.

Phylum Schizophyta. The bluegreen algae. Mostly bluegreen, but some becoming red. These grow rapidly where sewerage pollutes water. They have no nuclei in the plant cells.

Suggested research: Find an example of *Oscillatoria* species in the water of a pond or stream where they appear as slender, unbranched, long, tiny filaments of cells, blue-green in color (has to be seen under 10X magnifying power if possible). Bring to your home or laboratory in a large jar(s), and experiment with what kinds of polluted waters (garbage, sewerage, etc.) will cause them to grow, noting exactly how fast growth is hour by hour in your notebook, and associated with what kinds of pollution. Ask questions about this whole process and try to answer them from your observations and experiments.

Subdivision MYCOPHYTA—The fungi. No green in color and hence no chlorophyll. All live off dead or living plants. Includes rusts, smuts, mushrooms, puffballs, etc.

Class Basiodomycetes. Spores borne on clubs. Includes most mushrooms.

Suggested research: Study the sulphur polypore (*Polyporus sulphurus*), a yellow-colored bracket fungus that grows on both live and dead trees, liking conifers, oak, chestnut, walnut, apple, etc. It is a pest on living trees and kills them in time by running its mycelium threads down through wood and consuming it, changing it to a reddish-brown charcoal. Find out as much as possible the .

full story of how this plant destroys trees, and carefully check its growth in different kinds of trees to find if any have some resistance to it, and investigate if there are other fungi or bacteria that may attack and control this fungus. Ask as many questions as you can and try to find their answers by your research.

PHYLUM SPERMATOPHYTA—Seed-bearing plants.

Class Gymnospermae. Conifers and their relatives. Has ovules hidden inside an ovary, but born nakedly, usually in cones.

Order Coniferales. Conifers. Woody shrubs or trees with needle-like leaves.

Suggested research: If you live on the coast of Washington, Oregon, or northern California, study the maritime lodgepole pine or scrub pine (*Pinus contorta*). It has two comparatively short needles in each bunch, about 2 inches long, comes close over the seeds, often for many years, hence is called a closed-cone pine. Examine this pine to see how it has adapted to a maritime seashore habitat and in what ways, also checking from the literature and from observation how the closed cones operate to let the seeds free, and just what triggers this freeing. Hypothesize on the reasons for this and check against the facts from your observations and from those of others. Ask what questions you can and try to find the answers.

Class Angiospermae. Flowering plants, with completely enclosed ovaries; leaves parallel or net veined, and usually deciduous in temperate lands.

Subclass **Monocotyledonae.** The monocotyledons. Leaves with parallel veins; flower parts usually in threes; seeds with one cotyledon; stems hollow or with bundles scattered throughout.

Order Palmales. The palms. Foliage is palm-like and spreading; the leaves usually very large and stiff.

Suggested research: Study the palmetto palm (*Sabal palmetto*), a palm tree up to 80 feet high, with leaves up to 8 feet long, broad spreading; often forming dense thickets, especially when leveled by fire and regrown. Has twisted stems underground to preserve it from fires. This highly fire-adaptive tree can be found between North Carolina and Florida at low elevations near fresh or salt water where the soil is very sandy. Take a 1 kilometer long, ½ kilometer wide area that covers many palmettos and study their fire adaptation in the area by mapping and checking every tree, noting any fire effects and what they have caused. Determine how many have been struck by fire and what the percentage of this fire effect on them is. By inquiry of residents who have seen them struck by fire, and of botanists at a nearby university or college, determine how you can hypothesize the ways their fire resistance works, then check these hypotheses against any facts you can uncover. Ask questions and try to find the answers.

Order Orchidales. Orchids. Extremely irregular and beautiful flowers, the one to two stamens grown together with the pistil, making a column. Ovary inferior.

Suggested Research: Study the broad-lipped twayblade (*Ophyrys convallarioides*). This rather small flower is found in the Canadian Life Zone from Alaska to Newfoundland and south to Vermont and Michigan and to southern California in the mountains. Its two round oval or ovate leaves are three to nine nerved; the three to fifteen greenish-yellow flowers have very long, two-lobed lips. Research the relationship of these flowers to their insect pollinators, and how the flower is best adapted to fit a particular insect(s). How is the insect attracted—by smell, color, or other? Hypothesize the nature of the relationships and test against facts by observation and experiments.

Subclass **Dicotyledonae.** Net-veined plants or dicotyledons. Flowering parts generally in fives, rarely in fours; stems have the bundles arranged in rings around a pith, or they are woody with an outer bark; leaves are net veined; seeds have two cotyledons.

Order Fagales. Oaks and birches. Male or staminate flowers have tassel-like structures called aments; fruit usually an oval, hard nut with cap called an acorn; wood very hard.

Suggested research: Study the scarlet oak (*Quercus coccinea*). This very lovely tree is up to 100 feet or more in height, with 6-inch-long leaves, having seven to nine deep lobes ending in sharp points. The acorn is reddish-brown, shining on the deep bowl-like cap or cup. Investigate its freedom from insect pests, comparing with other oaks, and trying to find what exudates or other means the oak has to repel the pests. Hypothecate why it is so free from pests and check each hypothesis against the facts. Ask questions and try to find the answers.

Order Ranunculales. Buttercups and their relatives. Flower contains many single and distinct carpels, or carpels sometimes solitary or united; stamens more numerous than sepals.

Suggested research: Study the American lotus (*Nelumbo pentapetala*). This very distinctive plant is found from Nebraska, Minnesota, and southern Ontario south to the Gulf states. It has huge, shield-like leaves, 2 feet or more across, raised out of the surface of a pond, from an extraordinary root stock that may be more than 50 feet long. The flowers are pale yellow, lily-like and about 10 inches across with numerous petals. Research the potential of this plant as a food for mankind, studying the way it can be used, grown, and harvested. There is probably a food source here as yet little touched, as the root stocks, seeds, leaf stalks, and young leaves are all edible. Ask as many questions as you can and try to find the answers.

Order Ericales. Heaths, huckleberry, Indian pipe plants. Stamens do not touch the corolla. Perennial shrubs and herbs having mainly evergreen leaves; the Indian pipe is a white saprophytic plant that lives on dead organic matter, without using chlorophyll.

Suggested research: Study Indian pipe (*Monotropa uniflora*). Up to 10 inches high, white to pinkish when young, but turns blackish with age and then gradually brown; the long, slender stems support each a single drooping 1-inch long flower, which appears like a pipe, but gradually the flowers straighten as they get ready to produce capsule-like fruit. The roots actually get food from dead plants with the aid of the mycelium of a fungi that covers them in the rotting wood. This is a case of symbiosis between two entirely different kinds of plants, and could be researched to find out, if possible, why and how it happened, and exactly how the two plants help each other. Ask many questions about this and try to find the answers.

Order Campanulales. Bell flower and aster order. With rare exceptions the anthers are all united, and the petals are united into a sheath or bell. The aster or sunflower family usually has heads of many small flowers. Examples are gourds, pumpkins, lobelias, sunflowers.

Suggested research: Study gumweed (*Grindelia squarrosa*), a small herb to 2 feet high, found from New York to New Mexico and Manitoba. Leaves serrate, alternate, with clasping bases; flower head with yellow ray flower, each about 1 inch long, all having a sticky, gluey feel; fruits have two stiff awns on top. Commonly poisonous to stock where soil has selenium in it. Where found, the plant is supposed to be a good index species that shows overgrazing of pasture land. Research the plant's connection with the soil and other plants to find out just how good an index plant it is, including what are the best conditions for growth, and the effect of man and stock animals on it. Hypothesize how it operates in relation to overgrazing and test this with experiments and observations. Ask as many questions as you can and try to find the answers.

Part II

Major Habitats of North America and Their Exploration

INTRODUCTION TO
PART II

The remaining chapters deal with some of the major habitats of North America. To cover even one in any completeness would take a good-sized book, so these chapters are only introductions to the common animals and plants and the physiography of each habitat, giving you a few suggested ideas of how they can be profitably explored. An overview of the major habitats of our continent is of considerable benefit to the explorer of any single habitat so he can compare them with the one he is exploring and know which of the animals and plants he is watching have adapted to other habitats. Thus, as discussed earlier, the California ground squirrel of northwestern, mountainous California reacts in an almost opposite way to its environment than does the same species in the hot and dry, southern San Joaquin Valley area, and it is far more interesting and much more easy to understand the animal and its potentialities by seeing it as it has adapted to two or more habitats. How plants adapt to such different habitats is of similar interest in understanding the wonderful adaptiveness of life.

Since the basis of most habitats are the plant communities that set their major tone and character, it is vital for the explorer naturalist to learn more about how to identify plants, how to understand their place in each community, and how they affect the animal life. In the pages that follow pictures are given of several of the major habitats as if we were looking at all the common animals and plants at one time. This, of course, is impossible to see in the

140

natural situation, but is necessary in this book to get a beginning picture of the whole habitat. The artist has drawn the different animals and plants as much as possible in their natural part of the habitat.

In the chapters that follow it is necessary for the pictures to carry as much of the message about the appearance of the habitat as possible. Look them over carefully so you can grasp the general makeup of the habitat, and also study them as you read the suggested possible explorations of each habitat. These suggestions will necessarily be brief because of the need to keep this book as compact as possible, but you can refer to my earlier, more detailed descriptions of scientific projects to help you understand how to develop such projects with imagination and initiative.

Insects and other invertebrates are so numerous and of so many thousands of different species in these various habitats that it would take a complete and large book to cover even the common ones. Therefore, it is not possible here to do more than mention them in the suggested projects, but the Suggested References, Appendix C, lists other books that deal with them and will help you identify the common kinds. You will find, however, that even these books are only the beginning in an immense field, and that, if you deal very extensively with any invertebrates, you will need help in identifying them from the taxonomists at universities, colleges, and museums.

An exception to the above statement occurs in this book when I deal with life in a pond and along the seashore, as in these two habitats the invertebrates form the dominant life.

6

BRUSH OR SCRUB GROUP OF HABITATS, INCLUDING DESERTS

In North America the form of a brushland varies from the rather soft foliage of the coastal sage scrub and northwestern coast scrub, which are influenced by the almost daily moisture brought by fog from the Pacific Ocean, to the harsh, rigid, and thorn-like brush of the interior California chaparral, whose plants have to struggle to stay alive through the long, dry heat of summer and fall, to the still more spiny, but also more succulent desert scrub of the interior lowlands of the Southwest. The small leaves of most of these plants protect them from losing too much moisture to the heat of the sun, while the spines and thorns protect against their being browsed by deer, wild burros, and wild sheep. Only the chaparral and desert scrub are pictured and described in some detail.

WESTERN CHAPARRAL AND BRUSH COMMUNITIES

Northern Coastal Scrub

The northern coastal scrub extends along the coast from the neighborhood of San Francisco Bay north into Oregon and Washington. Rainfall is about 25 to 100 inches a year, with fog prevalent during the summer. Cow parsnip (*Heracleum lanatum*) and coyote brush (*Bacharis pilularis*) are two of the most common plants.

Coastal Sage Scrub

The coastal sage scrub habitat is along the coast from San Francisco south to Baja California. Rainfall ranges from 10 to 20 inches, but the almost-daily fog during the dry season keeps the brush better supplied with moisture than that of the true chaparral. Two of the dominant bushes are California sagebrush (*Artemisia californica*), and the California buckwheat brush (*Eriogonum fasiculatum*).

True Chaparral

The small, leathery leaves and the stiff, sometimes spine-like branches of this habitat are adapted to the very hot, dry conditions of the summer and fall when scarcely any moisture falls in this area. Many of the plants are fire resistant by having deep roots from which new plants can grow after a fire has passed over. Rainfall is about 10 to 25 inches and there is little or no fog. In southern California the chaparral covers most of the hills, with the larger bushes on the north sides, but in northern California and Oregon, the chaparral usually covers the south-facing slopes while oak woodlands or sometimes conifers are common on the north-facing slopes.

The western chaparral community is very different from somewhat similar brushlands in the higher mountains of the West and in the East due to the effect of the sharply marked, wet and dry seasons and the lack of severe cold or snow in the winter, although light snows occasionally fall on the higher hills. Thus, the main part of the rainy season from December to the end of February is more like a spring, because then the rains cause new plant growth and there are both cool and warm days. Birds and small mammals are active and not subdued as in the more wintery areas. From March through May the days become comparatively warm and mild, with only occasional rains, and this is the time of the greatest possible activity in the chaparral and should really be considered as equivalent to an eastern summer, for the birds are nesting and the mammals are most active of all, while the insects and reptiles swarm forth to their fullest in the dance of life. But the terrible heat and dryness of the June-to-August period subdues most life; many small mammals and many insects go underground, while most birds move to damper areas and the reptiles come out mainly at night. It can be thought of as a kind of fall. September, October, and November then appear to act like an odd, little winter, with life at a low ebb, waiting for the first rains. This makes the whole seasonal change around three months ahead of the East.

While most of the plants shown in figure 6–1 are definitely chaparral plants and rare elsewhere, most of the animal life overlaps into other habitats, the wren-tit alone being a completely chaparral creature, although the California striped whipsnake, too, likes mainly this habitat.

Suggested research: 1. Determine the insect and other invertebrate food on which the spotted skunk lives, the percentages of each kind, and how this animal may aid certain plants by killing their insect pests. Check this out in the brush.

2. Take two different 10-meter square areas in the chaparral and map them carefully for percentages of each kind of plant prevalent in each, the number of invertebrates per square meter on the average, and their distribution in relation to the plants in the four seasons of the year. From this hypothesize on the effects of the weather or climate at these different times of the year on both plant and invertebrate life. Ask questions and find the answers.

The Rocky Mountain Brushland

The Rocky Mountain brushland is made up of deciduous shrubs of 2 to 12 feet in height, appearing in some areas as scattered clumps and in others as solid masses. Rainfall ranges from about 10 to 20 inches, with most in summer, and with much more snow in winter than in the California chaparral. The mean temperature is about 44 degrees, with a maximum of around 98 degrees, and a minimum of around −32 degrees. Thus, life is greatly limited by the cold in winter, and summer is the most active time for life. A similar brushland is found in the Sierras and the Cascades, and in all three mountain ranges it is most likely to appear in areas burnt over by fires. The mountain mahoganies (*Cercocarpus* species) and various scrub oaks (*Quercus* species), are the most common plants.

Sagebrush and Shadscale Deserts of the Great Basin

Altitude in the sagebrush and shadscale deserts ranges from about 4,000 to 8,000 feet, with a low rainfall of around 4 to 8 inches, plus light snow in winter. Summer temperatures range past 100 degrees, with a winter low of around −10 degrees. Life is most active in these deserts when rains appear in the spring and summer; otherwise many creatures either migrate to higher areas in dry times or burrow in the ground. Common sagebrush (*Artemisia tridentata*) is the most common plant of the northern part of this desert, and furnishes both food and shelter for many animals, while the common shadscale (*Atriplex confertifolia*) is the dominant plant to the south and at lower elevations.

TRUE DESERT SCRUB COMMUNITY

Colorado-Sonora Desert

The Colorado-Sonora is the low desert (usually beneath 2,000 feet) of southeastern California and southwestern Arizona, but extending also down into northwestern Mexico mainly in the Province of Sonora. (See figure 6–2.) It has extreme heat, up to 135 degrees in summer, with practically no frost even in winter, although temperatures may drop rarely as low as 20 degrees. Precipitation is extremely low, but variable, from 0 to 8 inches, with the higher fall at the higher elevations, probably averaging around 4 inches a year. Thus, dryness and heat are the great limiters of life, and plants must find ways to store water as do the cacti, or use deep roots, as do the mesquites, to reach down to underground water sources that come from the mountains. Animals through much of the year escape the worst heat by coming out at dusk, at night, or in the very early morning, and many rodents get along without the need for drinking water, getting it instead by a special physiological process directly from plant foods, particularly seeds. Much life also concentrates around the few springs where such beautiful plants as the Washington palms grow. The winter is actually more like spring, as there is usually more moisture then, and the lesser amount of heat allows more life to be active during the day. Most birds begin to nest in February. There are sometimes summer thunderstorms that may bring quick torrents of rain that suddenly fill the dry, desert arroyos, and plants must adapt to withstand these floods, and animals to escape them quickly.

Figure 6–1. California chaparral, showing its common animals and plants. (Phyllis Thompson)

Turkey Vulture

Poor-will

Calif. Quail

Wren-Tit

Bewick Wren

Big-berried Manzanita

Calif. Thrasher

Gray Fox

Shaggy-barked Manzanita

Pileolated Warbler

Fox Sparrow

Calif. Mountain Mahogany

Spotted Towhee

Ring-tailed Cat

Western Rattlesnake

Bush-Tit

Opossum

Western Fence Lizard

Gopher Snake

Scrub Jay

Mountain Lion

Coast Horned Lizard

Calif. Ground Squirrel

Dusky-footed Woodrat

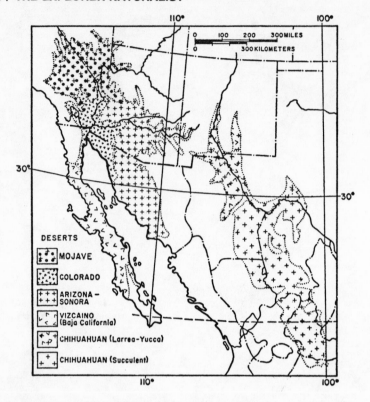

Figure 6–2. Map showing distribution of the hot deserts of the Southwest. (From Victor E. Shelford, *The Ecology of North America,* Urbana, Illinois: University of Illinois Press, 1963, with kind permission of the publishers.)

Common plants and animals of the Colorado (southeast California) branch of this desert are shown in figure 6–3.

Invertebrates are quite numerous at night or early morning, particularly large scorpions, large centipedes, solpugids or sun spiders, pseudo-scorpions, tarantulas and wolf spiders, numerous grasshoppers and desert katydids, ground and tiger beetles, tenebrionid or darkling beetles, plant bugs such as shield bugs and damsel bugs, mole crickets and other kinds of crickets, different kinds of harvester ants (mostly *Camponotus, Arphia, Myrmex,* and *Vermessor* species), numerous brightly colored flies and sand wasps (the latter digging holes in sandy places to put insect and spider prey they catch for their grubs), bright white, red, and orange or yellow velvet ants, many kinds of wild bees. etc.

Suggested research: 1. Take a flat, sandy area of about 30 square meters not too far from or too close to a water hole or spring and brush it clean of tracks every evening for one month, mapping the entire area over again each morning to show all the tracks made the night before. A *Field Guide to Animal Tracks*, by Olaus Murie,[1] will help you identify most of the tracks. Others you can make plaster casts of, or good sharp photographs, and send them to your nearest university or college biology department for identification (first asking permission). The daily mapping of track activity combined with some night study around the fringes of the area with a red, plastic-covered flashlight, watching the movements of creatures across the sand, will help you develop a series of patterns of night behavior of many different creatures that will give you keys to their lives. Describe everything observed carefully and at the close of your study, ask as many questions as you can; then try to answer them.

2. Make a comparative study of the hunting methods of the following invertebrate predators of the desert night: solpugids, scorpions, large centipedes, large hunting spiders and carabid beetles. This would have to be done mainly at night with a red-light flashlight, and wearing good boots for protection. Some questions to answer are: What are the favorite habitats and ecologic niches in which each kind of creature hunts? When the same kind of prey is attacked, how do their methods differ? What species seem to be the most successful hunter and why? Ask as many other questions as you can and try to answer them.

Mohave Desert

Elevation in the Mohave Desert is 1,500 to 4,000 feet; rainfall is less than 5 inches; temperature varies from 135 degrees in summer to 10 or 20 above in winter. There is very little snow. Winds are very strong in this desert, influencing life. Two outstanding plants are the Joshua tree (*Yucca brevifolia*) and the creosote bush (*Larrea divaricata*).

Sand Dune Deserts

The sand dune deserts form smaller enclaves inside all these

---

[1]Olaus J. Murie, *Field Guide to Animal Tracks* (Boston, Mass.: Houghton Mifflin Co., 1954).

Figure 6–3. General type of Colorado-Sonoran Desert, showing its common animals and plants. (Phyllis Thompson)

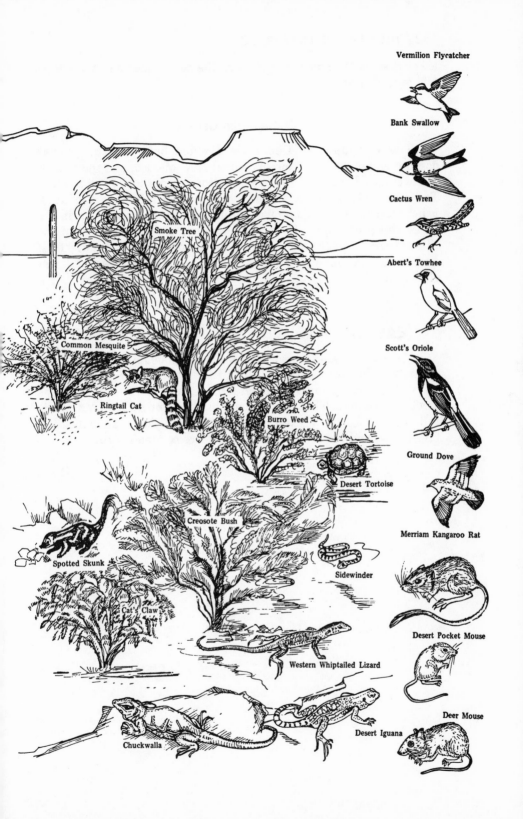

Vermilion Flycatcher

Bank Swallow

Cactus Wren

Abert's Towhee

Scott's Oriole

Ground Dove

Merriam Kangaroo Rat

Desert Pocket Mouse

Deer Mouse

Smoke Tree

Common Mesquite

Ringtail Cat

Burro Weed

Desert Tortoise

Creosote Bush

Spotted Skunk

Sidewinder

Cat's Claw

Western Whiptailed Lizard

Chuckwalla

Desert Iguana

lower deserts. Common animals are the sidewinder and the desert fringe-toed lizards.

Chihuahuan Desert

The Chihuahuan Desert is divided between the yucca-dominated northern section of central New Mexico, and the cactus- or succulent-dominated southern section in southern New Mexico, Texas west of the Pecos, and adjoining northern Mexico. Elevation is between 2,000 and 6,000 feet. Rainfall is between 3 inches in the lower elevations up to 16 inches at higher elevations. Most of the rainfall comes in the period from June through September; frost and occasional snow are prevalent in winter, but less at lower elevations.

EASTERN AND MIDWESTERN BRUSHLANDS

The eastern and midwestern brushlands usually move in temporarily in burnt or cut-over lands throughout the East and Midwest. They are so varied that no temperature or rainfall averages can be given here. They are favorite habitats for rabbits and, when tall enough, for the white-tailed deer. Hawthorns, crabapples, the black haw, and the scrub chestnut oak are common shrubs.

7

GRASSLAND GROUPS
OF HABITATS

The grassland habitats are more open than the others, with room for wide running as the antelope do, for high soaring by the hawks and eagles, with the special feel of vastness that is the Great Plains. In the grasslands animals and birds are less protected by cover, more on their own, dependent on their own powers in the open—swift running and swift flying. It is a place where the great herds and the great flocks used to be found, and where their remnants still call to us of past glories.

In this book I am arbitrarily making a boundary between eastern and midwestern grasslands on the one hand and western grasslands on the other hand: along the eastern edges of the Dakotas and Nebraska, swinging north in an arc to eastern Saskatchewan, while going south through the middle of Kansas, Oklahoma, and Texas. The basis for this division is that the plants to the west of this line are mainly xeric or short, dry country grasses, whereas the grasses to the east of this line are generally mesic-type, higher stemmed, and requiring moderate amounts of moisture most of the year. Actually the line is not that sharp and the mixed grass grasslands that extend for a hundred miles or more west of this border are made up of plants that are both xeric and mesic, so admittedly the division is very arbitrary. However, it is convenient for separating the mesic and xeric grasslands, for in this book my main descriptions combined with pictures are of the xeric, short grass grasslands of the Great Plains, and the mesic, tall grass

153

prairies of the Middle West, today mostly turned into farmlands. Other grasslands of North America are described briefly, but the connection of grasslands to animals is only dealt with in these two examples. (See figure 7–1.)

The grassland biome as a whole is quite different in its aspect and its effect on animal life over the forest biome, although not so

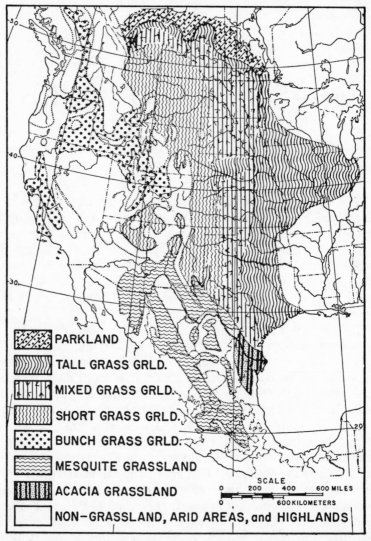

PARKLAND

TALL GRASS GRLD.

MIXED GRASS GRLD.

SHORT GRASS GRLD.

BUNCH GRASS GRLD.

MESQUITE GRASSLAND

ACACIA GRASSLAND

NON–GRASSLAND, ARID AREAS, and HIGHLANDS

SCALE
0 200 400 600 MILES
0 600 KILOMETERS

Figure 7–1. Map of the grassland communities of North America. (From Victor E. Shelford, *The Ecology of North America,* Urbana, Illinois: University of Illinois Press, 1963, p. 330, with kind permission of the publishers.)

widely separated from the brushland biome. It has a wider range of climate than the forest biome, including very cold, damp conditions in the north in Canada, where there may be only about three months of the year without frost, while far to the south in southwestern Texas and in Mexico or in California, there are grasslands with only a few days in the year when there is frost. It ranges from 40 inches or more of rainfall in the east to as little as 6 to 10 inches in parts of the Great Plains and in California.

In spite of this wide range in climate, the grasslands have a similar effect everywhere on animal life. In these wide-open spaces most large grassland animals, such as the antelope and buffalo, depend either on sharp eyesight and swift flight, as with the antelopes, or the protection of large size, horns, and numbers, as with the buffalo. Against high-powered rifles, of course, even the antelope have had little protection, while the buffalo were almost wiped from the surface of the earth. However, one animal that has swift running combined with the ability to hide in the grass is the jackrabbit, both black-tailed and white-tailed, which has been able to maintain its numbers despite man, and the clever coyote has done fairly well despite all the guns and traps and poison of man. The chief carnivore of the plains, however, the wolf, has almost completely disappeared from his ancient range, because although intelligent, he was too large to hide well and too dangerous to man's stock animals to be allowed to live.

The smaller mammals, particularly the rodents and the rabbits, have found the best escape from enemies in the grasslands and have been able to hide in holes in the ground, although two enemies, the weasel and the badger, have developed in one case a thin body form, and the other case, powerful digging legs to follow these creatures underground. The wise coyote follows the badger until the badger drives out a rabbit or ground squirrel from a hole and then seizes it. But it sometimes seems as though the coyote drives one of these animals into a hole where the badger is waiting his turn. If true, this would be called *mutualism*, a form of *commensalism* in which both animals benefit.

Birds in the grasslands are often swift and high fliers, particularly the swifts, swallows, and nighthawks that zoom through the air at high speed. Others are secretive hiders in the grass, like the longspurs and the sparrows, cleverly disguising their nests so they cannot be seen. Still others spend their nights in the woods along a stream, flying out into the grasslands during the day, as does the mourning dove. The burrowing owl goes underground with the rodents, sometimes perhaps eating them. Most of the hawks of this habitat are the buteos, usually having broad wings and broad, short tails that are meant for soaring while watching for prey far below out of sharp, far-seeing eyes. The other chief owl of the grasslands is the short-eared owl, who hunts by day, harrying rodents or rabbits. It prefers the marshlands where available along with the low-flying, longer-tailed marsh hawk. Another difference of the birds in the grasslands as opposed to those in the woods is that several grassland birds like to sing high in the air while flying, as does the horned lark, and the lark sparrow.

EASTERN AND MIDWESTERN GRASSLANDS

Tall and Mixed Grassland Prairies

The tall and mixed grassland prairies stretch from the western border of the eastern woodlands in Illinois and northwestern Indiana, as well as in northern and western Missouri, eastern Oklahoma and Texas, west to the eastern Dakotas, the northeast corner of Montana, the middle of Texas, Oklahoma, and Nebraska, and in a curve across central Saskatchewan and Alberta to the base of the Rockies. Annual precipitation of rain and snow varies from near 40 inches on its eastern boundary to an average of 20 inches in the west, but with only about 15 inches in the far northwest corner. Droughts, with their killing effect on much life, come more frequently in the west than in the east of this habitat. Temperature variations are much more extreme, from some −40 degrees and lower winter temperatures in the far north, to only about 10 degrees in lowest temperatures on a few days in the extreme south. Summer temperatures in most of the area frequently reach 100 degrees or over, but mostly in the south. Summers are also much more humid in the eastern half of this area, a good deal dryer to the west.

Common plants and animals of this grassland are shown in figure 7–2. Invertebrates, especially insects, are common during the summer.

Suggested research: 1. If you live near a game refuge, state park, abandoned farm, or other area where this grassland appears in its natural state, select a 50-square-meter area, and meticulously count the larger animals for the whole square, marking on a map where found, and also the larger plants, numbering and naming each. Do the same for the invertebrates and smaller plants for about five separate 1-meter-square areas, randomly selected (as described in chapter 1) in the same larger area. Find as nearby as you can a similar 50-meter square area that has been overgrazed by cattle or sheep, and make a similar check of the species found. Determine from this how overgrazing has changed the nature of the biotic community, and hypothesize why certain creatures become more populous in the overgrazed areas and others less so. Check these hypotheses against the facts of your observations.

2. Even though gophers eat plants, they also help break up and aerate the soil, which also helps improve plant growth. Take a 10-meter-square area where gophers are working, and study for at least a month the effect of gophers on the soil and on the plants. What are your conclusions about their effect on the habitat? Check against further observations, and describe in detail in your journal.

Eastern Meadowlands

The eastern meadows are usually caused by certain soil types on which mainly grass can grow, or the replacing of burnt or cut-down timber by a temporary grass subclimax. The climate and main animal and plant species are very similar to those in the tall grass prairie, but research will show a number of different species more typical of the East.

WESTERN GRASSLANDS

Short Grass Plains

A large area of short grass plains stretches from southern Alberta and southwestern Saskatchewan through the bulk of middle and eastern Montana, eastern Wyoming, the western Dakotas, western Nebraska, eastern Colorado, northwestern Texas, and western New Mexico. Climate ranges from a frost-free season of only three months or so in Alberta to a frost-free eight to nine months of the year in western Texas and New Mexico. Precipitation is around 10 to 15 inches a year, with winter snows and fairly regular summer thunderstorms except during very dry years. Strong winds cause much evaporation of moisture so plants must

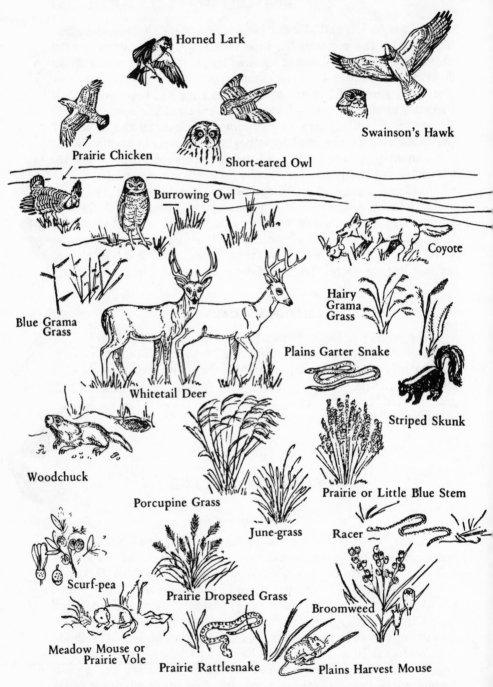

Figure 7–2. Typical tall grass prairie in Iowa, showing its common animals and plants. (Phyllis Thompson)

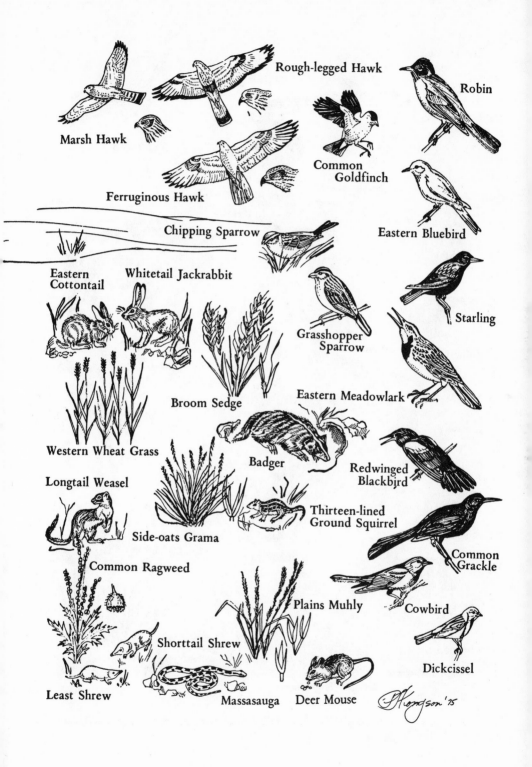

Rough-legged Hawk

Robin

Marsh Hawk

Common
Goldfinch

Ferruginous Hawk

Eastern Bluebird

Chipping Sparrow

Eastern
Cottontail

Whitetail Jackrabbit

Starling

Grasshopper
Sparrow

Broom Sedge

Eastern Meadowlark

Western Wheat Grass

Badger

Redwinged
Blackbird

Longtail Weasel

Side-oats Grama

Thirteen-lined
Ground Squirrel

Common
Grackle

Common Ragweed

Plains Muhly

Cowbird

Shorttail Shrew

Dickcissel

Least Shrew

Massasauga

Deer Mouse

Figure 7–3. Short grass plains in eastern Colorado, showing its common animals and plants. (Phyllis Thompson)

Horned Owl

Horned Lark

Ord Kangaroo Rat

McCown's Longspur

Chestnut-Collared
Longspur

Coyote

Western
Harvest
Mouse

Lark
Sparrow

Deer Mouse

Hispid Pocket Mouse

Western Rattlesnake

Whitetail
Deer

Lark
Bunting

Northern
Grasshopper
Mouse

Plains
Garter Snake

Sprague's Pipit

Mule Deer

Meadow
Jumping
Mouse

Brewer's
Sparrow

Yellow-bellied
Racer

Grasshopper
Sparrow

Western
Hognose Snake

Burrowing Owl

Blacktail Prairie Dog

Longtail Weasel

Western
Meadowlark

Blue Grama

Northern Pocket Gopher

Prairie Lizard

Plains
Pocket Gopher

Thirteen-lined Ground Squirrel

send roots deep to find it and most small mammals burrow holes in the ground.

In the old days the buffalo and antelope were the dominant, large herbivores, bothered by, but managing to handle fairly well, the buffalo wolves, but today the wolves and buffalo are mostly gone, with the antelopes still in fair number. The speed of the antelope, up to 55 miles per hour, preserves them from most predators, and their abilities to send signals to each other by flashing their white tails warns them ahead of time of danger. Once also vast prairie dog towns were found here, but most of these are long gone.

The common animals and plants of the short grass plains are shown in figure 7–3. It is interesting how the change from a wetter climate to a drouth condition affects these forms of life. In the wet years of the late 1920s the medium and tall grass moved westward and the plains became very lush, but the drouth of the 1930s not only wiped out the tall and medium grasses, but many of the short grasses, too. However, the tree cactus, *Opuntia macrohiza*, and various species of goosefoot (*Chenopodium*), and tumbleweeds (*Amaranthus*), with deep root systems, increased in number. Surprisingly the black-tailed jackrabbit population increased with the drouth, while the dicksissel and the prairie vole decreased, as evidently neither found enough water.

Suggested research project: Examine the adaptation of the reptiles and amphibians to the short grass plains, taking three sample amphibians and six sample reptile species and checking all their ways to exist in these plains, their food foraging behavior, their reactions to dry and wet weather and cold and heat, including what they do when conditions get unbearably cold, dry, or hot to continue to exist. Ask as many questions as possible and try to answer them.

Other western grasslands are only mentioned here. They are the *bunch grass grassland* of the mountain states and California, the *aspen and grass parkland* of the northern edge of the grasslands in western Canada, and the *mesquite grassland* of the four southwestern states and central Mexico. *Pine and oak savannahs* are found particularly in the Southeast, while *oak savannahs* are encountered in California and Oregon, with grass more dominant than trees.

8

DECIDUOUS WOODLAND GROUPS AND MIXED DECIDUOUS–CONIFEROUS WOODS

There are so many varied types of woods in this biome that it is impossible in the space allowed to do more than outline the larger and more important areas and show them on a map (figure 8–1). Two of these are described in this chapter, a typical deciduous woodland of the border between Midwest and East, and a southern, river bottom woodland partially combined with a cypress swamp. The mixed deciduous–coniferous woods have trees that are typical of both the purely coniferous forests that cover so much of Canada and the colder parts of the northern rim of the eastern half of the United States, and of the deciduous woods that lie to the south. Since they are hybrid between the two large biomes, with representatives of dominant tree species from each, I suggest you study the pictures of both the coniferous forest and the deciduous forest to see what is found in the mixed coniferous–deciduous border areas. Animals from both regions overlap and are represented in this middle ground.

Typical of the deciduous tree is its leaving in spring after a winter of barren branches, its flowering in early summer, its fruiting or nutting in late summer and early fall, and its brilliant coloring of dying leaves in the late fall. This ever-changing beauty of the deciduous woods is what makes life so pleasantly stimulating to those who dwell among these trees. You can even see in the bare-branched days of the white and snowy woods of winter much beauty from the hand and brush of the Master Artist. Through all

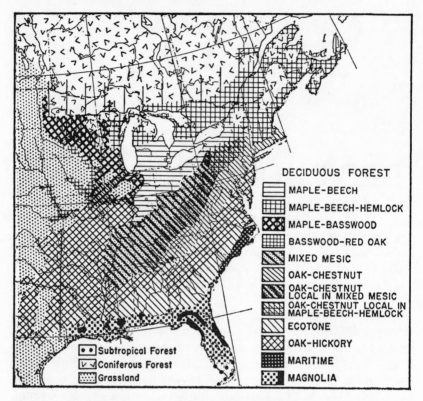

Figure 8–1. Map of the main deciduous forests of eastern North America as they were about 1800 A.D. (From Victor E. Shelford, *The Ecology of North America,* Urbana, Illinois: University of Illinois Press, 1963, p. 19, with kind permission of the publishers.)

these woods the mammals and birds, the reptiles and amphibians, the insects and others, merge by camouflage with their surroundings, a part of the leaf structure, both dead and living, and of the bark of the trees and the shadows of the forest floor. Once the Indian came here, silent as the wildcat, his skin the color of the brown earth and bark, and perhaps his spirit lingers in these lovely but too few remaining wilds to warn us that the white man cannot go on destroying the earth and its life without someday reaping the terrible consequences. If only we would heed that warning and learn to restore instead of destroy life.

The true temperate deciduous forest biome in days of old, including its hybrid northern edge of mixed deciduous and coniferous woods, covered most of the eastern part of North America from the edge of the western plains and prairies eastward to the Atlantic

Ocean, southward to the Gulf of Mexico, and northward to where the great Canadian spruce–fir forest comes down into the northern states and in a long thin line through the Appalachians. Today, of course, cities and farms have taken over vast areas, and in the south extensive cutting and fires have replaced many deciduous woods with subclimax pine forests and pine savannahs.

The annual precipitation of the whole area ranges from about 28 to 60 inches, and is different from all other parts of North America by being generally well distributed throughout much of the year, thus keeping the plants, especially the herbs and grasses, green over long periods. Rainfall in most areas comes near or better than equalling the evaporation, dropping to 80 percent on the western boundary. But river-skirting deciduous woods extend far into the plains and these, of course, have a lower evaporation–rainfall balance. Because of the high humidity and relative frequency of rain and streams, fires in these woods have been a good deal less dangerous than they are in western forests where there are long, dry spells.

The larger trees, such as oaks, maples, beeches, hickories, magnolias (in the South), basswoods, and hemlocks are dominant and form the main parts of the climax forest, which once included the chestnut before it was struck down by a fungus blight brought over from the Old World. Fires and cutting by men produce subclimaxes such as grassy meadows, pine woods, savannahs, brushlands, and clusters of minor trees such as scrub oaks, crabapple, and haws. These smaller trees, growing usually in poorer soil, act not only as soil improvers but as nurses to the new growing saplings of the major trees, which will eventually outshade and kill them.

The different ecologic niches and layers of life are numerous in these woods. The layers march from the subsoil, through the topsoil, the leaf mold, the herbs, the bushes, the smaller trees, the trunks of the great trees, their lower limbs, then their middle limbs, and finally up to the highest twigs and leaves of the forest tops. The shade from the upper leaves of summer filters down different amounts of sunlight, but less and less to the lower levels, where only shade-loving herbs can grow, and shade-loving animals such as snails and millipedes and forest mice swarm in and under the leaf mold. Very special ecologic niches are found in the tree cavities where enough water may accumulate to give life to aquatic creatures such as tree frogs and salamanders and water insects, while other sheltered hollows in the trees are taken by nesting birds, but the larger ones by tree squirrels and even creatures as large as wildcats and raccoons.

The high shrub layer is likely to have the paw-paw as its principal plant, while the spice bush may take over as the main plant in the low shrub layer, each kind of plant attracting its own particular kinds of insects, birds, and even mammals. The upper herb layer or tall herbs includes the sanicle, waterleaf, common nettle, and jewelweed as dominants, while the lower or small herb layer has such interesting and lovely plants as the different violets and the wild ginger, this level being especially noted for its large number of insects and snails, etc.

The following pages describe some of the main ecological divisions of this group of habitats, shown also on figure 8–1.

MIXED MESIC DECIDUOUS WOODS

The habitat of mixed mesic deciduous woods, shown on figure 8–2, with its common plants and animals, is particularly likely to contain most of the major trees of the temperate deciduous forest of North America, and is well-represented, particularly in the foothills of the Appalachians in western West Virginia and Eastern Kentucky. It also contains the major part of the animals typical of these deciduous woods. In figure 8–2 the animals are shown in relation to the different layers of forest life as much as possible.

Suggested research projects: 1. Study the relationship of deer to the growth of forest trees in a 1-kilometer square area of deciduous forest. Map the area and show the location of all young trees you find that are either browsed or not browsed by deer, choosing up to 26 common species of trees to watch and marking each species by letter and the individual trees of each species by number and letter, as A17, K3, and so forth. Study the effect of the deer browsing on these trees over a period of several months, recording in your notebook all changes, determining which plants most successfully resist the deer and which are most harmed by them. Try to ask all the questions you can about how and why these things happen. Test your answers.

2. Study all species of warblers you find in a square kilometer of woods, mapping and charting by tree layers the ecologic niches they are found in, and observing carefully for any overlapping or competition for the same area by two or more species. Add the vir-

eos, if you have the time and energy, so you can watch the interaction of these birds with the warblers in the treetops. It might be wise to build tree platforms with blinds in several places to do your watching. Ask many questions as you observe and see how many of these questions you can answer by further observation.

MAGNOLIA–LIVE OAK FOREST OF GULF COASTAL REGIONS PLUS PART OF A CYPRESS SWAMP

The lowland magnolia–live oak forest was once the dominant forest growth of much of this part of the South, but the effect of man's timber cutting and fire has left only scattered areas of this habitat, and has replaced it with cities, farms, and various stages of subclimax habitats such as xeric grasslands, brushlands, and groups of smaller trees, as well as pine savannahs. (See figure 8–1.) Much of the remaining climax forest occurs on somewhat raised ground or hammocks in the river bottoms, with magnolia, laurel oak, and red bay or beech the dominant plants, the red bay being confined mainly to Florida and the Atlantic coast of Georgia, with the beech found more to the west. Many of the main trees and about half of the understory plants are evergreen, due to the large number of frost-free days even in winter. The average rainfall of this forest ranges from 30 to 45 inches, and the average winter temperature is about 50 to 65 degrees. These thick forests, when large enough in size, give protection to a wide variety of animal life. Figure 8–3 shows most of the common plant and animal life in approximate ecologic niches.

Suggested research projects: 1. Take a single magnolia tree and study all the effects of life upon it that you can find, including how mammals, birds, insects, etc. react with it over a period of a year. Be able to pinpoint what life is doing the most damage to it and why, and what life is most beneficial to it, if any, and also what it is doing to the plants and animals around it with its shade, protection, and other influences. Develop some hypotheses to explain what happens in the life of this tree, and test them against continued observations.

2. Study the reptiles of this forest and of a cypress swamp, identifying all that you can; then pick a 100-meter square area and track down all their doings you can over a few months time, decid-

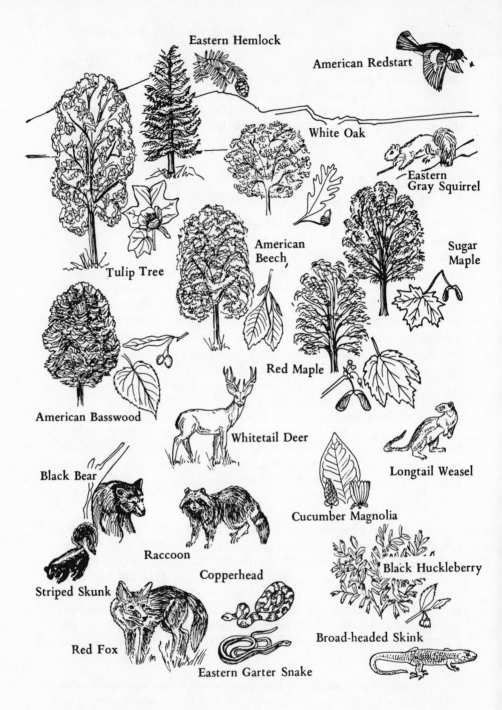

Figure 8–2. Mixed mesic deciduous woods of eastern Kentucky, showing its common animals and plants. (Phyllis Thompson)

Red-bellied Woodpecker

Ruffed Grouse

Sharp-shinned Hawk

Barred Owl

Red-eyed Vireo

Cooper's Hawk

Pawpaw

Eastern Fox Squirrel

Hairy Woodpecker

Oven-bird

Black and White Warbler

Scarlet Tanager

Wood Pewee

Sweet Buckeye

American Toad

Blue Jay

Opossum

Eastern Chipmunk

White-breasted Nuthatch

Red-spotted Newt (land form)

Red-backed Salamander

Wood Frog

Marginal Woodfern

Wood Thrush

Ebony Spleenwort

White-footed Mouse

Shorttail Shrew

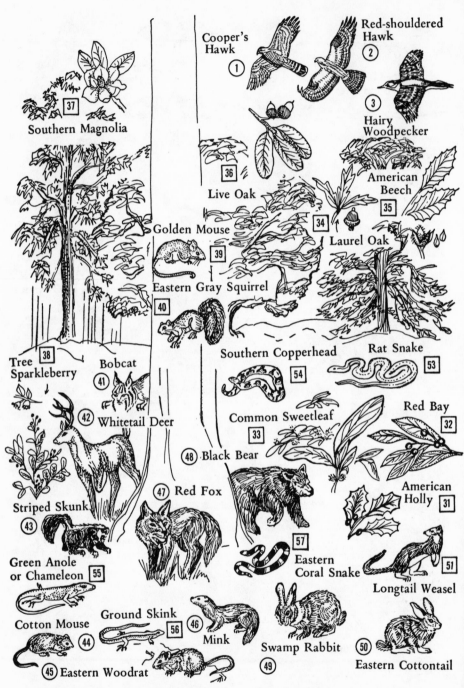

Cooper's Hawk ①
Red-shouldered Hawk ②
Hairy Woodpecker ③
Southern Magnolia 37
Live Oak 36
American Beech 35
Golden Mouse 39
Laurel Oak 34
Eastern Gray Squirrel 40
Tree Sparkleberry 38
Bobcat 41
Whitetail Deer 42
Southern Copperhead 54
Rat Snake 53
Common Sweetleaf 33
Red Bay 32
Black Bear 48
American Holly 31
Red Fox 47
Eastern Coral Snake 57
Striped Skunk 43
Longtail Weasel 51
Green Anole or Chameleon 55
Cotton Mouse 44
Ground Skink 56
Mink 46
Swamp Rabbit 49
Eastern Cottontail 50
Eastern Woodrat 45

Figure 8–3. Magnolia–live oak river-bottom forest, combined with part of cypress swamp, from Gulf Coast region, showing its common animals and plants. (Phyllis Thompson)

Belted Kingfisher 6

Osprey 7

8 Woodcock

Anhinga 4

25 Bald Cypress

Wood Ibis 5

Barred Owl 9

Spanish Moss
24

Red Maple 23

10 Chuck-will's-widow

Water-Locust 26

Box Elder
27

Acadian Flycatcher 11

22 Buttonbush

Planer-tree 29

Black Willow 28

Carolina Chickadee 12

Green Ash 30

Common Egret 20

Great Blue Heron 21

13 Blue-gray Gnatcatcher

14

52 Muskrat

Double-crested Cormorant 19

65 Southern Leopard Frog

Southern Parula Warbler

58 Black Racer

Green Treefrog 59

Pied-billed Grebe 18

15

Kentucky Warbler 16

61 Eastern Spadefoot Toad

60

Red- and Yellow-bellied Water Snakes 64

Cottonmouth

Black-crowned Night Heron

17

Eastern Garter Snake 62

63 Dusky Salamander

ing what ecologic niches suit each species best and how they have become adapted to them. If there are places they avoid in the forest or swamp, find out why if you can. What animals do they prey on, and what are the differences in their techniques of hunting. See if there is any evolutionary significance in these techniques as shown by related species. Ask questions and try to answer them.

OTHER BROAD-LEAVED WOODLAND HABITATS, AND ASSOCIATED SUBCLIMAXES

There are so many different broad-leaved woodland habitats and associated subclimaxes in the eastern half of North America that it is not possible to list more than the main ones here. Many of these are shown on figure 8-1. The *mixed coniferous–deciduous forest* is found mainly high in the Appalachian Mountains, and on the northern border of the main deciduous forests. Deciduous forests include: *maple–beech forest*; *maple–beech–hemlock*; *maple–basswood*; *basswood–red oak*; *ecotone* (a cross between several other forests); *oak–hickory*; *maritime live oak forest* (along Atlantic coast); *subclimax forests of southern pines*; *subtropical forest* of southern Florida; *streamside woodlands*, including mainly willows, alders, and cottonwoods. In the Appalachians there appear specialized communities of trees left as remnants from ancient times. These are called *coves* and are extremely interesting to explore.

In the west, *oak woodlands* of both live oaks and deciduous oak trees cover wide areas in California and Oregon, with smaller areas in New Mexico and Arizona.

9

CONIFEROUS FOREST HABITATS

Coniferous forests form probably the greatest forests of the world, stretching around the whole rim of the Northern Hemisphere and far down into the mountains of Central America. (See figure 9–1.) They form shelter for many animals, with the thicker-leaved trees such as firs forming especially thick leaf mats under which many creatures find shelter from winter storms. In winter many small, plant-feeding or omnivorous mammals, such as shrews and mice, find shelter by burrowing in the snow, also finding food where the snow has protected the plants.

Deer, elk, and moose, at the time of heavy snow, dig out trails and trampled-down areas with their hooves to find access to plant food and to give them room for flight from predators. The snowshoe rabbits on the other hand have developed such large and well-furred hind feet that they can hop about on top of the snow, and their white fur in winter gives them good camouflage.

The various carnivores also have to adapt themselves to the severe winter conditions. The Canada lynx, chief enemy of the snowshoe rabbit, also has wide-spread, furred feet for fast movement over the top of the snow. The red fox, on the contrary, hunts for his small, rodent prey by digging into the snow to find their tunnels, while the mountain lion (in the West) and wolves (in the North) prey on the large herbivores, the first by silent stalking, the second by hunting in packs.

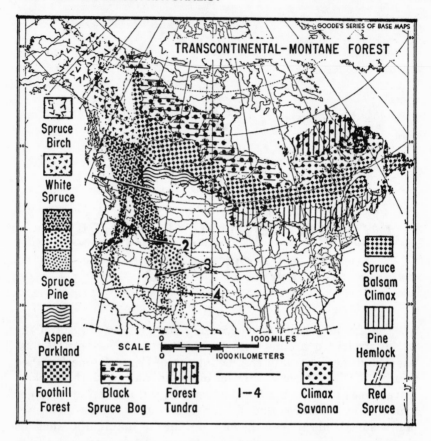

Figure 9–1. Map of transcontinental montane and northeastern coniferous forests of North America. (From Victor E. Shelford, *The Ecology of North America,* Urbana, Illinois: University of Illinois Press, 1963, p. 121, with kind permission of the publishers.)

The squirrels, particularly the red squirrel in the East and the chickaree in the West, are highly active tree climbers and store nuts and other food in hollows in the trees, and these supplies keep them in food all winter. But the marten is a member of the weasel family especially built for hunting squirrels by chasing them at high speed through the treetops. Often only when the squirrel can find a hole too small for the marten or perhaps leap from the top of a tree to the ground does he escape. Another animal with a plentiful food supply all year is the porcupine, who feeds on bark and protects himself against enemies with his spiny back and tail, although the fisher, another large, weasel-like fur bearer, has learned to turn the porcupine over with a quick undercut blow of his paw.

Some animals, such as the black bear, the grizzly bear, and the marmots, go into deep dens and sleep the cold months away. The beaver has the most successful plan of all, when man leaves him alone, for he builds a dam to create a pond, builds a stout house in the middle of his beaver pond out of logs, sticks, and mud and drags aspen and cottonwood saplings he has cut into his pond to store underwater and under the ice for winter food. The ice makes his house almost impenetrable even to the bear and he is usually quite safe and well fed until spring comes.

In late spring and summer, of course, the forest comes alive with new life, for the plants bring forth leaves and then flowers and fruit, the insects come out of winter dormancy, and many migratory birds, such as warblers, vireos, flycatchers, and thrushes, come winging in from the South or from lower altitudes, if the forest is in the mountains, to establish territories and nests and to rear families. The small mammals, forest voles, tree mice, wood rats, and many others, are very active on the ground and in the trees, but so are their predators, weasels and foxes, horned and barred owls, and the rest. Summer is also the time when insect pests, such as the spruce budworm, greatly increase in numbers and sometimes actually destroy wide areas of forestland. Man also comes to destroy.

Figure 9–1 shows the major coniferous forest areas of North America, of which four are pictured and described more fully in the remainder of this chapter.

NORTHERN SPRUCE–FIR FOREST

The two main trees of the northern spruce–fir forest are the balsam fir, with its delightful balsam odor, and the tall and stately white spruce. In the Appalachian extension of this same type of forest, rimming the crests of these southern mountains, these trees are supplanted as dominants by the Fraser fir and the red spruce. Height of the main northern forest is from sea level to about 1,200 feet, while in the extension in the North Carolina Appalachians it is from around 4,500 feet to 6,400. Animals in both places are very similar, although the bobcat takes the place of the lynx in the southern mountains, and the marten and fisher are absent. (See figure 9–2.)

In the far north of this forest in Canada there is permafrost in some areas in the forest floor, and mean January temperature averages around 5 degrees to −35 degrees or more, in fact sometimes dropping to a death-dealing −60 degrees. The snowfall may reach 200 inches in northern Ontario for the season. Annual rainfall for most of the forest is from 10 to 20 inches in the west, and from 20 to 50 inches in the east. In the summer temperatures rarely go much above 70 degrees.

The dominant and common trees, shrubs, and other plants of the forest, plus the common animal life are shown in figure 9–2. Remember that many of the birds disappear southward in winter, while the reptiles, amphibians, insects, and other invertebrates usually go underground or die. The large, plant-eating mammals that survive the winter have to scrounge very hard to find enough to live and some become quite specialized in their search, as does the caribou, feeding mainly on lichens.

Suggested research: 1. Study the behavior of the lynx, fox, snowshoe hare, and mice, as displayed in and under the snow. Map out an area about a kilometer square where they leave evidence in their tracks, or, in the case of mice, their tunnels, and during a winter map these tracks and tunnels into sets for each week, showing what happened in this day-by-day, life and death struggle and drama of the four kinds of animals. What are the differences in hunting techniques between the fox and the lynx, and what methods of evasion have been developed by the snowshoe hare and the mice? Develop hypotheses as to how these creatures stay in balance with the wilderness and with each other, and test them from observations of the facts.

2. In the summer study the tanagers, grosbeaks, and crossbills, all seed-eating birds, in the same area, who dwell in the treetops. How do they feed on seeds and other food and how is each different? What are the ecologic niches in which each is found, and what competition for food is there between them? Ask as many questions as possible and try to answer them through your research.

MONTANE FOREST OF THE SIERRA NEVADA

The montane forest of the Sierra Nevada includes two major forest habitats, the ponderosa or yellow pine forest of the lower slopes, and the red fir forest of the middle, higher areas. Figure 9–3 shows the common plants and animals of an area right along the border of these forests, thus combining elements of both habitats. The *ponderosa pine forest* is found from about 1,200 to 5,500 feet in the Mt. Lassen region, and around 2,500 to 6,000 feet high in the central Sierras. It is a typical mountain transition zone forest, fairly open and with comparatively little undergrowth. Precipitation is about 25 to 80 inches a year, with around 90 to 120 frost-free days; temperature in summer is around 80 to 90 degrees, while in winter it drops to a low of 0 degrees or lower. The dominant plants are ponderosa pine, black oak, white fir, and incense cedar.

The red fir forest is the dense, main forest of the Canadian life zone, but the red fir is commonest on the western slope of the Sierra, while the Jeffrey pine dominates the same zone on the steeper east slope. This forest is found on the west slope from about 6,000 feet to 9,000 feet in the central Sierras. The precipitation comes to about 35 to 65 inches a year with most of it in very heavy snow, often piling over 10 feet deep. The summer temperature averages around 75 to 85 degrees at midday, but in winter drops at the same time of day to 25 to 10 degrees, and much below zero at night. Frost-free days run from about 40 to 70.

In both forests, but mainly in the red fir forest, the marten is the common carnivore of the treetops, chasing the chickarees, chipmunks, and flying squirrels at high speed. The flying squirrels have the best escape method by gliding from a high tree to the lower trunk of another one. Most bird life in this forest moves lower in winter or flies south, while the mice burrow under the snow along with the shrews who hunt them. The ground squirrels, such as the golden mantled ground squirrel, the chipmunks, and the tree squirrels, all store nuts for the winter, while in the meadows the yellow-bellied marmot goes into a long sleep in his hole deep under a rock pile, as does the black bear. In the firs the blue grouse hides among the thick needles, on which it feeds, being one of the few birds that has plenty of food to last through the winter cold. But it has to keep a wary eye open for the horned owl by night and the equally fierce goshawk by day, each ready to strike when it grows careless.

In summer these forests teem with bird life, back from migration, and, of course, all the sleeping or hidden mammals of the snowtime, including the black bears and the marmots, come out of hiding and seek new food and life of the warm days. Many of these creatures, as well as the plants with which they are associated, can be seen in figure 9–3.

American Larch or Tamarack

White Spruce

Moose

Black Spruce

Whitetail Deer

Balsam Fir

Red Squirrel

Paper Birch

Woodland Caribou

Jack Pine

Black Bear

Bunchberry

Striped Skunk

Snowshoe Hare

Eastern
Garter Snake

Lynx

Figure 9–2. The northern spruce–fir forest of eastern and northern North America, showing its common animals and plants. (Phyllis Thompson)

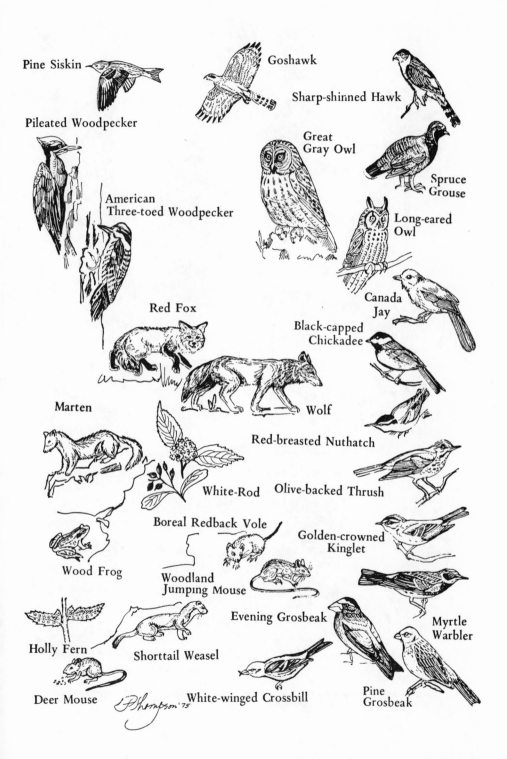

Pine Siskin

Goshawk

Sharp-shinned Hawk

Pileated Woodpecker

Great
Gray Owl

Spruce
Grouse

American
Three-toed Woodpecker

Long-eared
Owl

Canada
Jay

Red Fox

Black-capped
Chickadee

Marten

Wolf

Red-breasted Nuthatch

White-Rod

Olive-backed Thrush

Boreal Redback Vole

Golden-crowned
Kinglet

Wood Frog

Woodland
Jumping Mouse

Holly Fern

Shorttail Weasel

Evening Grosbeak

Myrtle
Warbler

Deer Mouse

LThompson '75

White-winged Crossbill

Pine
Grosbeak

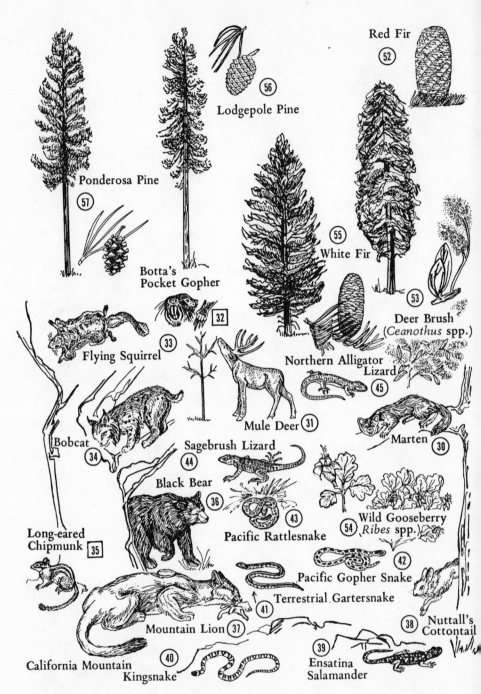

Red Fir
(52)

Lodgepole Pine
(56)

Ponderosa Pine
(57)

White Fir
(55)

Botta's
Pocket Gopher
(32)

Deer Brush
(Ceanothus spp.)
(53)

Flying Squirrel
(33)

Northern Alligator
Lizard
(45)

Mule Deer (31)

Marten
(30)

Bobcat
(34)

Sagebrush Lizard
(44)

Black Bear
(36)

Pacific Rattlesnake
(43)

Wild Gooseberry
(54) (Ribes spp.)

Long-eared
Chipmunk (35)

Pacific Gopher Snake
(42)

Terrestrial Gartersnake
(41)

Nuttall's
(38) Cottontail

Mountain Lion (37)

California Mountain
(40)
Kingsnake

Ensatina
(39) Salamander

Figure 9–3. Mixed ponderosa pine and red fir forest of Sierra Nevada, showing its common animals and plants. (Phyllis Thompson)

Common Nighthawk 1

Band-tailed Pigeon 2

Red-breasted Nuthatch 3

Purple Finch 4

Lincoln's Sparrow 5

Hammond's Flycatcher 6

Mountain Quail 7

Great Gray Owl 8

Pygmy Owl 9

Fox Sparrow 10

Blue Grouse 11

Calliope Hummingbird 12

Solitary Vireo 13

Incense Cedar 51

Western Hemlock 49

Black-throated Gray Warbler 14

Manzanita (*Arctostaphylos* spp.) 50

Nashville Warbler 15

Porcupine 29

Hermit Thrush 16

Winter Wren 17

Williamson's Sapsucker 18

Western Fence Lizard 46

Trowbridge Shrew 28

Pacific Tree Frog 47

Mountain Dogwood 48

White-headed Woodpecker 19

Mountain Chickadee 20

Coyote 25

Bushytail Woodrat 27

Ruby-crowned Kinglet 21

Audubon's Warbler 22

Brush Mouse 26

Golden-mantled Ground Squirrel 24

Pacific Jumping Mouse 23

Suggested research projects: 1. Study a small forest meadow with a small stream running through it to find the relationships between life in the forest and life in the meadow, such as what mammals and birds and other creatures use both the forest and the meadow for their livelihood and how they do this, how the meadow affects the behavior of forest creatures who enter it, and what plants form a border area between the forest and the meadow and how their growth is affected by both forest and meadow. Ask many questions about what you see and try to find the answers.

2. Study the life in a small stream that runs through both forest and meadow, determining how the forest and meadow may affect the life in the stream, including the plants that grow along it and in it. Draw diagrams or maps of the ecologic niches occupied by the different creatures that live in or on or near the stream, and study how they are adapted for these different niches. Develop hypotheses to explain the relationships of life in the stream and with the forest and meadow; check these against the facts of your observations.

HEMLOCK, CEDAR, SITKA SPRUCE, DOUGLAS FIR RAIN FOREST OF THE PACIFIC NORTHWEST

The main part of the general Northwest coast coniferous forest extends from Monterey County in California to the coast of southern Alaska. The redwood dominates this forest in northwestern California and southwestern Oregon. In the north, starting in northern British Columbia, the cedar fades away and is replaced by hemlocks and spruces northward into Alaska. In the main forest, about which I am speaking here, the Douglas fir is a fringe tree that sometimes becomes temporarily dominant when the other trees are cut down or destroyed by fire. (See figure 9–4.)

The trees in this forest are among the most massive in America, almost all over 125 feet high and quite a few passing 200 feet, some over 15 feet thick. They produce a canopy of leaves so thick that few rays of light reach the forest floor. The shade is indeed so deep that just a few ferns and herbs find growth on the forest floors, ones that are especially adapted to shade, while secondary trees and shrubs find it usually impossible to grow below these trees until one or more of the giants fall, leaving an opening in the canopy above through which some light can come. The layers of leaf mold and organic soil are necessarily very deep, as

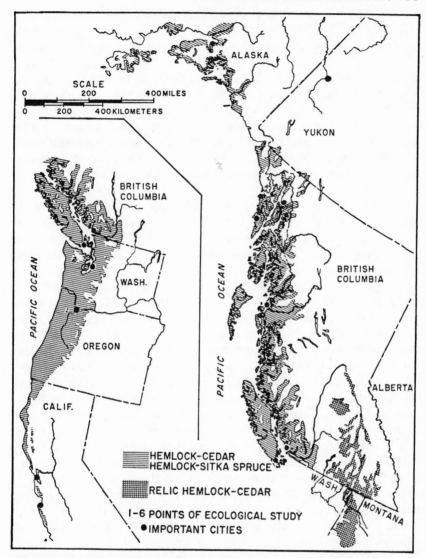

Figure 9–4. Map of the Pacific Coast coniferous forests. (From Victor E. Shelford, *The Ecology of North America,* Urbana, Illinois: University of Illinois Press, 1963, p. 212, with kind permission of the publishers.)

they have been laid down for many centuries. Beneath these great trees, especially in winter, there is an almost funereal quiet, in which the dripping of water from the leaves high above may be the only sound. Rainfall is heaviest in winter, but there is some even in summer, and total rainfall on parts of the Olympic Peninsula in

Washington may be as high as 130 inches and over. The forest at this point is frost free from 120 to 210 days, but there is more frost the farther inland you go. There is generally sunshine only about 50 percent of the year because of so much rain and fog. Mean annual temperature on the Washington coast is around 50 degrees, with temperatures dropping to around 30 degrees in mid-winter, but rarely rising higher than 75 degrees in the summer. The altitude of this forest ranges from sea level to 6,000 feet, with the giant cedar important in a belt from sea level to the mountainsides at 5,500 feet, while the Sitka spruce is more dominant in lower altitudes near the coast, and the hemlocks are found at most elevations.

Oregon grape, salal, and sword fern are three of the common plants found on the forest floor, but even they may avoid the darker parts of the wood where mosses and ferns seem to be the commonest plants. Oregon wood sorrel and vanilla leaf or deerfoot are common shade-loving herbs.

High in the treetops the blue grouse hides next to the trunks of the great firs or spruces, while far below the California red-back vole builds its tunnels through a decaying, moss-covered log. Along a creek that digs a shallow trench through the forest the ferns and other plants are thick because here a little more light penetrates the forest canopy, and here you may see some plants waving mysteriously until you see chewing at the base of one of them a strange animal, unknown to most humans—the aplodontia (sometimes miscalled a mountain beaver). Its squat, dark brown body with almost no tail merges best with the deep brown of the forest floor where, near the creek, it digs numerous underground tunnels. Along its surface trails in early fall wherever a bit of light strikes down through the great trees, you may see the aplodontia stacking or spreading out herbs and grass to dry. It harvests a form of hay that it makes and stores underground, probably under a huge rock where it is at least partly dry, to feed upon as a reserve food supply in winter.

In the higher meadows elk and mule deer may come, the latter more likely to wander down to the lower meadows in winter, the elk always there. The coyote and the wildcat come to these meadows, too, mostly hunting mice and bushy-tailed wood rats, the latter especially common near rock slides, but both predators keep an eye open for an abandoned or lost fawn or baby elk. But high in the trees of the deep forest the usual life and death game is played by the marten, long and brown and deadly, leaping from branch to branch after the chickarees by day and the flying squirrels by night.

The pictures of this forest in figure 9–5 are actually of the lowland forest near the sea, the dampest, thickest forest in America. Study it carefully to visualize this habitat.

Suggested research projects: 1. Examine the bark and surface wood of all the trees in an area 50 meters square, marked out with a line to keep the boundaries straight. Find out what insects are boring into the bark and into the wood of these trees and identify them so you can begin to classify them by name and also record the kind of damage each is doing to some tree. At the same time observe all the enemies you find they have that are trying to eat them or parasitize them, and discover how these enemies operate and which are the most successful and how and why they are. Keep careful notes for at least a month on all these observations, and then formulate hypotheses on what you think the long-range effect of these borers will be on the trees, and how their work can be stopped. Test each hypothesis with observations.

2. Do an ethogram, a complete life story, at least as far as possible, on the aplodontia, selecting one colony of these animals to observe. Watch them from blinds and by red flashlight at night, and perhaps keep some in captivity in conditions as natural as possible. Write out in detail this life story and get it checked by an interested mammalogist.

SUBALPINE FORESTS OF THE WEST

The subalpine forests of the West cover all the high mountains of the West, stretching from the upper border of the main mountain forests to the edge of timberline where the trees are so stunted and wind blown that they stretch almost flat to the ground. The topography often includes steep cliffs and large, rocky masses and slopes, but also the area is characterized by the presence in summer of many bogs and flowering mountain meadows. Figure 9–6 shows a subalpine forest and meadow in the high Cascades of Oregon. Plants vary from mountain range to mountain range, as shown by the lists below the main plants for each, but the animals are essentially the same for the subalpine forests, except that the grizzly bear is found mainly in the Rockies, the mountain goat and

Pileated Woodpecker

Douglas Fir

Flying Squirrel

Chickaree

Western Hemlock

Sitka Spruce

Giant Cedar

Marten

Red Alder

Black Huckleberry

Rubber Snake

Black-tailed Deer

Bushy-tailed Woodrat

Oregon Grape

W. Ring-necked Snake

Alligator Lizard

Roosevelt Elk

Figure 9–5. The hemlock, cedar, Sikta spruce, and Douglas fir rain forest of the Pacific Northwest coast, showing its common animals and plants. (Phyllis Thompson)

Hairy Woodpecker

Sharp-shinned Hawk

Blue Grouse

Pine Siskin

Horned Owl

Cedar Waxwing

Red Tree Mouse

Vaux Swift

Lowland Fir

Yellow-bellied Sapsucker

Striped Skunk

Black-throated Gray Warbler

W. Wood Peewee

Thimbleberry

Black Bear

Evening Grosbeak

Tailed Frog

Rough-skinned Newt

Steller Jay

Bobcat

Chestnut-backed Chickadee

Creeper

Beaver

Pacific Water Shrew

Red-breasted Nuthatch

Pac. Giant Salamander

Clouded Salamander

Russet-backed Thrush

Figure 9–6. Composite subalpine forest of mountaintops of the West, showing its common plants and animals. (Phyllis Thompson)

Sparrow Hawk

Common Nighthawk

Western Flycatcher

Clark's Nutcracker

Western Wood Peewee

Sooty or Blue Grouse

Horned Lark

Evening Grosbeak

Pine Grosbeak

Mountain Chickadee

Red-breasted Nuthatch

Yellow-haired Porcupine

Saw-whet Owl

Western Tanager

Cassin's Purple Finch

Winter Wren

Marten

Horned Owl

Mountain Bluebird

Oregon Junco

Black Bear

Lincoln Sparrow

Black-headed Three-toed Woodpecker

Townsend's Solitaire

Pipit

Williamson's Sapsucker

Audubon's Warbler

Sagebrush Lizard

Warbling Vireo

Thompson '75

hoary marmot in the Washington Cascades and the northern Rockies.

Here are the dominant trees for each area:

Sierra Nevada: White-bark pine, limber pine, foxtail pine, alpine willow.

Cascades: White-bark pine, lodgepole pine, western larch, Engelmann spruce, western hemlock, mountain hemlock, subalpine fir, alpine willow.

Northern Rocky Mountains: White-bark pine, dwarf juniper, alpine fir, Engelmann spruce, quaking aspen, alpine willow.

Southern Rocky Mountains: Subalpine fir, bog birch, Engelmann spruce, bristlecone pine, lodgepole pine, limber pine, quaking aspen, alpine willow.

In the subalpine biome life is so harsh in winter that most bird life, except the ptarmigan, either flees to lower levels or migrates completely out of the mountains. Even the mammals with their thick fur and warm blood often retreat below, although a few like the snowshoe hare and the white-haired mountain goat are so well adapted with thick hair to snow and cold that they can stay, and the goats can climb on icy rocks. Other mammals, like the pika and the marmot, gather food in the meadows in summer and fall and store some for winter in their rocky dens, the pika actually making hay.

Suggested research project: Study and compare the behavior of the pika and one or both of the marmot species (yellowbellied or hoary), seeing how they react to changes in the weather and to attacks by predators. If you find clear lines of difference between these different types of animals living in a similar habitat, see if you can discover the reasons for the differences and whether they keep the two different creatures from competing with each other for space or food. Study also their social behavior and communication to see which is the most effective. Ask many questions and try to find the answers.

Other coniferous forests communities include the following: the *southern pine forests*, the *pinyon–juniper woodlands* of the West, the *northern Rocky Mountain coniferous forest*, the *southern*

Rocky Mountain coniferous forest, the *redwood forest* of northwest California, the *hemlock–cedar, Douglas fir forest* of the west slopes of the Cascades, the *forest tundra* of northern Canada just south of the true tundra of the Arctic slope, the *white spruce forest* of Yukon Territory, the *pine–hemlock forest* of southeastern Canada and the northern tier of states from Minnesota to Maine, the *spruce–birch forest* of central eastern Alaska, and the *black spruce bogs* that mix with the forest tundra of northern Canada. These are shown on the map, figure 9–1.

10

MISCELLANEOUS GROUPS OF HABITATS

Two habitats are considered in this chapter: an eastern pond, and a western rocky ocean shore, and others are mentioned briefly to give you some concept of the whole.

WATER HABITATS

Fresh water and marine habitats cover over 75 percent of the earth's surface, so that the great bulk of life is found in these habitats. There are thus probably at least three times as many projects for exploration in these waters as there are in the rest of the world. Think of this, and, as you develop your abilities, I hope you will find excitement and adventure in seeking truth and vital discovery in the many liquid worlds to be explored.

Fresh Water Habitats

Fresh water habitats include fresh water marshes, swamps, streams and rivers, ponds and lakes. Fresh water has at least two qualities that are different from those of salt water: First, fresh water is less buoyant than salt water so that animals either have to swim more rapidly to stay afloat in fresh water, or develop methods of carrying extra air either inside or outside to give them greater buoyancy. Second, fresh water does not sting or irritate the eyes as does salt water so no special covers for the eyes are needed by fresh water animals.

Water has special effects on animals that make life in water very different from that on land.

1. Water in winter forms ice on the top only, although to increasing depths as the cold increases, thus allowing animals to continue to live at just slightly above-freezing temperatures in the water below the ice.

2. As the ice forms there is usually a little air under the surface that allows the smaller creatures at least to find air and sometimes even animals as large as otters can find enough air to live for a while under the ice. This air is also absorbed into the water to supply oxygen to fish. However, if the ice lasts too long over the water, and the lake or pond is small, all the oxygen may be used by the creatures under the ice and most of them will die. A few may survive by burying themselves in the mud and going into a state of near-suspended animation in which little oxygen is needed.

3. Water is a much heavier medium than air so that creatures can be suspended in it more easily than air without the need of wings and thus can actually live suspended in and swimming through water for all their lives.

4. Water can become destructive to life if it moves too much as it does in waves or swift rapids. Where this happens life must either perish or adjust to such drastic changes (as, for example, caddis fly larvae do in swift currents by clinging to the undersides of rocks with a strong silk and glue they manufacture).

5. The amount of oxygen in water is a good deal less concentrated than it is in the air so that aquatic animals usually have to have special adaptations (gills) for taking oxygen from water as fish do, or for getting it at the surface and then storing it for a time in the body as do turtles, or taking bubbles below under their wing covers as do water beetles.

6. Since water is an excellent solvent for various chemicals aquatic animals have to be able to detect those that are beneficial, such as nitrates and vitamins, and make use of them while avoiding water that has dangerous chemicals in it, such as copper sulphates, mercury, and other poisons.

7. The high heat capacity of water—that is, its ability to hold heat for a long time—causes aquatic habitats to be much less influenced by cold than land habitats.

8. Water refracts light in a different way than air so that you see differently and not nearly as far under water.

9. Sound travels much faster under water than in air and also much farther so that communication can be made over long distances.

All these and other qualities of water should be studied and appreciated as you investigate aquatic life and see how it affects animal ife and how the animals and plants adapt to it. Books dealing with aquatic life are listed in the Suggested References, Appendix C.

An Eastern Pond: A pond of water goes through an evolution over a period of many years in which it changes greatly. It often starts as a clear pond with no life in it, caused by some sudden change such as the flooding of a small area by a storm or by a stream diversion. This is its infancy, but in youth it gradually sees the growth of such plants as submerged pond weeds, and some hornworts and stoneworts, adding a few amphibians at the same time. Soon after this come insects, crustaceans, and snails, which, finding lots of room, soon become very abundant. As floating plants and partly underwater shoreline plants begin to come, the pond enters its height in its population of living things and becomes middle-aged. Increasingly the water becomes less well oxygenated, as it becomes too populated and the water also becomes more muddy, all signs that the pond is entering into old age. Now shoreline plants are heavily encroaching on the water and the pond becomes shallower and smaller as it becomes filled with detritus, and eventually it dies as a pond but lives on for a while as a marsh or swamp that eventually turns into woods growing on dry land.

The pond shown in figure 10–1 has reached maturity, but not yet started on the downgrade of old age. Many common plants and animals of an eastern state's pond are shown in the pictures, but this is only an inkling of the incredible diversity and richness of life in such a pond. Below that surface are a dozen different kinds of jungles filled with underwater tigers and a chain(s) of life that includes myriads that eat plants, and others that eat the plant eaters, and larger meat eaters that eat the smaller meat eaters, until you come to the great blue heron who stalks the waters with his long legs and spears with his long bill the large fish.

Suggested research projects: 1. Build a waterproof box with glass or plastic bottom through which you can see clearly, and attach this to four strong stakes driven into the water on the edge of a good pond where the most underwater life can be seen; fasten the box in place so the glass bottom is about 3 inches or slightly more below the surface. Make a platform of 2 by 4's and boards over the water so you can lie flat on your belly, on a foam rubber pad if you want comfort, and peer through the glass bottom down through the water-weed jungle below. With the aid of the proper book identify the water plants you can see in this place; also continue to identify the creatures you see and can capture from books, or by sending specimens to a museum or college biology department, as already described in chapter 2, to be identified.

Carefully study the life you observe through the glass bottom on a regular daily basis if possible, and also at night, using a red, plastic-covered, waterproof flashlight, attached to a stake or the sides of your box so it will light the underwater area. Make a population count of all species present, and try to place each species in its ecologic niche as you observe it. Ask as many questions as you can about the life you see, and try to find the answers by further observations. Give a full report in your journal.

2. Select two species of animals in the water, one a predator and the other an animal that it feeds on, and follow their lives as closely as possible, taking notes and photographs, too, when you can, of all phases of their interrelations and behavior patterns. Compare their lives and the effects the plants have on them, and develop several hypotheses to explain their actions, checking each with observations and experiments.

MARINE HABITATS

Marine habitats include salt water marshes and estuaries, tidal mud flats, bay rocky shores, bay muddy beaches, bay sandy beaches, bay eel grass tidal areas, bay pilings and wharfs, sandy ocean beaches, muddy ocean beaches, salt water lagoons along the ocean shore, rocky ocean beaches, rocky sea caves, pelagic or coastal waters, and deep sea. Here is a description of a Pacific ocean rocky beach near San Francisco.

Figure 10-2 shows the tide zones, a tide pool among the rocks, and some of the common animals and plants of the different tide zones. Notice that many animals hide among the seaweeds to escape being seen, while others who are heavily armored or spined cling tightly to the rocks so that their soft undersides are protected.

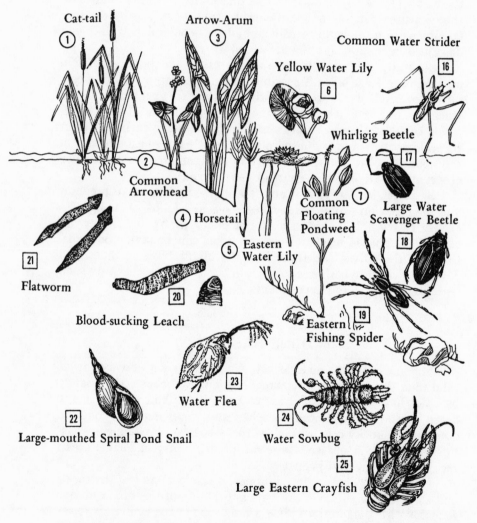

Cat-tail
①
Arrow-Arum
③
Common Water Strider
16
Yellow Water Lily
6
Whirligig Beetle
17
②
Common
Arrowhead
④ Horsetail
Common
Floating
Pondweed
⑦
Large Water
Scavenger Beetle
18
⑤ Eastern
Water Lily
21
Flatworm
20
Blood-sucking Leach
19
Eastern
Fishing Spider
23
Water Flea
22
Large-mouthed Spiral Pond Snail
24
Water Sowbug
25
Large Eastern Crayfish

Figure 10–1. A typical shallow pond of the eastern states, showing its common animals and plants. (Phyllis Thompson)

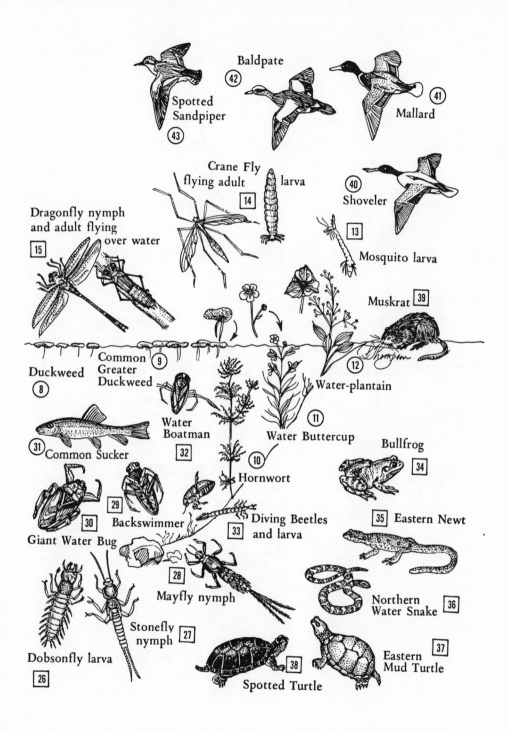

Baldpate 42

Spotted Sandpiper 43

Mallard 41

Crane Fly flying adult 14 larva

Shoveler 40

Mosquito larva 13

Dragonfly nymph and adult flying over water 15

Muskrat 39

Duckweed 8

Common Greater Duckweed 9

Water-plantain 12

Water Boatman 32

Water Buttercup 11

Common Sucker 31

Hornwort 10

Bullfrog 34

Backswimmer 29

Giant Water Bug 30

Diving Beetles and larva 33

Eastern Newt 35

Mayfly nymph 28

Northern Water Snake 36

Dobsonfly larva 26

Stonefly nymph 27

Spotted Turtle 38

Eastern Mud Turtle 37

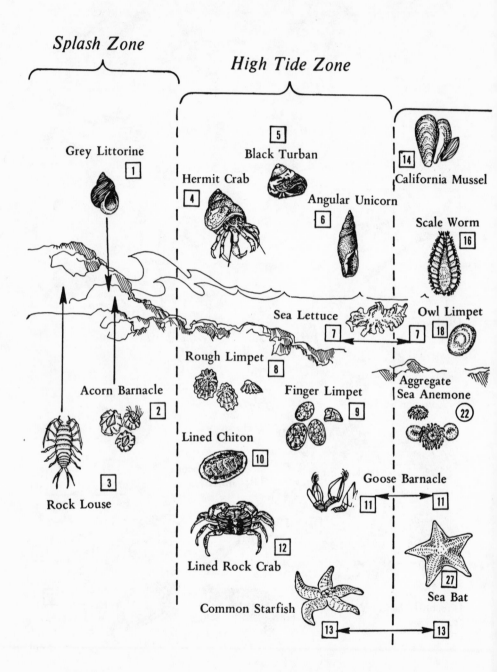

Splash Zone

High Tide Zone

Grey Littorine 1

Black Turban 5

Hermit Crab 4

Angular Unicorn 6

California Mussel 14

Scale Worm 16

Sea Lettuce 7 7 Owl Limpet 18

Rough Limpet 8

Finger Limpet 9

Aggregate Sea Anemone 22

Acorn Barnacle 2

Lined Chiton 10

Goose Barnacle 11 11

Rock Louse 3

Lined Rock Crab 12

Common Starfish 13 13

Sea Bat 27

Figure 10–2. A sheltered rocky beach on the Pacific Coast, showing its common animals and plants. (Phyllis Thompson)

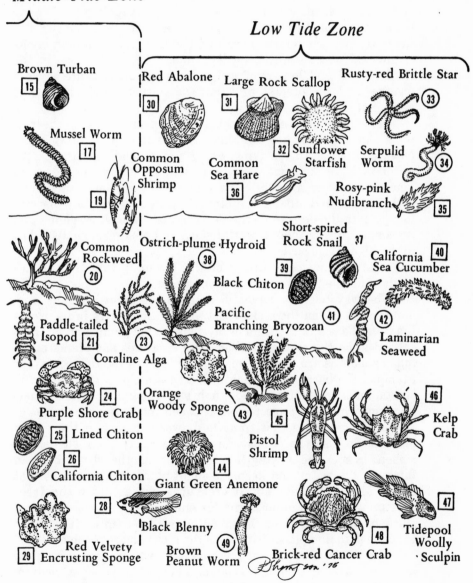

Middle Tide Zone

Low Tide Zone

Brown Turban
15

Red Abalone
30

Large Rock Scallop
31

Rusty-red Brittle Star
33

Mussel Worm
17

Common
Opposum
Shrimp
19

Common
Sea Hare
36

32 Sunflower
Starfish

Serpulid
Worm
34

Rosy-pink
Nudibranch
35

Short-spired
Rock Snail 37

Common
Rockweed
20

Ostrich-plume Hydroid
38

Black Chiton
39

California
Sea Cucumber
40

Paddle-tailed
Isopod
21

23

Coraline Alga

Pacific
Branching Bryozoan
41

42

Laminarian
Seaweed

Purple Shore Crab
24

Orange
Woody Sponge
43

45

46

Kelp
Crab

25 Lined Chiton

Pistol
Shrimp

26

California Chiton

28

44

Giant Green Anemone

47

29

Red Velvety
Encrusting Sponge

Black Blenny

Brown
Peanut Worm
49

48

Brick-red Cancer Crab

Tidepool
Woolly
Sculpin

The sea urchins even dig with the aid of their chelicerae or tiny chitinous mouth parts, plus an acid they secrete, holes or hollows into the rock so they are more protected against their enemies, the starfish. Notice that the starfish, who are probably the major predators of the rocky shore tide zones, move about slowly, unlike most predators on land, who move swiftly to catch their prey. This is because most of their prey also move slowly or are so anchored to the rock that they do not move at all. When starfish attack banks of mussels they usually attack the outer fringes because in the thick matted middle part of such a bank the mussels are so close together and anchored so well that the starfish have a hard time getting at them.

However, there are more fast-moving predators in the tide pools. Among these are the blennies, fish that chase down swift-moving prey like the shrimps, which hurl themselves through the water by leg-jerking movements, much as a grasshopper does on land. The blenny must also move fast to escape large predators, such as gulls and other shore birds that try to seize them out of a tide pool. In the deep pools the larger crabs are both predators and scavengers, using their powerful claws to break open shells, while in the higher tide pools and among the rocks the smaller rock crabs are pure scavengers, waiting for the incoming tide to bring all kinds of dead and dying things from the sea.

The way the tide comes in daily is the great rhythmic regulator of all life on the rocky coast. As the tide moves in its brings life from the sea in the form of myriads of tiny plants and animals carried in on the waves, and for these creatures and plants many hungry mouths are waiting on the rocks and in the tide pools. For example, the barnacles, which look like sea shells but are really crustaceans, are waiting inside their shells to unfold their feather-like legs, which are projected out between their armor ready to net any small creatures that come and sweep them into their open mouths. So also the clams and mussels ready their shells and siphons to suck the moving tide into their mouths where they can filter out the water and keep the small plants and creatures that come. Many of these small creatures are actually the free-swimming young of other barnacles and mussels, also of crabs and starfish, who spend their first months in the ocean until they are old enough to find places to cling to the rocks and so become adult.

The tide first covers the low-tide zone, where it stays for quite a while, then the middle-tide zone, where it stays for a medium amount of time, then the high-tide zone, which it completely covers for only half an hour or so, while the last zone of all, the splash zone, feels only the splashing drops flung upon it from the highest waves. Yet, even in this ultimate zone there is found life dependent upon the gifts from the sea, particularly the rock louse, *Lygia occidentalis*, which hides deeply in the high cracks during the dry part of the day, conserving its moisture, and waiting for the highest waves to splash it for a few minutes and throw it living things it can eat from the sea. Although it has to wait a long time, it demonstrates how some life seeks safety before plenty of food, for in the splash zone there are very few predators to bother the rock louse.

As you go down toward the sea from the splash zone through the different lower zones, life increases in complexity and number, so that in the lowest zone there is the most food of all and also the most creatures to eat and be eaten, a veritable jungle where life is a constant struggle and where there are many dramatic escapes from death. But the low-tide zone does have some advantages over the higher zones, as it is not so exposed to the dessicating heat of the sun, and there is less danger from such predators as the sea birds and man.

Suggested research projects: 1. Select a plant of a tide pool and an animal that seems to use it as its ecolgic niche, as, for example, a ruffled purple rockweed, *Porphryra perforata*, and a common kelp crab, *Pugetia producta*, which often lives under this rockweed, and study their relationship over a period of a month. Try to answer such questions as the following: How long does the rock weed fasten itself to the rock and how strong is this hold to withstand the force of the waves? What proportion of the average day does the kelp crab spend in hiding under the plant, and how good is its camouflage to appear like the plant? Does this ability to camouflage itself to appear like the plant vary? Does the crab use the plant as a hiding place from which to attack prey, or does it use it entirely for a hiding place to escape enemies? What does the crab eat and how? What does the kelp crab do under different circumstances of danger from predators, as from man, sea bird, larger crab, etc.? Ask many other similar questions and try to answer them by observations and experiments. Keep careful notes. (Warning: Kelp crabs have very powerful pincers.)

2. The worst enemy of the sea urchin is the common starfish; yet, the sea urchin is generally quite numerous on the beach. Observe over a period of a month the variations and patterns of be-

havior that happen between starfish and sea urchin, and see if you can find what behavior of the sea urchin best preserves him from starfish attack, and what behavior does the opposite. Is there any evidence that as sea urchins grow older and larger that they learn behavior that helps them prevent or escape from the attacks of starfish? Ask other questions. Try to find the answers.

GEOLOGIC HABITATS

Geologic habitats are mainly rock piles, rocky cliffs, rock slides, sand dunes, and caves in which very little, but often interesting, life is found.

11

FAR FRONTIERS AND
THE VAST UNKNOWN

It almost seems as if the human race is in a gigantic contest to gain sufficient understanding of this planet, its life, and of man himself to bring the whole fragile ecosystem of our world into balance before it is too late. On the frontiers of this exploration and conflict are (1) the scientists, who are aware of the dangers of destruction of all we hold dear, and also the opportunities we have to make a beautiful and harmonious world, and (2) all people who are awakening to the need for mankind to come to grips with our high destiny. We can no longer drift in the delusive dreams of selfishness and pride, thinking that exploitation and pollution of the earth are a necessary part of our "progress." We must somehow come to understand that there is something far bigger and more important for us to do: to come into harmony with the creative force and beauty of the universe.

The explorer naturalist needs to realize that to truly explore the natural world is to be involved in its triumphs and disasters, the latter at least in an understanding way, and to enter into a communion with the life he contacts and watches in a deeper way than just the uncovering of surface facts. There are scientists who may tell you that such involvement is too anthropomorphic, too emotional, and, therefore, unscientific, but there are others who will agree that keeping a clear head and an open mind in one's investigations are not at all incompatible with seeing and feeling and in other ways sensing an animal's sensitivity to life, even its

204 / THE EXPLORER NATURALIST

moods, and its flashes of intuition and understanding. Someday we may possibly be able to have a similar sense of communion with plants and know how they, also, as living things, may have certain sensations at present beyond our knowledge. It is indeed necessary at all times to control one's desire to read human feelings and thoughts into other living things, and to maintain the critical attitude of the scientist towards our own and others' observations and theories, but it is still possible to feel deeply and positively and keenly one's kinship with all life.

If you have read this book with keen interest and a seeking mind and can use it with wisdom and energy as a guide into the world of the natural scientist, you are only at the beginning of a long trail that leads to the far frontiers of the vast unknown. After a while you will leave this part of the journey far behind you and I hope you will find your way into a knowledge and insight far beyond mine. To join the ranks of the true explorers, however, will mean a dedication of the heart and the mind and the body that never ends as long as you can live and think. Never be content with your work, but always strive to make it better, always seek new ways, new observations, new experiments, and new planning to uncover the truth, trying over and over again, never discouraged, until your goal is reached.

Remember that other scientists will rarely think your work is as important as theirs, but do not let this bother you. In fact, if you can keep a sense of humor and proportion about the whole matter, as the best scientists do, that is, stay relaxed and never jealous or unhappy with other people, everyone will benefit. May your journey be a long and successful one, and filled with many rewards of discovery.

Appendixes

Appendix A

GLOSSARY OF COMMON ECOLOGIC TERMS

Acclimatization: The heredity of a given animal or plant determines its acclimatization or limits of tolerance to a special factor in the environment such as the temperature. For example, in one species, if the temperature drops below −10 degrees C it will die, so it is acclimatized only down to this temperature.

Adaptations: Animals and plants succeed in life mainly by how well they adapt themselves to different effects in their environment. Thus, a rose bush is adapted to the attacks of deer and other plant-eating animals by having thorns that protect many of its branches and leaves.

Adaptive radiation: Animals or plants may become adapted to new conditions or unused areas in their environment where there is room to grow and find new kinds of food. Thus, when by some freak or transportation over the sea, a pair or more of honey creepers (family *Drepaniidae*) came to Hawaii, they found all kinds of potential food supplies that no other birds were using, but their descendants had to adapt themselves to such foods over a long period to make use of them. Some developed bills, apparently by natural selection, that could open nuts or cut up fruits. Some even became scavengers and carnivores with appropriate bills to fill niches in life on the islands that no one before them had filled. This is what is called *adaptive radiation*.

Aerial community: A group of creatures flying in association in the sky. They can be of one species or several, and in cooperation or not.

Aestivation: The deep sleep into which some animals go in underground burrows during the hottest and dryest times of the year, as in the

206

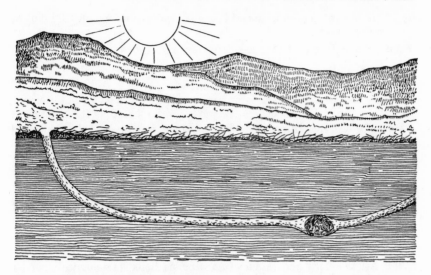

Figure A–1. Rodent aestivating in a state of dormancy or deep sleep in burrow during hot summer to avoid heat and dryness. (Judith Hennessey)

hotter parts of California and Arizona. It is a way to resist or avoid being active when living is difficult and is similar to hibernation. (See figure A–1.)

Aggregation: A group of individual plants or animals that are found closely together. It can be a social group or nonsocial; all of one sex or mixed sexes; one species, two, or many; cooperative or noncooperative.

Alien species: Spoken of mainly in regard to territoriality. A male bird singing in its territory, for example, repels males of its own species from the territory, but rarely bothers alien species that may enter it.

Aquatic communities: Communities in either fresh or salt water, including pelagic (or open water sea) communities, littoral communities (found along shores), abbysal or benthos communities (at the bottom of the sea or a deep lake), running water communities, and so on.

Aspection: Deals with changes of the seasons, as vernal aspect (springtime), autumnal aspect (autumn), aestival and serotinal (two phases of summer), and hiemal (winter), including the changes in the composition, activity, and appearance of different organisms at these different times of the year.

Association: A group of similar-type plants associated together, as, for example, a short grass association, an oak woodland, a chaparral or brushland association. In the large regional area called a biotic province, one such association will probably occur as a series of irregular patches, each called a *strand*. There are also animal associations, often thought of as integrated with a plant association or community.

Band: In general, a distinct social group of two or more moving animals of a single species.

Behavior: See chapter 4, Animal Behavior, and Appendix B.

Biocenosis: European ecologists use this term to cover more or less the same meaning as an association.

Biomass: Includes all the living organisms present at a particular moment in time in a described area. Biomass can be stated as the amount of weight of living things per unit of surface area in one habitat. It does not include nonliving but biological material such as shells or skeletons. Sometimes used to cover just certain living things in an area, not all, as, for example, all the ants.

Biome: A major area or ecologic community distinguished by a similar outward appearance of its plant climaxes. It is usually composed of two or more similar-looking associations. Typical biomes in North America are the grama grass-antelope biome of the Great Plains and prairies, and the deciduous forest biome of the eastern states.

Biota: All the flora and fauna of an area as listed taxonomically or by genus and species.

Biotic district: Subdivisions of some biotic provinces caused by lesser differences in the plant communities than those that separate the provinces. For example, the Californian Biotic Province is divided into the Coastal, Great Valley, Southern Californian, and Sierran biotic districts.

Biotic province: A large geographical area or region characterized by one or more large ecologic associations that largely differ in species makeup from those found in neighboring biotic provinces. (See figure A–2.) It usually includes an area with similar climatic factors and similar physiography or terrain of mountains, valleys, etc. The Californian Biotic Province is somewhat unusual in that it covers such different plant communities as the coastal oak woodlands, the great valley dry grasslands, and the Sierran coniferous forests, but it is held together by the fact that it is in general in the same drainage system from mountain crests to the Pacific Ocean. Most other biotic provinces are more uniform in plant community types.

Biotope: Sometimes considered simply another name for an ecologic niche, such as the life found under a flat rock in a meadow, but by other ecologists considered as the next size up from an ecologic niche in area, as, for example, an area of a stream bed that is defined by boundaries, but includes several niches.

Carrying capacity: Generally means how many animals of a particular species can exist in a specific plant community using the food that is available, but sometimes may also be dependent upon the amount of breeding places and shelter available, since this can limit population in a different way. Measuring this capacity is very difficult, as it var-

Figure A–2. Biotic provinces of North America. (From Lee R. Dice, *Natural Communities*, Ann Arbor, Michigan: University of Michigan Press, 1968, with kind permission of the publishers.)

ies with the seasons, and the food demands of individual animals change with growth, number of young to be fed, and so on. Also, changes in dryness and moisture, effects of wind, etc., may change the amount of food available in a short time.

Center of differentiation: A key meaning that applies to biotic provinces, as each is often a center of differentiation for certain species of animals and plants, so being different from those in surrounding provinces.

Characteristic species: Species that are sure to be found in a particular community no matter whether they are abundant or scarce, but applying more strongly to the abundant ones.

Child family: A group of mostly almost-grown offspring that has been driven out of a nest or den by the parents, but which holds together for mutual protection or comfort.

Clan: A group or society composed of several related families of the same species, usually descended from the same grandparents or great grandparents.

Climatic cycles: There is no question that climate moves in cycles in different regions, but there is little agreement on the exact causes, and they seem to be more irregular than regular, although some scientists believe an 11-year cycle is the most common, with a series of dry years following wet years.

Climax, climatic: The highest state of succession or stage that can exist in a given area or region, determined by climate and physiography.

Climax communities: Those that are most likely to be permanent, ending a sere or succession of less permanent communities that evolve toward a climax. The signs of a good climax forest community, for example, are the appearance in the understory below the adult trees of young trees of the same species, growing up to replace them, as young redwoods under the adult redwoods of the mature forest.

Climax community, criteria of: Usually in a true forest climax community young growing plants of the climax species are found in the understory, and the stand is of all ages of the same general dominant species.

Climax plants and animals: Those animals and plants that are usually strongly characteristic of a climax community.

Climaxes, classification of: *Aquatic*, a climax found in water, the most stable over long periods being those found in oceans and large lakes, since small lakes and ponds change in time to land and land climaxes take over. Sometimes water takes over land and forms aquatic climaxes because of wave action or constant flooding. *Edaphic*, a subclimax that may become rather permanent because of factors in the soil that keep a real climax from growing there. Some southern pine forests are examples. *Subclimax*, the succession of plants and animals in a community before the climax. *Topographic*, a climax caused by the nature of the topography, as with a steep mountain slope facing north and always with deep shade allowing only certain shade-requiring trees to grow. (These are a few of the different types of climaxes.)

Coactions: Interactions or contacts between species and individuals, generally including physical contact in part or whole.

Colony: A gathering of the individuals of one species that has a fairly permanent location in a plant or other type of community, as, for example, a colony of bank or rough-winged swallows in their holes in a steep creek bank, which they occupy together for the warmer parts of the year. Colonies may have a fixed position, but the individuals may go off on foraging expeditions during the day or night, as with a bee colony.

Commensals: Two or more animals or plants living in nonharmful association with each other.

Community: Can be as simple as one animal and one plant together in association, as a single kangaroo rat hiding under a cholla cactus, or can mean the community of all the life of an entire continent. A plant community usually has an animal community coexisting with it, the two intertwined with the rest of their environment as an ecosystem.

Community development: The process of change by succession that leads to a climax plant community.

Critical periods: This applies to those times in the life of a given species when it is in greatest danger of local destruction due to severe climatic conditions.

Dominants: Plants that dominate other plants by their shade or other abilities to control growth of the lesser plants, and animals that have a strong effect on the plants and other animals of their community. Deer, for example, may kill some plants by overbrowsing, but the stronger plants survive.

Ecologic equilibrium: A state of balance in a community, which is dynamic rather than rigid, different species ebbing and flowing in numbers, but none taking over at the expense of others, and the whole appearing to be generally in a state more of cooperation than disharmony. For example, the mountain lion may keep the deer in equilibrium by killing off enough to keep the population at a level.

Ecosystem: A combination of the plant and animal communities with the bare habitat of rock and soil on which they live. The name *community* means a community of living things only.

Ecotone: Where two plant communities approach each other there is usually a narrow-to-broad strip of plants that indicate the transition between the two communities. Thus, where a forest touches a grassland there is often a border of low shrubs. This is also called a *tension zone* because plants from the two communities compete together along it.

Ecotypes: Species or individuals that show a distinctive kind of appearance as well as the internal nature of their physiology that suits them for living in a certain ecosystem. Thus, one species of plant may have a very short, quick-growing life, suiting it for living on the tops of high mountains, while another plant is suited for living in warm meadows far below where there are longer summers. (See figure A–3.)

Environment: Covers all the living beings and nonliving objects that surround an individual organism or group of organisms. The living parts are called the *biotic environment* and the nonliving the *physical environment*.

Exclusiveness: Some species are restricted in distribution to just one or two communities in a given area. This is called exclusiveness.

Faciation: The name for a subdivision of a climax association where certain plant species are found together rather than in other parts of the association.

Facies: In most *stands* (the name for a local integrated plant community) there are usually two or more notable species that act as dominants in

Figure A–3. Saguaro cactus, an example of an ecotype that has adapted to hot desert living with very little rainfall. (Judith Hennessey)

each stand. Thus, the white spruce and the balsam fir are dominants in the main boreal forest of Canada. But in more western parts of the range the balsam fir becomes much scarcer, and other trees such as the lodgepole pine and the black spruce and birch take its place. Each such variation or change in the relative abundance of an important species like this is called a *facies*. Such facies are more numerous in areas where habitats change frequently, as in the mountains.

Food cycle: The food chain, which usually begins with a plant that may be eaten by a small animal like a mouse, which is caught and eaten by a fox, which in turn may be caught and eaten by a lynx or mountain lion, which may be killed by man and then eaten by scavengers such as crows or vultures, other parts decaying under the work of bacteria and merging with the earth to make soil from which new plants grow. Thus, such food chains may have many branches and several food circles or cycles are created. (See figure A–4.)

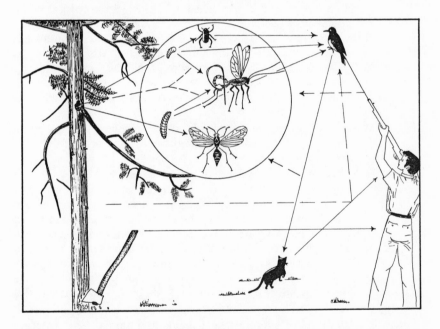

Figure A–4. Food cycle and ecologic linkage between many different creatures. Solid lines show connection between aggressor or carnivore and his prey or victim, with arrow pointing to one who benefits. Dashed lines point to those who benefit unknowingly from aggression or predation. Thus, the insects who lay eggs under the bark of the tree that produce grubs which may hurt or destroy the tree are helped when a man or cat kills a woodpecker. But man, who may want to keep the tree alive as a future source of wood, benefits when the woodpecker or the ichneumon wasp (the one with the long tail) destroys the harmful insects. We need to know what our place is in the food cycle and when we are helped or harmed by what we do, often out of ignorance. (Judith Hennessey, after Don Greame Kelley, in Vinson Brown, *The Amateur Naturalist's Handbook*, Boston, Massachusetts: Little, Brown and Co., 1948.)

Frequency index: A mathematical computation of the percentage of frequency of a particular species of plant or animal in any sampling of species taken in a specific area by a naturalist, or the percentage from a specified number of such samplings. It is derived as follows: Frequency index = $\dfrac{\text{Number of samples in which the species is present}}{\text{Total number of samples examined}}$

Habitat: A hard word to define as it has been given different meanings by many biologists. Originally it was considered just the physical features surrounding a species of plant or animal, but more often it is considered to mean all the features in its near surroundings or even farther, including rocks and soil, topography, whether hilly or level, water, climate, and all the surrounding other forms of life, but with particular emphasis on the plants. Most often a habitat is named as a particular plant community, such as the habitat of the black-tailed jackrabbit in Nevada, which is called the sagebrush community. But sometimes a topography is mentioned, too, as when the habitat of the kaibab tassle-eared squirrel is said to be in the yellow pine commu-ity of the southern Rocky Mountains. Sometimes a plant community is not mentioned at all, as when the habitat of the rock wren is said to be among rocks and cliffs. Some very specific habitats are named, as when the habitat of a dog flea is said to be a dog. The tape worm, however, may have two or three different host habitats during its lifetime, such as man and pig.

Hibernation: Found among some animals in cold climates that go into a state of dormancy during the cold months of the winter to avoid life's rigors. (See *Aestivation*.)

Homeostasis: Happens when an individual, a community, or a society of animals regulates itself to continue to exist successfully in a frequently changing environment, as in an area where there are extremes of cold and heat. A mammal, for example, such as a long-tailed weasel, has the usual ability of mammals to keep its internal temperature high despite the cold, but also, as winter approaches, its coat of hair becomes thicker and gradually changes to white (figure A-5), protecting it by both greater warmth and a camouflaging color in the snow, hiding it from both its enemies and its prey. This is also called *community or individual regulation*.

Indicator communities: Communities of plants and animals that indicate by their existence the maximum stability for the kind of climate and habitat in which they are found. These are usually climax communities. Thus, the redwood community indicates a foggy climate.

Influent: A member of a community that may change the well-being or abundance of other members of its community. A *major influent* is generally a large animal, while a *minor influent* is a small animal. A bear, being a major influent, may disrupt and even destroy the lives of

Figure A–5. Weasel changing color from brown to piebald to almost completely white as fall changes into winter. This change, which keeps the weasel in tune with and protected by its environment, is called *homeostasis*. (Judith Hennessey)

many small creatures when it uproots and tears apart a rotting log looking for grubs.

Intergradation between communities: Where two natural communities come together, intermingling their species, and where there may also be some plants and animals that are typical of such bordering areas. These areas of intergradation may be broad or narrow or in between.

Life belt: A life belt appears as a subdivision of a life zone usually in a mountainous area. It may appear at several or many different places on the mountainsides of a biotic province. Very similar life belts are found in neighboring biotic provinces, although some of their species are usually different. Thus, there is a ponderosa or yellow pine life belt on the western slopes of the Sierra Nevada Mountains of the Californian Biotic Province and a similar yellow pine life belt in the Coloradan Biotic Province of the southern Rockies.

Life zones: Somewhat broader bands of life than the life belts that are generally based on the mean annual and extremes of temperature for which the area is noted. In North America the life zones most commonly used are the Tropical, Lower Austral, Upper Austral, Transition, Canadian, Hudsonian, and Arctic or Arctic–alpine. In the West the Austral zones are more likely to be called Lower Sonoran and Upper Sonoran (figure A–6). A typical series of life zones found on the slopes of the California Sierras are here illustrated. Unlike a life belt, several communities are likely to be found in a life zone. Thus, in California, grasslands and low deserts are both found in the Lower Sonoran Life Zone.

Limiting factors: Any factor in the environment of a community that prevents some species from living there, such as low temperature, dryness, or a predator. For example, the California gray squirrel is commonly found in the oak wood belt of the Sierras, but is not able to establish itself for long in the coniferous forest above this belt due to the pine marten that is too successful in chasing and catching it. Thus, the marten is a limiting factor. The *law of the limiting factor* means that the ability of a species of animal or plant to live in a particular community will be limited by any one factor that approaches too closely to its limit of toleration, either up or down.

Marginal community: Applies to communities or associations of plants that are hard to define as distinct communities, and may be simply intergradations between more distinct communities. The ecologist generally refuses to admit such a marginal community to full community status until it shows a distinctive pattern of species covering a fairly wide area.

Microassociation: If several similar microstands are found in a community they are usually called a microassociation. (See *microstand*.)

Microclimates: In almost any area of a generally similar climate there are usually pockets we can call microclimates because they are different

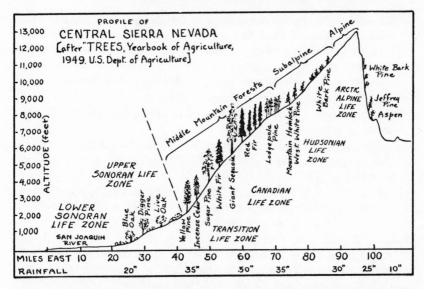

Figure A–6. Life zones are demonstrated in this profile of the Sierra Nevada in central eastern California. Each life zone has different types of trees and other plants that are distinctive to it, and also distinctive animals, each adapted to its zone.(Adapted from "Trees," *Yearbook of Agriculture,* Washington, D.C.: U.S. Department of Agriculture, 1949.)

from the general climate of the area. Thus, south-facing slopes of hills usually have a warmer than usual climate for the area, while north-facing slopes have a colder climate. Large bodies of water also create damper and less cold areas nearby. These produce several microclimates, each of which usually has distinctive plants and animals present.

Microsere: A miniature succession of plant and animal life that takes place in a small part of a major community, such as the succession found in a decaying log that is attractive to a series of different organisms as it reaches different stages in its decomposition.

Microstand: A group of associated plants and animals found within a larger stand or plant community. An example is the group of plants and animals found on or in a large piece of animal dung such as a cow pie.

Niche, ecologic: A term having several meanings to different ecologists, defined by Dice as "the ecologic position that a species occupies in a particular ecosystem," or as "the habitat that the species concerned occupies for shelter, for breeding sites, and for other activities, the food it eats, and all the other features of the ecosystem that it utilizes."[1]

---

[1]Lee R. Dice, *Natural Communities* (Ann Arbor, Mich.: University of Michigan Press, 1968).

Oscillations of abundance: Occur mainly between prey species and their predators. Thus, in Canadian coniferous forests both lynx and snowshoe hare oscillate between periods of great abundance, about once in ten years, and periods of great scarcity. Sometimes such an oscillation is caused by the coming and going of a widespread disease.

Parasites: See *Symbiotic relationships*.

Pelagic community: A community of animals and plants found in the open ocean.

Permeants: Animals found entering a climax community and all or most of its stages and faciations as a part of their day-by-day or week-by-week movements.

Reproductive potential: Also called the *breeding potential*, meaning the highest possible increase a given species can make to the population in a given year and in a particular ecosystem.

Rhythms: Repeated regular changes in the patterns of life. Animals and plants have daily rhythms, monthly rhythms (based on the moon), yearly rhythms (based on the seasons), tidal rhythms, and so forth. Different animals and plants have their rhythms controlled in different ways by the same factor. For example, most flowers open their petals when the sun comes out, but some, like the evening primrose, open them in the twilight. Most mice come out at night; most squirrels like daylight.

Seasonal aspect: The appearance of a community at a particular time of the year, such as winter, spring, summer, fall, as in North America.

Sere: Any continuous succession of stages of plant life, starting from a definite beginning, such as bare rock or earth, and ending, after several stages, in a climax or permanent association of plants and animals. The *xerosere* leads from bare rock to such a climax, while the *hydrosere* shows a series of stages leading from open water in a pond, for example, to its gradual filling up with soil and ending in a dry land climax.

Society: A plant society can be considered simply as an association of plants together, as in a plant community, but also as in microstands. This does not imply any direct cooperation. But an animal society is usually defined differently, as a group or gathering of members of a particular species, coming together for mutual benefit.

Stages: This term can mean the stages of succession in a sere of plant communities, or the stages in the life history of a plant or animal, as when a butterfly goes through egg, larval, pupal, and adult, winged stages of metamorphosis.

Stratification: Includes (1) *thermal*, happening in deep lakes or oceans where water is stratified by different layers of warmth and cold (see *thermocline*); (2) *pressure*, happening also in deep lakes or ocean by increasing layers of pressure as you descend into the depths, with only specially adapted animals able to stand the heavy pressures; (3) *shade*, happening in forests where different strata of shade under the forest canopy determine what plants will live in each stratum of shade.

Stratum: A usually horizontal or near-horizontal layer or division of a stand or association. Strata show best in forests where you have sub-soil, surface soil, leaf mold, low plants, most herbs, bushes, low trees, medium-sized trees (or mid-part of branches of big trees), and tops of tall trees, each forming a different stratum.

Subclimax: Any succession of plant communities will have subclimax states before the climax.

Succession of communities: Many plant communities are mainly tempo-rary in nature, and are part of a sere or succession of communities, one following another until the climatic climax community is reached, which usually remains comparatively stable for some time until ended by some catastrophe such as a flood or forest fire or the cutting down of trees by man. After a severe fire succession will begin with tiny plants like mosses, then grasses, herbs, shrubs, small softwood trees, and so on until a climax forest is reached. Some *causes of succession* are: (1) physiographic processes such as soil erosion, major earth movements, etc.; (2) catastrophes such as fires or floods; (3) climatic changes, as the coming of an ice age or a desert; (4) changes in re-gional biota (plant and animal life) by invasions of destructive species, such as the mongoose in the Hawaiian Islands or the rabbit in Au-stralia; and (5) evolutionary changes in species. *Factors that control succession* are: (1) climate control, which will allow only those plants and animals to grow that can meet the extremes of climate in that area; (2) physiographic control, which limits plant growth or develop-ment by things such as heavily shaded north slopes and rocky areas; (3) soil control which is determined by the nature of the soil, such as very acidic or very alkaline soil, clay soil or sandy soil, being favorable to only certain plants; (4) wave control, as found along shores of lakes and oceans where only specially adapted plants and animals can stand the waves; (5) plant control, as when tall, large-leaved or thick-leaved plants so shade the area below them that only shade-loving kinds can grow there; and (6) animal control, as when large animals such as large herbivores like buffalo or caribou eat some plants to the point of extinction while allowing others to grow, or rodents, such as gophers, break up the soil and help plant growth, or sea birds start plant growth on bare rocks because of their increasing droppings.

Symbiosis: Involves two or more different species of organisms living to-gether. Each individual of such a relationship is called a *symbiont*. The relationship may be harmful to one side if one symbiont is a para-site, or it may be beneficial or at least neutral if both are commensals.

Symbiotic relationships: (1) *Conjunctive symbiosis* means two individuals of different species associate in such close bodily contact that they cannot be separated without injury to one or both, as happens when algae and a fungus form together a lichen, or an insect forms a gall on a tree in which the larva must live; (2) *disjunctive symbiosis* means two or more individuals of separate species are often found in contact, but are also free to go separately. Most of the plants and animals in a stand are in disjunctive symbiosis with each other. (3) *Food relation symbiosis* simply means eating another species or being eaten by it. The pine marten feeds mainly on tree squirrels, for example, and is in close symbiotic relationship with them. (4) *Parasitism* involves a plant or animal that lives by feeding on a different plant or animal without immediately killing it, as a flea does to a wolf. Parasites that kill their hosts rather quickly are usually newcomers in this field, as to become a truly successful parasite they should be able to feed on their host without doing it any long-range harm. Some parasitic plants, like the mistletoe, derive only part of their food from their host plant, the oak, having chlorophyll in their leaves to manufacture their own food; other plant parasites like the dodder are much more harmful to the plants they feed on as they take all their food from them. *Obligate parasites* live only on one kind of host during a major stage of their life history. *Facultative parasites* can live on two or more host species during the same stage. (5) *Beneficial conjunctive symbiosis* happens when both symbionts help each other, as the algae does the fungus in the lichen, the first making food from the air and sun, the second furnishing support, and when they do it while closely attached. *Beneficial disjunctive symbiosis* occurs, for example, when tick-eating birds fly about large mammals, such as the rhinoceros, and pick and eat the ticks from their hides, both animals being separate (figure A–7). (6) *Pollination of flowers by animals* occurs when bees get nectar in exchange for working as flower pollinators. (7) *Spreading of plant seeds by animals* happens when birds eat berries and spread the seeds widely in their droppings. (8) *Removal of sick or wounded birds or animals by predators* results, for example, when mountain lions keep deer herds healthy by killing and eating the sick and wounded. (9) *Special services between species that are beneficially symbiotic* are numerous. For example, the blackberry bramble of heavily thorned bushes not only protects the plants with which the blackberry is associated, but also the rabbits and mice that hide under it. Jays give alarm notes when they see a man approaching, which is helpful to other creatures.

Territories and home ranges: Many birds and animals, including fish and some insects, have special territories or home ranges. (See the explanation of this in the glossary, Appendix B.

Thermocline: In certain middle sizes of lakes only the water in the upper portion of the lake is influenced by wind, causing movement that circulates the water and brings oxygen to several layers. But below these

Figure A–7. An example of beneficial disjunctive symbiosis occurs when a cowbird rides on the back of a cow and helps rid her of ticks and flies, both cow and cowbird benefiting from the exchange.

areas, where there is no such circulation, the oxygen becomes too little to support much life. The line between these two areas in the water is called the *thermocline*. Heavy storms in autumn, however, may break up the thermocline, allowing water and oxygen to circulate to the bottom of the lake once more. (See figure A–8.)

Threshold of activity: This describes the point, usually involving temperature or humidity or both, at which an organism, either plant or animal, becomes active. Thus, the sap begins to rise in a maple tree when the outside temperature on a sunny day after a frost reaches a certain point.

Threshold of reproduction: Animals and plants tend to reproduce their kind at those times of the year when conditions are best for raising young. Thus, young animals are generally born in the spring in North America when food becomes most plentiful. But the time when actual conception occurs must be synchronized to happen so the birth comes

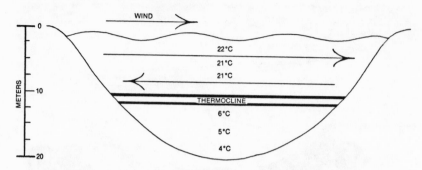

Figure A–8. Diagram of thermocline in deep lake. Above the thermocline the water is circulating so that oxygen is drawn into it, but below the thermocline the water is still so that no new oxygen is added, and fish below the line may die or be driven higher. (Judith Hennessey)

at the right time. This is why deer and elk, for example, have their rutting season in the fall, giving time for the fertilized eggs to bring new young animals to birth in the following spring. Plants also become fertilized and produce flowers and seeds at a time when it is best for them to do so.

Toleration, limits of: The maximum and minimum limits of temperature, humidity, and so forth, within which an animal or plant can live successfully.

Variations in territories and home ranges: One clue to the different ecologic niches of different species can be the differences in sizes and shapes of

Figure A–9. Example of variations or different adaptations in home range. California quail has grassy open areas for feeding, bushes for hiding during the day when enemies are approaching, and low tree for roosting at night. (Judith Hennessey)

their home ranges or territories. However, even a single species may have considerable variation in this field and many interesting scientific investigations could be made of this subject. A territory can be compact as one unit, or it can be divided into two or more different areas for different purposes, one area, for example, being for food gathering, while another area is for nesting or denning. Narrow home ranges are found along the shores of lakes or streams, while wide home ranges are found in large, grassy areas. (See figure A–9.)

Appendix B

Abberant behavior: Behavior that is unadaptive, that is, without evident value to the organism using it.

Action specific energy: An idea of Konrad Lorenz that the energy building up for a specific action in an animal's central nervous system is controlled or inhibited by the lack of a releaser until a releaser appears, which triggers the release of the energy in an appropriate manner. For example, a male deer at the proper time of the year, fall, is caused by the feel of the environment and the release of certain glandular hormones from the gonads, or male sex glands, to build up energy for both courting and mating with a female, and also for repelling another buck deer. This energy buildup may not be evident on the surface until the female appears, which triggers courting behavior. Fighting energy is also building up, which is triggered into fighting action when another buck comes and challenges the first. If neither comes very soon, however, the rising energy may eventually spill over into aggressive action with the horns against a tree or bush.

Activity, displacement: When energy building up toward a specific behavior finds no immediate release from the environment, but becomes so great that it spills over into another form of activity. If this activity is another form of purposeful activity, such as nest-building for a bird, then it is displacement activity.

Activity, vacuum: Activity due to too much energy buildup without a proper release from the environment, so that the energy spills over into activity without essential purpose, as, for example, the deer buck mentioned under *Action specific energy* who attacks a bush with his horns because no opposing buck is available.

224

Adaptation: The way a species or an individual becomes in harmony with its environment for maximum effectiveness in living and reproducing. However, there are nonadaptive as well as adaptive patterns of behavior, and careful observation is usually necessary to determine how adaptive a particular pattern will become.

Adaptive radiation: The splitting up of a species or group of similar animals into different ways of life, as sometimes happens when a climate radically changes due to increased dryness, wetness, or coldness, and causes different populations of the species to move into new environments where new adaptations are needed to stay alive. If allowed to continue long enough, new and different species may be formed from the original species due to different kinds of environments producing different adaptations of body form and behavior through natural selection.

Affection: Develops early in the life of most of the higher animals when the young animal clings to its mother and is protected by her. It is evidently an innate characteristic in mammals and birds. In social animals and birds this affection towards others often returns later in life through experience in social action and helps hold a social bird or mammal group together.

Aggregations: Groups of animals, ranging from completely nonsocial gatherings, such as a particular species of insects coming together at a new food source for purposes of consuming the food alone, to highly integrated animal societies such as an ant city or a baboon troop. *Social types*: (1) Mateships or pairs for reproduction; (2) family or enlarged family, usually centering around a mother or grandmother, but sometimes around a father or grandfather (as among men); (3) herds, packs, schools, hives, etc. *Tropistic or kinetic*: When aggregations form to reach a place of maximum humidity (as in wood lice), or are drawn together by light (moths to a lamp), etc.

Aggression: Usually triggered in defense of territory or a mate, battles between males or between females, and so on. In nature it is often toned down from outright aggression by aggressive signals that prevent real battle, such as the stiff hairs on a dog's back, the yawn to show the large fangs in a male baboon, etc., which often inhibit real aggression and so prevent unnecessary injury or death that would harm the species. It is wise to understand, however, that all aggression is not necessarily competitive, and that all competition is not necessarily aggressive. There are two major kinds of aggression: *intraspecific aggression* (between members of the same species), and *interspecific aggression* (between members of different species). In regard to the latter, the attack of a predator on a prey animal to kill it for food is not normally considered a true aggression because no anger is involved, just a desire for food, but if an angry mother deer turns on an attacking mountain lion and strikes it with her sharp hooves, this is true aggression.

Alarm signals: Many kinds, as between parents and young to warn of approaching predators, within a species to warn a group of the approach of a predator, and even between species, as when jays warn deer and other herbivores of the approach of a mountain lion. Alarm signals can also be general as when a strange scent is caught by a dog and it begins barking, or highly specific as when a hen stretches its head to the sky and gives the high-pitched alarm cry that means "hawk!" Alarm signals usually rise in intensity and pitch as the object of the alarm comes closer. (See figure B–1.)

Allopatric or allopatry: When the geographic ranges of two or more related species do not overlap.

Altruism: Usually defined as help given to another animal(s) without any return or expectation of a return of the favor, and often to the disadvantage of the altruistic animal. An example is when three male baboons attack and kill an attacking leopard to save their troop, but themselves are severely injured in the combat. This is rather rare among mammals, except in the higher forms, although very common among social insects, such as the termites, ants, and bees.

Ambivalent behavior: A changing between two or more incompletely expressed drives or instinctive behavior patterns. Successive ambivalent behavior means a continuous zig-zagging between the two, as in an animal that one moment starts to attack and then retreats from an enemy, repeating this.

Appetitive and consummatory behavior: Illustrates how instinctive behavior, or behavior with which an animal is born, becomes developed through learning into a series of hierarchical (ranked in order) patterns leading to a consummatory act. For example, a fox is a hunting animal and is born with the instinct to hunt and even when young will try to jump and seize a moving mouse. But its first movements are mainly ineffective until it learns from watching older foxes hunt and then learns from experience. As an experienced fox hunts, its

Figure B–1. Steller's jay giving alarm signal. (Jerry Buzzell)

movements at first are very general as it trots along, casting from side to side, looking for movements in the bushes or grass. Suddenly it sees a mouse, but the mouse disappears into a hole, and the fox's movements stop being general and become specifically centered on this mouse. It moves behind the mouse hole so it can watch the entrance without being seen from inside, and here it crouches. Now it is especially necessary to be patient and watch for a long time, a pattern of behavior a young fox finds hard to learn. Up to now this has been all *appetitive (preparatory) behavior*, but, if it is patient enough, at last the mouse comes out of the hole again, and the fox pounces forward and seizes it. This is the *consummatory behavior*, the final act in the hunting drama, and the most effective kind of pounce probably has to be learned.

Assembly of association area neurons: A group of neurons (nerve cells) in the brain that act as a unit in forming reverberatory networks, or closed systems, which continue to react for some time after the effect of an original stimulus. This forms a *memory bank* somewhere in the brain, which can be called on by the animal when it again meets the same stimulus. Thus, if a grebe has managed to escape a hawk by suddenly turning in flight around a tree and then diving into the water of a pond, the associate area neurons may keep repeating the thought of this escape until it becomes memorized.

Autonomous development of stereotyped motor patterns: The internal development of behavioral actions that become frozen in one form and then repeated over and over, as, for example, the repeated hostile reaction of a male robin on seeing anything that looks like the red breast of another male robin.

Autophasing: The timing of a rhythm in animal life, using a 24-hour clock, but usually with a somewhat different timing than the exact 24 hours.

Behavior patterns: Usually arise as a series from each major instinct or drive. Thus, the reproductive instinct would have associated with it behavioral patterns such as establishing territory, fighting or threatening to fight other males to preserve it, courting female, mating, nesting or denning, and gathering food for young. While the basis of each pattern would be instinctive, parts of the pattern would be learned as the individual reacted with the environment and with other members of his species, perhaps learning traditions from them. There is much more to be discovered in this field.

Behavioral context: How an animal behaves in reaction to a stimulus often changes when the context of the stimulus changes. Thus, when a male bird enters another male bird's territory, the second bird reacts with hostility, but if a female enters he probably acts with courting behavior. The context has changed.

Behavioral control: The control of an animal's behavior is regulated by an extremely complex nervous system and associated organs of the body.

Scientists have found that they can study the control system involved much as is done in the sciences of mathematics and electronics in a combined general theory of control called *cybernetics*, especially as this applies to electronic calculators and similar complicated machines. This method of study of animal behavioral control breaks it down into these divisions: (1) transformations and feedbacks, (2) the theory of detection, and (3) the measurement of information. Let us follow the behavior of an animal and see how this operates. A fox cub comes out of its den at the call of its mother. The call is a stimulus input to the cub, which the cub transforms into a response output by climbing out of the den into the open. This act stimulates the mother to lay before the cub a rabbit she has caught and killed, another transformation of energy. The act of the cub has become a stimulus input by bringing food before it, and it transforms this into a new response output by starting to eat. In this case each part of the cub's behavior furnishes feedback to the other parts. The eating (response input) feeds back to the environment by changing the stimulus (now a response output) to "no rabbit" because the fox cub has eaten it. If the rabbit were alive, the fox cub might spring at it and miss it through clumsiness, and there would be another kind of transformation and feedback. To understand this further, we need to visualize four factors in behavior control: (1) The animal senses a stimulation, and the sense organ transforms this to nerve impulses, which, in the process may be filtered or changed in various ways. (2) By a complex method further impulses are started in second-order neurons and the sensory information is moved through the many paths necessary for the animal to come to a conclusion about how to react. (3) Effector nerves bring the message from the higher nerve center to the muscles and glands, which transform it into mechanical or chemical energy. (4) This action or feedback either changes the environment (gets rid of the food) or changes the relation of the animal to the environment (loses the food) and ends the process. At this point the scientist uses the theory of detection to try to find out by experiment and observation why and how the fox cub acts as it does, while the measurement of the information is done by putting the facts received into a visible measurement device such as a graph, and by diagrams that show the actions and reactions much as we would see it in the diagram of the actions and reactions of an electronic calculator. (For a fuller understanding of this see some of the modern books on animal behavior listed in the Suggested References, Appendix C.)

Behavioral inheritance: Experiments and research have shown that inheritance of behavioral patterns, such as preferences for certain habitats or certain ways of hunting, occurs, but that it does not fit simple Mendealian ratios of factors inherited. This is because each behavioral pattern usually involves too many different genes combined with environmental influences that would take a lot of research to classify. This field is thus wide open for extensive exploration.

Biogenic law: States that *ontogeny* (the life story of the individual animal) recapitulates (repeats) its *phylogeny* (evolutionary history of its species).

Biological clocks: Each clock is a rhythm of behavior and action lasting for so many seasons, days, hours, or minutes, based usually on the physiologic reaction of the animal as associated with repeated natural cycles, such as the changing seasons, day and night, and ebb and flow of tides. A circadian clock, for example, is a biological rhythm associated more or less closely with a 24-hour day.

Biological rhythms: Animal rhythms are of many kinds, extending from very simple rhythms such as the daily activity of a squirrel gathering food, to the very complex rhythms involved in long and complicated migrations.

Biotelemetry: The science of using instruments to check the daily movements of a wild animal or bird in the field, using miniaturized electronic circuits to transmit radio signals that tell about these movements to a remote observer.

Brain stimulation: Experiments have been made to show how the central nervous system directs an animal to react to various stimuli. This is done by placing wired electrodes into different parts of the brain and stimulating with light electrical shocks. For example, it was found that when one part of the brain was stimulated in a cat it would act as if it wanted to start hunting; another place in the brain would make it act aggressively, particularly if another cat or stuffed cat were placed near, and so on. Much further research in this line with many creatures is needed.

CCCC principle: "Complete competitors cannot coexist." For a more complete explanation, see *Gause's hypothesis*.

Central filters: Occur in the central nervous system where a wide variety of environmental signals are filtered out and only one kind of signal is acted upon. If a mother fur seal, for example, is trying to find her pup in a noisy rookery, she filters out of the paths to her brain all the other sounds she hears except the cry of her child.

Chemical trails of ants: Ant scouts who discover a new food supply mark the route to it by leaving chemical exudates or smells that lead other ants to the find. These chemicals are fairly stable and give out smells for a long time.

Chemoreceptors: Cells in the nose that have fine filaments in a mucous layer where they pick up different smells and analyze them. Similar cells are found in the taste buds of the tongue. Such cells are also found in the antennae of insects, and in their hairs, proboscis, and feet, etc.

Climate and weather, effect on behavior: Their effect is much greater on animal behavior in the temperate zone, because of the great difference between the usually cold and stormy winters and the rest of the year. In winter animal life is put under severe stress and each species must find ways of behavior to keep alive so as to pass the germ of live on to the next generation. Wide fluctuations in populations are evident in such times, and ways to conserve energy and heat must constantly be sought.

Color preferences: Some birds and insects respond to certain colors more than others. Thus, certain gull chicks respond by opening their bills for food only on seeing the red spots on the bills of their parents. Such a species' specific response to a color keeps the young birds oriented towards their own kind, which protects them. Bees are lured to certain flowers by color, while turning away from others.

Commensalism: A close relationship between two organisms, from which at least one benefits, while the other neither benefits nor is harmed.

Communication, acoustic: How sounds are used for communications are quite different among different kinds of animals. Sounds are mainly important to arthropods (insects, spiders, etc.) and the higher vertebrates, while the hisses of reptiles are little more than warning signals (except for the geckos who make several other sounds), while the calls of frogs and toads are entirely to draw mates together. Sounds of arthropods are found mainly among insects, but are more limited in their dimensions than among mammals and birds. Insects lack much melody or rhythmic fluctuations, and depend more on the distribution in time of their sound pulses instead of having different pitches and tones as birds and mammals do. Mammals and birds alone seem to use sounds for extended communications.

Communication, chemical: Includes taste and smell, and is used mainly for communication by most mammals, some snakes, amphibians and fish, and numerous insects. Many male mammals leave scent signs all over their territories to warn other males or attract females. Insects also leave scent chemically about for communication (see *Pheromones*). Bees can discriminate about 43 different scents and can use these scents to tell other bees of the availability of nectar from certain flowers. Noxious chemicals are used by skunks and certain insects to say "No!" to predators.

Communication, levels of: Include: (1) inadvertent and unspecific signaling that happens, for example, when one animal sees another attacked by a wildcat and thereafter stays away from that area. This is the lowest level of communication. (2) A higher level of communication is seen in a flock of birds when one bird sees the movements of the other birds in the flock and stays in tune with them. (3) A higher and more complex level occurs when a specific signal is given for which another animal has a special response, as when an antelope flashes its brilliantly white tail like a mirror and other antelope hundreds of yards away catch the signal by eye and immediately know it means danger and also from which direction the enemy is coming (figure B–2). (4) The highest levels of communication are found among primates and whales and dolphins, which all have subtle and complex ways to signal each other. For example, dolphins can signal other dolphins of the approach of sharks at the time when a dolphin baby is being born, and at the same time call them together in defense of the baby.

Communication, social: Social communication naturally becomes much deeper and richer among social animals than among comparatively nonsocial animals. But there are wide differences in communication between social groups. Groups that move together for companionship but are not organized either for defense against predators or cooperative gathering of food have lower levels of communication than groups like a baboon troop, or a bee hive, that are organized for defense and also for food gathering.

Communication, visual: Most prevalent among primates, birds, fishes, lizards, and many diurnal and a few nocturnal insects. However, even mammals that use mainly smell for communication often have important visual signals, as when the dominant wolf of a pack takes the stiff-legged stance, with hackles raised and canine teeth bared, that usually cows other wolves into immediate submission. Visual signals

Figure B–2. Pronghorn antelope, showing white expanse of rump, made whiter by raising hairs, and so used in signaling. (Phyllis Thompson)

are specially useful in carrying complex messages because of the four basic ways in which they can be used: (1) movement, (2) timing, (3) posture or form, and (4) color.

Comparative studies: Scientists, when they find by observation the behavior of one type of animal in a particular habitat, like to compare this with the behavior of a similar type of animal in the same kind of habitat elsewhere. This reinforces the first observations and often helps prove or disprove the validity of any hypotheses made about them. For example, both the howling monkeys of American jungles, and gibbons of Asian jungles live in the same kind of habitat and use loud voices for both aggression and defense as well as in mating behavior (figure B–3). A comparative study of the two types of primates has been made by Dr. C. R. Carpenter, but much more of this kind of study is needed.

Competitive exclusion principle: See *Gause's hypothesis.*

Conditioned reflex: Happens when an animal becomes conditioned to expect something pleasant like food whenever a special signal is given, as when a bell is rung. At such time the mouth begins to salivate and the animal looks around for the food. The word should really be "conditional," as the behavior is conditioned by the environment. The bell is the conditioned stimulus while the food is an unconditional stimulus. The bell reinforces the conditioned response, which is salivation in the mouth.

Figure B–3. Gibbon, of Southeast Asia, a long-armed and loud-voiced primate with a habitat and behavior comparative to the long-armed, loud-voiced howling monkey of the Central and South American jungles. (Phyllis Thompson)

Conditioning: An animal can be conditioned by a happening in its environment to act in one specific way by a particular stimulus, as a dolphin becomes conditioned to leap high from the water to seize a fish from a man's hand if the man trains it to do so by lifting his hand higher and higher over time.

Consummatory (behavior) stimulus: Also a part of the "fixed action pattern," this stimulus triggers the final consummatory act in a pattern of behavior. Thus, a marsh hawk, for example, has been flying low over a fleeing rabbit, chivvying it from side to side with what is called appetitive behavior and getting it so filled with fear that it makes a mistake and slams into a wire fence where it is temporarily held. This is the stimulus to the hawk to make its consummatory act, which is to dive straight at the rabbit and strike it with its talons. (See figure B–4.)

Contact animals: Baboons, chimpanzees, and gorillas, as well as prairie dogs and otters, are contact animals because they constantly must touch, groom, and rub against each other. This builds the social bond and cooperation between them.

Critical periods in animal life: Such periods in a monkey's life, for example, are (1) the few minutes after birth when the image of his mother imprints itself upon him as the one he must follow and turn to for comfort and protection; (2) the time when he temporarily leaves his mother and integrates into a group of other young monkeys by learning to play with them; (3) the time when he becomes an adolescent and learns to assert his individuality by fighting or by threat; and (4) the time when he realizes he is an adult and begins to seek a mate and find one. If the monkey is not properly stimulated in a normal way at

Figure B–4. Marsh hawk showing consummatory behavior in catching rabbit. (Jerry Buzzell)

234 / THE EXPLORER NATURALIST

these times, he will usually become abnormal or strange in his actions.

Crossbreeding experiments and behavior: Some such experiments have shown that if two related species are hybridized through interspecies breeding, the hybrids will carry the behavior patterns that are common to both parents, while in behavior patterns that are quantitatively different (number of times, form, etc.), the hybrid children will show a behavior half way between the parents. If, on the other hand, there are qualitative differences, such as wildness, which is a more ancient character of behavior, the hybrid is most likely to be like the parent who shows wildness in behavior. Another example: when there is difference in timing and complication, as between the more sophisticated *Bembix pruinosa* (sand wasp), which lays an egg in a cell first and then deposits a paralyzed fly to be fed on by the hatching larva, or the simpler *Bembix spinolae*, which brings in the paralyzed fly first and then lays the egg, which allows the fly often to decay before the egg hatches, the hybrid between these species is more likely to follow the simpler but less effective way.

Cybernetics: Science of comparing complex electronic computers to the human and animal nervous systems; also called *control theory*.

Darling effect: A hypothesis that, if a breeding population of colonial birds drops below a certain level, it will tend to have inadequate stimulation and this will lead to reproductive failure, whereas, at above the minimum level, reproduction will start more quickly and the breeding season will be shortened, giving more protection to the species.

Defensive aggregates: The simplest aggregates of this type do not consciously seem to be defensive but give an implication of something dangerous to a predator by their very mass, preventing it from attacking. Thus, a school of fish closely massed together may look large and dangerous to an approaching seal and he will avoid them. A true, defensive aggregate would be something similar to a herd of musk-oxen who form a complete circle for protection against wolves, with the large bulls on the outer fringe of the herd, horns pointed outward.

Dispersion: To prevent overcrowding most animals tend to disperse so the numbers are spread into wider areas. Thus, young spiders, not too long after birth, often make long journeys by the aid of silken filaments of spider thread that are caught and carried by the wind, spreading their species into new areas instead of keeping them crowded into one.

Displacement activities: Seem to occur in animals when competing stimuli are received, as, for example, the desire to attack and the desire to flee. Instead of either fleeing or attacking, the animal may start grooming itself, or the bird may bend and pick up grass or pebbles, as if it were going to build a nest. There are many such so-called "displacement activities" but we have to be careful not to make their explanation too simple. Much more research is needed.

Display: Many kinds of animals, from cephalopods and insects to birds and mammals, have males and sometimes females (phalaropes, for example) that put on courtship and territorial displays. The spreading of wings and tail and the drumming on a log by a male ruffed grouse is an example of such display (figure B–5). Scientists feel we must be careful how we interpret the meanings of different displays, and much careful research will be necessary to understand them thoroughly.

Distance animals: Animals that keep a certain distance between themselves and other animals, and this may occur in flocks or herds, as with starlings and some antelopes. See also *Contact animals.*

Dominance: Among many animals dominance is important in maintaining rank and in preventing too much fighting. Thus, in a flock of birds there is often a peck order in which one bird pecks all the rest, and a second bird pecks all but number one, and so on down to one that can peck no one. In polygamous animal societies dominance in males means access to more females. There is usually a pattern of dominance among the females too, but in some species, such as the baboons, females may increase their rank by being associated with dominant males. In some cases dominance is won by bluff alone, as when a smart chimpanzee, watched by Jane Van Lawick-Goodall in Africa,

Figure B–5. Male ruffed grouse displaying tail feathers and drumming on a log to show off to female. (Jerry Buzzell)

banged together some large cans to scare other male chimpanzees into awarding him dominance in the group.

Drives: Sometimes considered as simply another word for instincts. Certainly the primary drives, such as hunger, thirst, desire for warmth, and desire for contact, can be called instinctive in that most animals are born with the urge to find some or all of them. But other kinds of drives are often too complex and too little understood as yet to be put into simple terms. They are generally considered to be states of activity in the nervous system that interact with outside stimulations to bring about responsive behavior. Such states, for example, would be the sex drive or the drive to dominate other animals, and most such drives in higher animals cannot be acted upon efficiently until they are learned by watching other individuals.

Echolocation: A method used by animals, such as bats, dolphins, sealions, a few birds, and some shrews and mice, to locate objects or creatures in their surroundings by repeated, usually high-pitched sounds of very short duration, which bounce back by echo when they strike something, and are processed in the brain in such a way that the animal using them can judge fairly precisely where each object or creature located by an echo is. Bats can move freely in pitch blackness without hitting obstructions by using this method, as can dolphins and porpoises in murky water.

Ecological aggressiveness: Commonly aggressive and adaptable animals, such as the starling and the Norway rat, become ecologically aggressive by invading and colonizing new ecological areas.

Electric fields in fish: Several fish, including the electric eel, can induce electric charges in their bodies, usually from organs in their tails, and these also produce electric fields around their bodies, which they can use to locate both creatures they prey on and those that may attack them. They can also communicate with their electric fields.

Electromagnetic fields: It has been suggested by some scientists that birds and possibly other animals, including fish and mammals, may be able to detect the electromagnetic fields that surround the earth and use them to help in migration and in homing from far distances.

Electrophysiological studies: See *Brain stimulation*.

Emitted-energy orientation: Different kinds of animals, particularly bats, porpoises, electric fish, and water beetles, but also some birds, emit energy into their surroundings in order to determine how to move from one place to another or to orient themselves in regard to their surroundings or to each other. Echolocation and electric fields that do this have already been mentioned. Another method is that of whirligig beetles, whirling on the water surface to create vibrating waves on the water that feed back energy and/or orientation to the beetles.

Emotions: Divided into *concurrent emotions* (gratification versus dissatisfaction), and *prospective emotions* (optimism versus pessimism). The former are the ones in constant use. If the input or stimulus from the environment, such as food, sex, or comfort, satisfies or gratifies an emotion, then the emotion subsides. If not, the emotion seeks another input from another source until it is either satisfied or becomes frustrated and gives up for the time being. (See books on animal behavior listed in Appendix C.)

Enzymes: Complex proteins that act as chemical catalysts, each for a different chemical reaction involving specific substances, and greatly speeding up their reactions. They may be catalyzers of biological clocks or have some other influences over the rhythms of the body and of behavior, but not enough is known about this yet. They do aid digestion.

Equipotentiality and mass action: The equal capacities of different parts of the cortex in the brain and their capability of substituting for each other. There is evidence that if different parts of the brain were removed, other parts could still carry on a mass action to replace them.

Ethogram: A complete behavioral record of a species under study.

Evoked potentials: Potentials of hearing or other sensations evoked by external stimuli. Thus, the human ear can hear only a limited number of sound vibrations and this is its complete potential in hearing. Much sound stimuli it does not hear.

Evolution, genetics and: To the ethologist it is vital to learn if behavioral patterns are inherited, and if so, how they have developed. But units of behavior are hard to find and observe since many patterns of behavior grade into each other or gradually change to others. This is why a truly exhaustive study of an animal's life and its whole physiology, with particular emphasis on the nervous system and the operation of the endocrine glands, is necessary in order to know what produces what operation in behavior and why, so some kind of balanced judgment of the animal's complete behavior can be made and some real facts and theories established. In time we should be able to know fairly accurately what genes influence what behavior, although knowing how they do it will probably take a much longer time to learn. Then there is yet to be studied in any depth the effect mutations of the genes have on behavior.

Evolutionary selective advantage: See *Natural selection*.

Experimental neuroses: Produced in dogs and other animals when an experimenter shows the animals two different symbols, such as a square and a triangle and gives a reward when one appears, but gives a mild electric shock with the other. Gradually the two shapes are brought closer together in appearance, until the animal cannot be sure which is which, a situation that may make it neurotic.

Extraoptic photoreceptors: These areas of light sensitivity other than the eyes are found in the center of the forehead of southern cricket frogs

(*Acris*), and are probably associated with what has sometimes been called the *third eye or pineal gland*. They may exist in other animals too.

Fighting: *Intraspecific fighting* is dangerous to the species, and has been changed in many species to tournament fighting, in which the movements are so ritualized that there is little danger of real injury, or to vocal or visual displays in which one male outbluffs the other by the loud noise he makes or the ferocious appearance he gives, which allows no one to get hurt. In other cases, once fighting establishes a hierarchy of rank, little more fighting is necessary. Superior fighting or display ability generally gives the superior male more territory or more access to females or both. *Interspecific fighting* may occur between two predators, as between a lynx and a wolf over food, or an attack by a mother bear against a man in defense of her young, or between a predator and a prey animal when a prey animal such as a wild pig resists furiously when it is attacked by a leopard.

Filtering mechanisms: Usually found in the central nervous system where stimuli are filtered out by special nerve concentrations when these stimuli are considered not important. Thus, a frog will pay no attention to wind-moved leaves, but will pay attention to and try to capture a moving insect. However, there is also some evidence that perhaps the whole nervous and sensory system acts together in filtering.

Fixed action pattern: An action such as the final spring of a fox to seize a mouse, which is nearly always the same, but his preliminary movements to prepare for this leap are usually selective and will vary according to each situation. See also *Taxes*.

Foraging: Food foraging gives rise to competition, which is prevented from becoming too bad by related species foraging in different habitats or different parts of one habitat. Foraging, particularly in fruit-eating birds, is usually helped by flocking, as the flock can cover a wider area to seek for widely separated fruit trees.

Form preferences in reaction to vision stimuli: When observing its environment, an animal is more likely to respond by reaction to certain forms it sees rather than others. Thus, a toad will react quickly to a form that looks like a fly, but will ignore shapes like balls or blocks.

Gas microchromatography: The study of how microchromatophores in the membranes of an animal's nose respond to different gaseous smells. An attempt is made to pinpoint how the shapes of gaseous molecules are attuned to the shapes of the chromatophores in the nose and so influence them to respond by detecting a smell.

Gause's hypothesis: States that complete competitors cannot long coexist in the same ecologic niche, as one usually drives out the other. So in parts of Europe and America the more aggressive Norway rat has driven the closely related black rat out of areas where it formerly lived because the competition between the two is too intense.

Genetic drift: The idea that in a comparatively small, isolated population of animals the acquiring of different genetic properties over time is caused by random mutations producing a genetic drift in which such characters may not have special survival value. However, some ethologists are wary of this general view because of hidden benefits or regressions we may not see on the surface, and therefore they restrict the use of the idea of genetic drift to those genetic influences that are definitely harmful to the animal. These make themselves obvious in morphological structures or behavioral patterns.

Genetic variations: With rare exceptions, single genes changed by mutation seem to have little effect in producing variations in behavior, but these changes seem to come from many factors in the genes and outside. This many-factor relationship is proved by hybrids between two related species, which usually showed about equal amounts of inheritance of quantitative behavior traits from both sides.

Geographic ranges: Each species usually occupies a distinctive geographic range, which changes over time by expansion on the part of a dynamic species seeking new territory (the coyote's recent spread into the eastern states), or retraction on the part of a species unable to adapt to new conditions (the ivory-billed woodpeckers, whose primeval forest habitats were largely destroyed by man). If geographic ranges of related species do not overlap, this is called *allopatry*; if they do overlap, it is called *sympatry*, whereas two exactly bordering each other is called *parapatry*. The latter is unusual and is likely to be caused by equal antagonism along a common border, as with some species of baboons in Africa, and with the red squirrel and the chickaree in America.

Geotropism: Movements caused by response to the forces of gravity. Thus, the flying squirrel is forced by gravity to glide from a tree to the ground or to a lower point on another tree.

Grooming: Many animals and birds, particularly many primates, rats, prairie dogs, herons, geese, etc., groom each other, often to seek out parasites, but it is also a social habit that brings out greater social cohesiveness.

Group selection hypothesis: The idea is that environmental selection acts on groups, selecting for success in living those groups whose social behavior is most adaptive to the environment such as by better resistance to predators and parasites and increased ease of finding food. Thus, the crow, by constant posting of sentinels to watch for predators, particularly man, has been able to adapt its flocks very well to man-influenced habitats, such as farms.

Habitat preferences: In any geographical range an animal stays most of the time in those preferred habitats where it feels most at home and where food is plentiful and predators not too dangerous. What places animals may like depends on the structure of their bodies. A powerful bill, for example, influences the woodpecker's preference for the trunks of trees. Other preferences depend on how they have been imprinted or conditioned by others of their species. Thus, a wolf has been conditioned at an early age to run in packs through forests.

Habituation: Animals become so habituated to certain noises, smells, and sights that are repeated over and over that they cease to notice them. But if some of these are taken away, they suddenly become alert that something is wrong in their environment. For example, in a certain small area of New York City its inhabitants rather suddenly began having a hard time sleeping at night and became very nervous and upset. The doctors who examined them could not figure out what was wrong until one noted that the tracks of an elevated train that for many years had run through their neighborhood had been torn down. Although they had long become habituated to the loud noise of this train, when the source of noise was removed, the neighborhood became strange and frightening to them. Animals react the same way under similar conditions.

Heterogeneous summation, law of: This has to do with the stimuli that release instinctive behavior in animals and are called *releasers*. For example, a bull fur seal invading the territory of a bull harem master releases the instinctive action to fight in the harem bull and this bull's first act is to move towards the invader. If the invading bull not only invades, but advances towards the harem bull, this releases a still stronger urge to fight. If the invading bull then raises his front body and head high and turns sideways to the harem master, this is the final signal or releaser to the harem master and a vicious fight almost immediately follows. Any of the signals alone may provoke a fight, but the three together produce one much more dramatically and quickly; so this is the summation of the three parts of the challenge, each addition making a fight more inevitable and ferocious.

Hierarchical system: Ethologists postulate a series of levels or a hierarchical system in a particular behavioral drive started by a basic instinct, such as reproduction or food foraging. The animal goes up through different levels of appetitive behavior that are generalized in structure, leading to the fixed pattern of a consummatory act. Thus, a hunting pack of wolves starts out hunting on an evening, acting as a unit, but with the wolves spread out to find a good scent trail. They reject the trail of a large, adult bull moose because they can tell from the scent and the trail that he is too strong for them. But they find the trail of an older moose that shows he is acting wobbly as if he is tired or sick or has been bested in a fight, and they take up his trail. As they close in on him after a chase, he stands at bay, and the wolves circle him, leaping in and out as they try to hamstring him with a slash of powerful teeth and jaws. When the hamstringing is accomplished, his hind quarters are brought low. Up to this time hierarchical patterns of behavior have been generalized and appetitive, but now comes the final consummative act. The pack leader leaps for the throat and, if successful, slashes the jugular vein so the blood rushes out and the bull moose soon dies. This is one form of heirarchical system, the levels of action in a hunting pack; another form is the one involving rank in an animal group. In a crow flock, for example, there is usually a wise and powerful leader, followed in hierarchical rank by other crows, depending on their fighting abilities.

Holistic or Gestalt nature of signs and signals: Means that the signs and signals given by animals and birds to communicate should be considered as parts of the whole animal and the whole group, as the parts cannot be well understood alone without some understanding of the whole.

Home range: The total area covered by an animal or by a pair while feeding and rearing young, whereas *territory* means only the area that is actively patrolled and defended to keep other animals of the species away.

Homeostasis: A word coined in 1915 by the physiologist Dr. Walter Cannon, meaning that all the parts found in an animal's controlling physiological system must be self-regulating and interrelated. More recent research into the way hormones secreted by the endocrine glands control and cause feedbacks in the body to create behavior when stimulated by the environment have strengthened this analysis.

Homing: The ability of birds or animals to return to their homes from some distance. This ability varies greatly among individuals of a species and among species, with some able to home much more accurately and quickly than others. Most homing pigeons, for example, need to be trained to home by gradual lengthening of the distance at which they are released. A few learn to home very rapidly and expertly; some never seem to learn. Experiments indicate there is some dependence on recognized landmarks. Wild seabirds, however, are much more expert at homing than pigeons, probably because natural selection has continually chosen fine homers from those that lived through great ocean storms, which caused many to perish that lost their way. Some of these birds have homed from as much or more than 4,000 miles across oceans, so that their ability must be due to reasons other than recognizing landmarks. See also *Migration*, *Navigation*, and *Sun-arc hypothesis*.

Homology of behavior: Indicates that similar behavior in related animals can be traced to a common ancestor and that the basic instincts behind all behavior probably go back to a common ancestral vertebrate and/or invertebrate. While there is some evidence for this hypothesis, it is very far from complete. Obviously more closely related species show much more homology of behavior than those of widely separate orders or even families. One problem is that ethologists are not always agreed on what constitutes valid behavioral characteristics for the study of their homology.

Hormones: Very complicated molecules that act as chemical messengers and persuaders inside the body. They are excreted by the endocrine glands.

Imitation: When young animals imitate older ones of the same species this is a way of learning the patterns of behavior of the species and their traditions. When one animal introduces a new form of behavior, imitation increases the complexity of behavior of the group unless the new idea simply replaces an old one. An example is the invention by a young female Japanese macaque monkey in 1952 of a method of washing sand and dirt off her potatoes before eating. Other young individuals imitated this until it eventually spread to most of this species present in Japan.

Immigration sampling (or Founder effect): When small populations or a population of a particular species becomes isolated from a larger main population, as can be caused by advancing glaciers or deserts, etc., a sampling of behavior of each isolated group usually shows variants in behavior from that of the main population and these will increase as time passes, producing in time a new species or even a new genus.

Imprinting: Soon after birth young animals see the largest living thing near them, which is usually one of their parents, and become imprinted with a strong attachment to the parent, which grows with further association. My wife and I hatched a female gosling from one egg we had kept warm in our bed, and it was imprinted soon after hatching with our image, thereafter following us as if we were its parents. However, when it became nearly adult, we gradually introduced it to other geese, whom it at first rejected, but, in time, learned to accept. When it mated with a gander, our imprinting left it for the most part and it then thought of itself as a goose rather than a human being.

Individual distance: In many animal species individuals maintain a certain distance from other members of the same species, except at mating time. Pairs during nesting or denning also maintain a habitual distance from other pairs even in large dense colonies of birds. See *Distance animals*.

Inertial theories of celestial bird migration: There have been several theories or hypotheses that birds migrate correctly to reach home by noting the position of the sun in the sky at noon and relating this to the position it would be in at home on the same day and at the same time, so that they know whether they are north or south of home or east or west and approximately how far. If birds can do this, then they can find their way home by the sun. Another theory refers to night birds using the stars in the same way, noting the positions of the constellations. Experimental evidence may in time prove these theories true. The cerebellums of migratory pigeons have been found to respond to a peculiar electrical pattern when the birds are rotated in a cage, which did not happen with nonmigratory pigeons, which may be some evidence in this regard.

Infrared sensing in pit vipers: Pit vipers have small hole-like pits back of their nasal openings, and these have been found to have thousands of heat-sensing cells in their linings. With these they can sense the approach of warm-blooded animals and even follow their tracks by this sense, coming close enough to strike them with their poisoned fangs.

Inhibitors: Patterns of behavior and of nervous control that inhibit such drives as aggressiveness, fear, and hunger. In dogs and wolves a posture of crouching inhibits the aggressiveness of a dominant dog or wolf towards a lesser one. Knowing the other is female inhibits a male's attack.

Innate behavior pattern: A behavior pattern that derives from inheritance, not learning. See also *Fixed action pattern* and *Instinct*.

Innate perceptual mechanisms: Natural selection has probably selected certain innate (inherited) ways of perceiving the outside world for different animals and emphasized those traits that were most helpful to survival until they became quite fixed in all their descendants. Some of these traits in a new environment, however, can become positively harmful. For example, western gray squirrels have a trick of running into the middle of a road when a car is coming and then dashing in one direction, but immediately reversing and dashing in the opposite direction. In the wild such a trait would probably confuse a predator, but with a fast-moving car it often proves fatal, as I have seen.

Innate releasing mechanism: Originally conceived as a special center in the brain that released action on the part of an animal in response to certain outside stimuli, such as the attack of a predator, but now considered to come from a larger area of several interacting nerve centers.

Insight: The sudden perceiving by an animal of relationships in its environment that help it in the fulfillment of one of its drives. Thus, if an animal wishes to escape from a cage and suddenly sees how to do it by lifting a gate latch or breaking out through a loose place in the wire, this is called *insight*. Insight also comes from trial-and-error learning, in which futile attempts suddenly lead to insight as to the correct method or way to go. Expectancy has a great deal to do with insight learning, as when an animal expects to see some object or some particular action soon, which prepares it for the change that is coming and gives it much quicker insight to know what to do when the change comes.

Instinct: Also called *inherited behavior* and *innate behavior pattern*. The word instinct has been somewhat misused at times, so that some ethologists and psychologists shy away from it. The behaviorists of the early twentieth century believed that most behavior among animals except that of man was instinctive, that is, predetermined by inheritance. More recent research had tended to prove instinctive behavior may be the basis of most behavior, but that most behavior is modified and improved by learning, even in such creatures as insects and other invertebrates. There may even be some behavioral patterns in which neither instinct nor learning are present. Some instinctive patterns of behavior are not present at birth at all, but appear at certain critical periods in the life of the individual animal. See *Critical periods in animal life*. The gene of inheritance behind an instinct was once regarded as a blueprint of future action after birth, but it is now more likely to be regarded as an information-generating neural influence, which prepares the animal for responding in the most fruitful way to the common events of its life. For example, it gives the animal the instinctive response of fear and flight when it is attacked by a predator, a response that could save its life, but that is more certain to save it if it has fruitfully learned to improve its escape technique from experience.

Intensity of behavioral pattern: The intensity of such a pattern depends on how much *action specific energy* has been accumulated, and this is an important consideration in understanding behavior. For example, if a young mountain lion has had a few failures in trying to catch deer, the energy for the specific act of leaping on a deer to catch it accumulates to a higher state because of these frustrations, so that if suddenly the lion sees a good opportunity to leap on a deer and kill it, it will seize on this opportunity with great intensity and probably be successful.

Intention movements: Movements of very low intensity, also called *incipient movements*, usually made at the start of what may be a long action. For example, a bee may start on a hunt for flowers in early spring and not really know where to go yet; so its movements may be hesitant and weak until it really makes up its mind.

Interface of nerves and behavior: The line of meeting of nerves with the behavior they produce, a field of research that seems to be undergoing constant change. Two of many important questions to be answered in this field are: What is the foundation for memory, and if the central nervous system influences perception, how does it do it?

Irradiation: A term that applies to the influence of conditioned reflexes on other parts of the body than that which is conditioned. Thus, if you tap a shoulder and a minute later pop a delicious piece of candy into the mouth of a child you have tapped, and do this several times during a week, you will condition the child to start salivating every time you touch its shoulder. Then, if you tap the hand instead of the shoulder and the child also salivates, this shows irradiation of the effect of the conditioned reflex from the shoulder to the hand.

Irruptions: The mass movements of lower ranked individuals in territorial animal species to areas on the fringes of the main territories in order to escape too much pressure from the dominant individuals.

Isolating mechanisms, ecological: This happens in regard to closely related species who live in the same general habitat, but have ecological isolating mechanisms as a part of their behavior that prevent them from coming into direct competition or too close contact so that crossbreeding occurs. Thus, several species of American vireos are all woodland birds, but each species occupies a different level in the trees than the other species so that they rarely come into close contact.

Kineses: Undirected reactions with random movements brought about by such drives as (1) a desire for frequency or speed of movement (*ortho-kinesis*), or (2) a desire for frequency of turning or other bodily adaptation (*klino-kinesis*). See also *Taxes*.

Kinship altruism: Prevalent in social insects, such as bees, wasps, ants, and termites, where all are usually the descendants of one queen. An ant, for example, may throw herself in defense against even the largest enemies with no thought of herself but only of saving the society. Such altruism may happen among advanced mammal and bird societies also.

Law of exercise: If an animal responds to a stimulus frequently, the strength of its attachment to the stimulus will grow in proportion to the number of times this behavior occurs. Thus, habits are formed.

Leadership: Usually manifests itself in one individual animal who directs the movement of a group, often sets its mood, and determines defense or feeding behavior. Sometimes leadership is divided by different animals having different roles. Dominant males may act as leaders during the breeding season, whereas an older female may lead a migration or direct feeding behavior or defense. In some groups leadership is simply taken over at a particular moment by the one animal who moves most purposely in any direction.

Learning: A subject of conflicting views among scientists, and many are justifiably suspicious of animal learning ability until thoroughly proved by extensive tests and observations. It has been found, for example, that some domestic animals are so attuned to their masters that they copy some of their mannerisms and ways without really understanding them, and often without even the master knowing what has happened. Thus, they may seem to be acting with great intelligence when really it is only a form of imitation.

Learning, latent: An example of this is letting a rat run loose in a maze and explore it without any reward, but later testing the rat for the time he takes to find his way through the maze to a reward. The knowledge already gained by the rat about the maze, *latent learning*, helps it figure out the maze much more quickly.

Learning traditions: Tradition learning happens mainly among the more intelligent mammals and birds in social groups, where the traditions of the group that help its cooperation and ecologic success are passed down from generation to generation. Baboons, for example, pass down traditions about how to avoid and defend against leopards from one generation to the next.

Magnetism, sensing: See *Electromagnetic fields*.

Maze learning: Mazes are used as simple-to-complicated tests of animal intelligence and learning ability. How fast an animal learns to figure out a maze and reach a goal (usually food) helps determine its relative intelligence. (See figure B-6.)

Mechanoreceptors: Nerve endings scattered over the body that respond to touch.

Memory storage: There are hypotheses about memory storage in the brain based on the association of complicated molecules, such as the RNA (Ribo-nucleic acid) molecule and certain other chemicals, which help the brain cells to form banks for memory storage, but the only certain thing is that somewhere memories are stored. The complexity of the system involved is so great that only a small beginning has been made in understanding it.

Migration: It seems fairly certain that the increase of sunlight and temperature in the springtime and possibly other climatic effects cause the gonads (sex glands) of migratory creatures, particularly birds, to

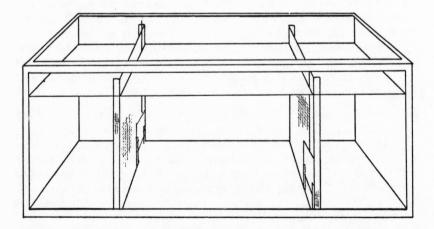

Figure B-6. Aquarium-type maze in which fish learn to find their way from compartment to compartment through doors, which can be changed to vary the maze, thus testing their intelligence. Glass partitions keep fish trying to find food until they take correct path. (Judith Hennessey)

give off secretions that stimulate migration northwards to the breeding and nesting grounds, while an opposite decrease in light and temperature in the fall causes the gonads to decrease in size and stimulates a southward migration. The secretions of the pituitary glands may also have some effect on migration. In any case, in the Northern Hemisphere such migration moves northward in springtime and southward in fall, while the opposite effect occurs in the Southern Hemisphere. The Arctic tern is something of an exception as it flies to the north polar regions in spring, but clear to the south polar regions in fall (actually springtime in the south), a migration of over 10,000 miles. Birds usually prepare for migration by building up a store of fat to be burned by the energy used in long flights. (See figure B-7.)

Mimicry: In some cases mimicry is a form of camouflage, as when the leopard's spots make him look like the leaves and shadows of a forest, while the leaf butterfly avoids enemies by looking like an individual leaf (figure B-8). Another form of mimicry is when one creature imitates or mimics in appearance and actions a dangerous creature such as a wasp or one that is poisonous to eat such as a monarch butterfly. This mimicry is a way of communicating: "Don't touch me, or you will wish you hadn't!" Some insects mimic the appearance and actions of ants to gain admittance to their colonies, sometimes for nefarious purposes such as parasitism or predation.

Monogamy: Strict monogamy, or one male and one female mating for life, is rather rare, but somewhat commoner among birds (geese, hawks, eagles, for example) than among mammals (river otters and wolves). But simply monogamy for a period of a year, with mates inclining to be changed again in a new year, is quite common among both birds and mammals.

Mortality: Populations of animals are controlled by mortality due to predators, diseases, parasitism, climatic change, and aging. *Abiotic control* of populations functions largely through the change of the seasons in temperate areas, as winter destroys large numbers of a particular species while a few continue to exist under special circumstances to renew the species in the springtime. Thus, social wasps increase greatly in number in summer, but all die in the fall except for a few young queens who store fat in their bodies and go into underground hiding places and wait for spring. In other cases extreme drouth may create the same kind of abiotic control, by destroying frog populations, but allowing a few who are buried deep in drying mud to exist at a low level of life until water comes again. *Biotic control* is the limiting of populations by predators, parasites, and disease.

Multifactorial control of behavior: The concept that most forms and patterns of behavior are controlled by not one but many factors.

Mutual stimulation and parental care: Many animals, but particularly monkeys, apes and prairie dogs, use much mutual stimulation, includ-

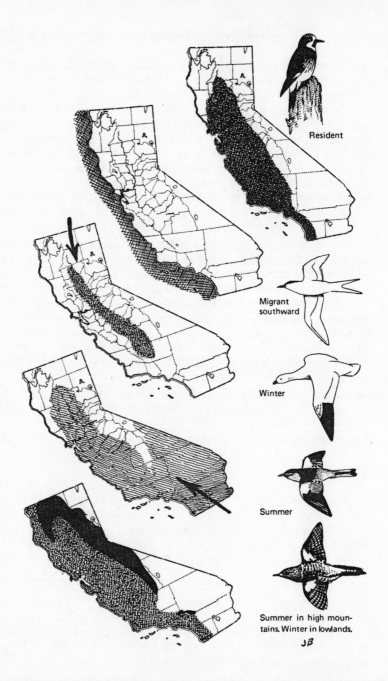

Figure B–7. Types of migration and nonmigration of birds in California. *From top to bottom:* acorn woodpecker, arctic tern, snow goose, Bullock's oriole, red-breasted sapsucker. (From Vinson Brown and Henry Weston, Jr., *Handbook of California Birds,* 2nd rev. ed., Healdsburg, California: Naturegraph Publishers, Inc., 1973. Illustration by Jerry Buzzell. Courtesy of Naturegraph Publishers, Inc.)

Figure B–8. Clapper rail mimics appearance of marsh grass in its coloration in order to camouflage itself from enemies. (Jerry Buzzell)

ing grooming, nuzzling, and kissing, to reinforce the bonds of the family, and also of the society, when carried over to other members of the social group.

Mutualism: When animals of two different species act together in such a way as to be mutually helpful, it is called *mutualism*, and is a form of symbiosis. An example is when crabs carry about on their carapaces barnacles or sea anemones. The crab is camouflaged and its armor strengthened by these other animals, while they get a free ride and a place to cling to from which they can get plentiful food.

Natural selection: Based on variations in structure and physiology and behavior in each group or species of animals. Sometimes these variations are produced by new mutations, sometimes in other ways. Natural selection acts by selecting for early mortality those individuals whose variations are least adaptable to the environment, since they are more easily killed by predators, disease, or stress of other kinds. It selects for long life and high production of progeny those individuals whose variations are most adaptive to the environment, giving these individuals protection against predation and disease. (See figure B–9.) Thus, in the wild, a species generally becomes changed and improved by this constant selection towards higher adaptiveness. If this does not happen, the species may become extinct. An example of high adaptiveness in which natural selection played a part is *Bembix pruinosa*, a sand wasp that digs its complicated nest in the deep sand of dunes. The wasp shows an extraordinary ability to find its nests in these shifting sands, as there are no obvious landmarks available. What form of natural selection caused her ancestors to develop this habit

Figure B–9. Example of natural selection. Moth, by zig-zag evasive action, avoids attack of bat. Moths that learn this live, while moths that do not are eaten. Eventually this ability may be passed on by inheritance. (Judith Hennessey)

over the centuries? We know that members of the *Bembix* genus are bothered greatly by parasitic flies and wingless wasps (called velvet ants) that lay their eggs in the nests and consume all the captured and paralyzed flies the wasp brings for her larvae before the larvae have a chance to eat them. We know also that the *Bembix* wasps have been driven by this to seek more isolated or difficult places to build their nests in order to escape these parasites. Evidently over the years *Bembix pruinosa* was flexible enough to develop a totally new place and method of building a nest, as she not only found escape from the parasites by going to the hot and trackless sand dunes where the flies have a hard time finding her nest, but also hid the nest even further by making a fake preliminary burrow and backtracking under the sand to clog it up, then, still under the sand, starting a new and completely hidden burrow. Even more apparently intelligent is her laying of the egg in this chamber and not moving from it until the egg is ready to hatch, so she can bring the newly hatched grub a completely fresh fly and with only one going and coming from the hidden burrow in order to fool the parasites. By all these maneuvers, including carefully disguising the nest hole with sand when she comes out, she cuts way down the possibility of parasites and so increases the chances of her young to live. This kind of behavior has probably developed by natural selection over a long period, plus a long series of graduated acts that became more and more adapted to overcoming the dangers to her young—a clear case of evolutionary excellence.

Nature–nurture controversy: Scientists are human beings and subject like all of us to be emotionally attached to ideas. The nature–nurture controversy between two large groups of scientists illustrates this. One group maintains that *nature*, that is, inheritance, decides almost completely the behavior of the individual animal, while the other group equally vehemently says that *nurture*, that is, experience and learning, provides the major part of behavior. There is another group of scientists who have been working for moderation and cooperation between the two views. There is growing evidence that inherited behavior in animals is modified by learning and sometimes also by those individuals who possess unusual perceptions and set the pace for a species. Much more research is needed.

Navigation: The study of animal migration and the navigation used to effect it and other travels of different creatures is still in its infancy. Essentially animal navigation has the following divisions: (1) *Navigation by landmarks*: Most birds, mammals, and insects navigate by landmarks, but this seems to be mainly over short distances where they know the landmarks well. Landmarks are of little use in long flights over the sea. (2) *Navigation by stellar objects such as sun, moon, and stars*. See *Inertial theories of celestial bird migration*, and *Sun-arc hypothesis*. (3) *Navigation by the earth's magnetic force*. See *Electromagnetic fields*. (4) *Navigation by emitted energy orientation*. See *Emitted energy orientation*. (5) *The unknown sense*. So amazing are some of the feats of navigation, especially by sea birds, over thousands of miles of oceans, and in the face of great storms, and also some of the feats of domestic mammals, such as cats and dogs, in finding their way back to homes over hundreds of miles of unknown territory, that we are tempted to theorize that there is still some undiscovered sense used in animal navigation that we know nothing about. This we can only call the *unknown sense*.

Nesting: Where nests are made varies among different species of birds according to their needs. Most offshore feeders nest on inaccessible cliffs or on large rocks out in the sea, all places where most predators cannot reach. In such cases, the nests and eggs are usually plain to see. Inland birds, however, generally hide their nests and have eggs that are mottled to camouflage them. However, woodpeckers and a few other birds, such as cliff swallows, whose eggs are hidden in tree holes or other well-covered sites, have white eggs.

Niche, ecologic: The ecologic niche of a species of animal or plant can be defined rather loosely as the sum total of the areas in which it lives. This can include many different habitats, as with a coyote or robin, or just one part of one habitat, as with a brine shrimp in the salt pool of a desert or a termite in the wood of a dead forest tree. (*See* Appendix A.)

Nongenetic heritability: Goes back to the old evolutionary theory of Lamarck called "the inheritance of acquired characteristics." In the first half of the twentieth century this was believed by scientists to be completely disproven, but more recent research has shown that (1) there may be some inheritance of emotional states through influence of the endocrine system and its glandular excretions; and (2) there may be some inheritance of learned behavior by taking into the body certain nucleic acid fractions. Thus, mice have been subjected to stress by crowding, which changed the secretions of adrenal glands, producing offspring with different emotional states from mice in less crowded surroundings, even though the offspring were given plenty of space. Experiments in the second type of transmission of nongenetic traits, which still needs proving, are still going on.

Nonsense orientation: When a bird or bat starts on a journey, to go home, for example, from a far away place, it often appears to start in the wrong direction. This is called *nonsense orientation*, but is usually used simply for the bird or bat to get its bearings and then redirect itself in the right direction, perhaps by locking in its sensitive nervous system to some steering force like the magnetic lines of force that surround the earth.

Olfactory communication: See *Communication, chemical*.

Ontogeny: Life cycle of a single organism. See also *Phylogeny*.

Ontogeny of behavior: The development of behavior during the lifetime of a single animal, starting with the instinctive patterns of behavior with which it is born and continuing with the modifications of this behavior by learning from the mother and others and by experience.

Ontogeny of sociality: (1) Self-reinforcement of beginning responses, such as imprinting of newborn by presence and actions of parents. (2) Contact with peers, such as two kittens playing together. (3) Increasing social discrimination, as between a dominant male and other leaders or juveniles. (4) Social guidance by family. (5) Separation from society and reintegration when animal rejoins group.

Operant conditioning: A variant of trial-and-error learning by reward in which the scientist has a box (Skinner's box) in which is an object, such as a lever (for a rat) or a disk or key (for a bird), that the animal or bird can press or peck in order to receive a reward. A food box is attached that can be opened to give the animal food only if the lever or disk is struck or depressed. The animal is conditioned first to expect a reward with each press of the lever, but later the number of times the lever must be pressed to obtain food is increased, or a definite time interval may be arranged, so that the animal can be conditioned in various other ways to test its learning ability. In this conditioning the new word *reinforcement* replaces the earlier word *reward*. Reinforcement may be defined as that which changes the probability of the response.

Oscilloscope: A kind of instrument that visually shows an electrical wave on a fluorescent screen, using a cathode ray tube. It is valuable in the study of ultrasonic sounds in animals as used in echolocation by showing their variations in wave shape. These can be photographed for comparison.

Parasitism: A parasite is generally an animal that derives a benefit from a host species, but at the expense of the host. Some parasites are so tiny or so innocuous that they do little damage to the host species, while others cause such injury as to eventually cause death. In many cases a weakened host fails to reproduce offspring, or becomes an easy prey to predators, so that the parasite itself suffers. Usually a parasite that causes too much harm to its host can be considered as having been fairly recently introduced to it. The parasite has not yet learned how to get along with its host on a long-time basis, and the host has not yet built up any defenses against the parasite. The cowbird, for example, which parasitizes the nests of other birds by laying her eggs in them to be raised by the other mother birds may cause the young of the other birds to die because the cowbird young monopolizes the food. If this is done too much it is harmful to the cowbird because she cuts down on future birds to be parasitized.

Parental care: Has evolved mainly among more complex animals with larger brains, especially where the young are born comparatively helpless and need time to be trained how to deal with the world. In feeding the young there is a direct communication between parents and young that draws them together in a common bond that becomes the basic unit of many bird and mammal social systems. Fish, in some cases, care for their young after they have hatched, but for a comparatively short time (figure B–10). Most reptiles lay their eggs and then leave them, although many, like the turtles, bury them in sand, and the American alligator mother keeps her eggs warm by burying them in decaying vegetation and may even stand guard over them. Among most animals that take care of their young it is only one parent, usually the mother, that does the caring, but occasionally, as in the phalaropes, and the stickleback fish, it is the father that makes the nest and rears the young. Among birds both parents and the young often pass back and forth signals to start feeding behavior, sometimes with bright colors in the mouth or on the bill.

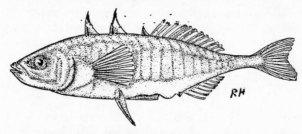

Figure B–10. Male three-spined stickleback takes care of eggs and young. (Rune Hapness)

Perceptions, unitary and serial: Young animals are considered to start their perceptions of the world one part at a time, or serially, but they learn gradually to perceive a whole object or creature as a unit. Then they take each of these units serially, finally seeing their world around them as a whole—the Gestalt perception. As we study animals we also need to see them and their worlds as a whole more important than the parts.

Period: The length of time to complete one cycle in the rhythm of a biological clock.

Peripheral sensory filters: Filter systems of neurons in the spinal cord or lower brain that filter out stimuli considered of no importance for cortical (higher brain) sensing.

Phase: A specific part of a cycle (a 24-hour cycle, for example) in the biological clock, as, for example, when the organism is feeding. *Lability*: a change in the phase due to a resetting of the biological clock, as can be done experimentally in the laboratory by changing a "day" artifically to, say, 18 hours instead of 24. *Relationships*: The enzymes and other energy sources of the body appear in properly arranged sequences or phases to help the body coordinate as a whole. For example, crabs are scavengers and the times of their greatest activity occur at night when the tide goes out, exposing food left by the waves; so these phases are in tune with the moon and the tides, but they also have a day phase and night phase of activity in tune with the movements of the sun. *Entrainment*: The changing of a phase by the application of an outside force, such as light or dryness. *Shifting*: The phase makes a definite shift after entrainment has been applied for some time. *Synchrony*: Occurs when a particular phase of reproduction happens to all members of a species at the same time at a particular latitude and place. Thus, the male, orange-crowned warblers arrive in Sonoma County, California about the same time in mid-February and all start singing as a preliminary of courtship and to establish territories.

Pheromones: Hormones or smell molecules that carry messages between individuals of a given species outside the body. They are particularly used by ants in their communications along trails, but also by some other insects, and even mammals. Specific behavior patterns are released by these pheromones, such as running to look for food, or preparing to fight in defense of a colony.

Photoperiod effect: The effect of increasing daylight in the springtime, starting animals to prepare for migration or the raising of young. Decreasing daylight in fall triggers the fall migration, or hibernation.

Phylogeny: The story of the evolution of a particular kind of plant or animal, or of a genus, family, or order, or even of animals as a whole, as shown in their history written in the rocks by fossils.

Plumage as releasers of behavior: In many birds males have different kinds of plumage from females, and both from juveniles. This is because each type of plumage has a different effect on the behavior of other birds. Thus, the breast of a male robin induces another male robin to flee or attack, depending on which side of a territorial boundary the first male is standing. The female's lack of a red breast induces a male to start courting her. The plainer coloration of young birds, also usually more speckled, prevents them from being attacked by older birds and also camouflages them. (See figure B–11.)

Polyandry: A form of mating in which the female (usually in birds) acts as dominant towards the male in courtship and may even take several mates during the mating season. As in the phalaropes, the female in such cases usually has more colorful plumage than the male. She may even allow the male to build the nest and take care of the eggs.

Figure B–11. Male red-shafted flicker displays orange wing linings and bright red mark on cheek that threatens rival male while attracting female.

Polygamy: Occurs where a male mates with several females in the mating season. Usually these males are much larger and more conspicuous and colorful than the females. Polygamy among birds usually occurs more often in grassland areas where there is more food available than in forests. Some male mammals, such as the fur seal, have large harems in which the male dominates jealously over the females, and surplus males with less fighting ability are driven off to live as bachelors.

Populations of animals: See *Dispersion*, *Mortality*.

Preadaptation: Occurs when representatives of a particular species enter a new area, as when some land birds are carried by a storm or on a raft to an island where their genus has not been before. If the birds have learned certain adaptations on the mainland, such as boring in dead trees for insect grubs as a woodpecker does, then they are preadapted for finding the same kinds of food on the island even though the insects are different.

Protection in groups: Ranges from protection against the weather or non-living hazards, as when penguins or buffalo come close together to protect each other against storms, through protection by the simple power of numbers to confuse or frighten a predator, to cooperative defense with horns as with musk-oxen against wolves, or teeth as with baboons against leopards, or to flocks of birds that actually mob a predator. A higher form of protection is shown when one or more animals try to rescue another, as when porpoises come to the rescue of a friend from sharks.

Receptor filtering: Happens when the receptor itself, such as the ear, filters out in a female bird, for example, at mating time, all sounds except those made by the male to whom she is receptive.

Recognition: Is divided into: (1) *Species recognition*, or the recognition of one's own species by its marks, colors, sounds, and smells, etc.; the original imprinting of this recognition usually happens right after birth when the young creature recognizes its parents. Proper recognition of one's species prevents interspecies mating. (2) *Population recognition*: Happens within a species when one recognizes his own particular group as friends, but outsiders of the same species may be recognized as possible enemies. Thus, one baboon band will fight another over territory, knowing the other band is different by its smell, appearance, and sounds. (3) *Individual recognition*: Happens among most species, with each individual in a group being recognized as different by the others, even though to a man they may seem all exactly alike.

Recognition signals: Used by the more advanced organisms to make sure they respect with association only those of their own species or group. Where members of a species are so close together in appearance and action to another species that recognition signals do not work, trouble may take place, as when a *Formica rufa* queen ant enters the nest of

Formica fusca, and gets them to accept her because her recognition signals are the same. She kills the *fusca* queen and then acts as queen until her own progeny eventually take over the nest. The more successful species are those whose recognition signals have such a special code that other species, particularly those who are parasitic, cannot break the code, and thus are rejected and defended against successfully. Thus, some beehives reject and kill the parasitic bee moth, while other hives do not and are parasitized and destroyed.

Recruitment: Happens in a population of a particular species, such as the fur seals, when males that have been driven away from the rookeries by the larger and more fierce harem bulls form a reserve pool of males that could be drawn on if anything happened, such as the killing of many of the harem bulls by men, to replace the harem bulls by recruitment.

Redirected behavior: Happens when an animal has one drive within it overruled by another. Thus, a combative elephant seal male may have its drive to attack another male suddenly overruled by finding itself facing a much larger and noisier bull and will turn away in fear.

Reflexive selection: A principle of animal behavior that is the opposite of mimicry. Instead of trying to look like some other creature, members of a particular species will have varied and different appearances, as is found in some species of brittle stars, so that the predators do not get a visual image of one type of animal they are looking for to eat, are disturbed by the different types they see, and leave most of them alone.

Reinforcement or reward in learning: If an action of an animal helps or relieves bodily needs, the animal is likely to repeat such action, thus reinforcing the action so it becomes a habit that helps the animal cope more successfully with its environment. Thus, some ancestor of the barn owl found that nesting in barns not only protected the owls from the weather but gave them a fine, daily source of mice for food. This new lesson gradually spread to other barn owls, because such owls had a better chance to continue to live and reproduce, until it became very widespread in the species. It was *reinforced*.

Releasers: Certain things in the environment surrounding an animal act as stimuli for instinctive actions or drives and are called *releasers*. They may sometimes be different from what would stimulate a human being. Thus, a human mother seeing her baby hurt would not have to hear it crying to rush to its rescue, but chicken-like birds are not stimulated by such a sign, as they have to hear a young bird cry for help before they go to the rescue. There are thus several different releasers for each kind of animal, and different animals may have different kinds. The sight or sound or smell of a predator causes a deer to run, whereas a wolf pack seeing a deer running is instinctively stimulated to chase after it. However, there are certain releasers that act only at certain times of the year or under special circumstances. Mating behavior is released in many animals and birds only at the proper time of the year to produce offspring when the most food is available to feed them. Hunting behavior by a peregrine falcon or duck hawk is released in the hawk when it sees a flock of ducks in flight below it in the air, but may not be released at all by seeing ducks feeding in the reeds of a lake.

Releasing mechanisms: See *Innate releasing mechanism.*

Reproduction, sociality of: Social gatherings or organizations of the individuals of a species may influence reproduction in the following ways: (1) Just gathering together brings males and females together and increases the chances of reproduction, so bettering the species' chances of survival. (2) Sociality by increasing the chance of seeing other individuals mating or courting influences other pairs to court and mate. So dependent is the reproductive behavior of some species on these releasers produced by social gatherings that without them females may refuse to mate, or if reproduction does take place, they may destroy or void the fetus. (4) There is considerable stimulation of breeding behavior in animals that converge at the mating season for special display dances or formal courting. This happens, for example, at the *leks* or great display dances of such birds as the male prairie chickens, turkeys, herons, and cranes. (5) Building nests or dens or other special places for rearing young, when done socially, influences others of the same species to join in the work, which is soon followed by mating and egg laying. (6) In large colonies of breeding animals, competition between males or between pairs for the best breeding or nesting sites not only stimulates other reproductive behavior but acts as a selector of the most powerful and adaptive blood lines for the production of the most progeny, thus improving the genetic development of the species. There is a great deal of research to be done in this field.

Reproductive behavior: Establishing of territory by males and their courting of females are both preliminary forms of reproductive behavior in many animals as well as the usual rivalry between males. See also *Display* and *Fighting.* Males particularly, but also females, often go through special maneuvers before the mating act is released for their particular species, maneuvers that are generally different for each species. This helps prevent interbreeding with related species. The making of nests or dens is done either by both sexes working together or by one alone, and the same situation holds for the raising of young, at least among the birds and mammals. Among most of the lower animals, with a few exceptions such as the stickleback fish, the male has little if any rearing duties, while the female often finishes her duty to the next generation by laying eggs in a comparatively safe place. See *Nesting.*

Response output: What the animal does in response to a stimulus input by an outside source into the nervous system. If this response changes the nature of the stimulus from the environment, as when a bull moose reacts so strongly to the attack of a wolf pack as to discourage the attack, this new transformation becomes a *response input* and the stimulus becomes an *output* by the wolves running away.

Responsiveness to stimulation: This is tied to a threshold of response. In some species or individuals the threshold is high, in others low. For example young cheetahs or lions may attempt to attack a rhinoceros out of youthful ignorance, but suddenly find themselves facing a large and dangerous animal with a very low threshold of response to an attack (i.e., a very low boiling point). Cheetahs and lions either learn very quickly not to attack rhinoceroses or they die. A small antelope, on the other hand, is conditioned from a very early age to run from any lion or cheetah. It has a high level of flight response to such a stimulation. Most young animals or birds react with fear or flight to most strange stimuli in their environment. As they grow older, however, they learn which are really dangerous and which are not, and so become more discriminating in their responses.

Reward in learning: See *Reinforcement or reward in learning*.

Ritual fighting: Ritual, ceremonial, and tournament fighting are more or less the same thing. They usually help a species hold the fighting between males (or females in some cases) down to a level where it is not too destructive to the species. In such fighting the males go through ritual forms that are copied by all young animals as they grow up watching their elders. Thus, two buck antelope, fighting over a territory or females, will use horns against horns, pushing and shoving, but rarely use them as they could for sudden lunges with the horns against the midsection, which could lead to fatal wounds. Thus, the one who shoves hardest wins, but the loser is not killed or wounded.

Ritualization: A complex development of behavior, derived from innate forms or patterns, which develops over a long period into stereotyped (rigidly repeated) reactions to certain stimuli. For example, a wolf who is about to be attacked by a dominant wolf in the pack rolls over onto his back and exposes his throat and belly, which effectively stops the dominant wolf from attacking. This prevents injury and so maintains the strength of the pack, a useful adaptation and now ritualized into a form of behavior repeated from generation to generation. Ritualization is also believed to occur through a displacement activity, as when a male gull who is threatened with attack does not attack back but picks up straws as if building a nest. This is usually done at a boundary line between the territories of two pairs around their nests, and indicates to the attacker that the first bird will fight if pressed too far. This helps establish a boundary between the two nest territories without the need for actual fighting, and so is an example of where the nest-building activity, which would otherwise be futile (nonadaptive to real nest building), becomes adaptive as a communicative device in its ritualization to establish a boundary and prevent fighting.

RNA molecules: Molecules of ribonucleic acid are believed, as the result of recent experiments, to be the key memory-inducing chemicals in the brain or in the central nervous systems of many animals. See *Memory storage*. Research showed that planarians (flatworms) whose heads were cut off and then grew new heads retained memories that were held by the original animal if there were RNA molecules in the body, but if the RNA molecules were destroyed, the planarians lost these memories. This proved a connection between these complex molecules and memory.

Role assignment in social life: This concept involving the social organization and behavior of the higher animals, such as crows, baboons, and dolphins, has begun to take the place of dominance as a major factor in understanding animal social behavior. In an immensely complex baboon society, for example, animals play different roles and these roles may change dramatically. Since understanding such roles depends upon knowing the meaning of many signals that are exchanged between the animals, signals that may be very hard to detect by human beings, it is understandable that research in this line is very difficult. Thus, Dr. Shirley Strum spent 16 months practically living with a baboon troop in the grassy plains and rocky escarpments in the veld of Kenya, and learned things about them unknown before. These troops of olive baboons (*Papio anubis*) had long been considered ruled by a dominant oligarchy of powerful males, 75 pounds or more in weight, and with long knife-like fangs. But careful observation over a long period showed that the troop was kept together as a unit and guided more by the older females than by the large males. These females formed the stable friendships with other females and with males around which the whole troop circled. The relations of these females with the males were far from being just sexual, but were more important as examples of deep respect on the part of the males and guidance on the part of the older females. Between the males, on the contrary, there was constant rivalry, although not necessarily fighting, and they fairly often changed from one troop to another. It was true the males formed the fighting front of the troop when attacked by a predator, and this was their major leadership role, but otherwise the older females had the superior role of guiding their families, planning the troop foraging behavior, and finding shelter for the night. This particular troop illustrated also what could be a changing role for a whole species. For centuries these baboons had been mainly vegetarian, eating meat they caught only occasionally, but, as their natural enemies, the leopards, lions, and hyenas, were killed by men to protect domestic animals, the baboons appeared to learn increasingly how to become successful predators of antelopes and other grazing animals, somewhat replacing the great carnivores in the role of meat eaters in the ecology of the veld.

Search image: If a predator catches a number of prey animals of a particular species whose taste it likes, it forms a search image of this kind of animal and searches for it frequently. If a member of this species has a color pattern different from the usual one, it may escape this predator because it will not be noticed, and this would influence a greater variety of color patterns in future generations by natural selection, as these variations in pattern would encourage a better chance of surviving.

Selection, directional: In natural selection of a species population that has a variation from light to dark individuals, if the environment becomes increasingly dark because of the increase of shading trees, natural selection will begin to choose the darker individuals for longer life and more progeny, causing a directional selection in favor of the dark colors.

Selection, group: Animals in a group that cooperate for mutual success in foraging and in defense against predators are selected *in* if they conform to the group rules of cooperation and if they understand and follow the social signals, but are selected *out* if they stray too far from the group, or misunderstand signals that demand cooperation, for predators will soon seize them. There is also selection as regards groups as a whole, those groups maintaining their populations and growing in strength that learn to avoid environmental dangers, as successful crow flocks do when they avoid men with guns long before they get close to the flocks. On the other hand, groups who fail to adapt well to changing environments become weaker in numbers and finally vanish, as did the great flocks of passenger pigeons who never learned to adapt to the danger of men and their guns.

Selection, sexual: See *Sexual dimorphism*. In some species great danger from predators has apparently eliminated sexual dimorphism, and both males and females have been selected who were best camouflaged in their environment; so they tended to look alike instead of different.

Selection, stabilizing: When selection of individuals from a species population tends to select for favorable adaptation to the environment those individuals who are near the mean between two extremes, such as between boldness or fear towards sharks on the part of porpoises, then this is called a *stabilizing selection*.

Selection for territoriality: How natural selection selects territoriality as a good adaptive behavior pattern in certain species and ignores it in others is not always clear, but there is some evidence that territoriality is more adaptive for species that need more room to act in, such species whose pairs are the fundamental basis of their sociality, but that in highly integrated and populous communities, such as those of the crows and starlings, territoriality becomes nonadaptive and group cooperation for food foraging becomes a stronger necessity.

Selective pressures of the environment: When two different but closely related species occupy partly the same territory, selective pressures of the environment are likely to force them to become different in how they use the habitats available for food foraging. If not, one species will probably gradually force the other out. See *Gause's hypothesis*.

Semiotics: A comparatively new term meaning the marriage or cooperation of many different scientific disciplines, such as physiology, ethology, climatology, cybernetics, mathematics, and ecology, to get a look at the whole meaning of animal behavior, as seen from different angles, but all brought into harmony.

Sensory coding: As the physiologists and psychologists got deeper into their research into the physiological basis of behavior, they found the picture growing more and more complex. Sensory coding, which is the way the various sensory cells, such as the cells in the retina of the eye, combine with the deeper layers of nerve cells in the brain of an animal to encode or translate to the brain the sensory stimuli, shows an extraordinary complexity. This is due to both the sensory cells, and the main nerve cells of the brain dividing up special duties in the process of encoding stimuli, some, for example, acting to carry and encode a bright light stimulus, and others a dark one. This coding is necessary in order to enable the animal to act quickly in a way to cope with whatever changes appear in its environment, and not waste time on inconsequential actions. Thus, the frog must be able to select quickly the proper motions to make when a fly passes near, and, perhaps, at the same fraction of a second, avoid swallowing a similar-looking bee. At the same time the sensory cells and nerve cells connected with the frog's ears are encoding the sounds of footsteps approaching, and it must determine quickly the moment it would be wise to jump into the pond and disappear among the thick growth of the water plants. Electrophysiological machines and methods are being used by scientists to unravel how the different cells act in this sensory coding.

Sensory feedback: Happens when an animal transforms a stimulus input into a response output, which changes the nature of the environment, as in the catching and eating of a mouse by a barn owl, which produces a response input and a stimulus output (no mouse). The last half of this process is the feedback to the first stimulus.

Sex differences in behavior: The two sexes of any species usually have certain different behavior patterns. In a maze male rats usually quickly find the way to a female in heat, but the female will do the same with either a sexually passive or active male. Sometimes a female will be of different size than a male, as a female woodpecker will have a different-sized bill so that her behavior in food foraging is different from that of the male. She cannot dig as deeply into wood so must find different insect food.

Sexual dimorphism: Differences between the sexes in appearance and actions and in sexual selection (figure B–12). Sexes usually differ in behavior in one or more of the following ways: (1) When the male is larger he tends to act more domineering and aggressive. (2) The male will often have larger and more beautiful feathers in birds, which means he will do a lot more strutting, posturing, and other kinds of display. (3) If the male has more dangerous fighting weapons such as horns in a male deer or long, sharp tusks in a baboon or wild boar, he will use these to threaten or actually fight with other males much more than the female would. Sometimes these patterns are reversed, as in phalaropes, where the female has the beautiful feathers and does the displaying. There are many other differences.

Skinner's box: See *Operant conditioning.*

Smell receptors, primary (theory of J. E. Amoore): (1) Camphoraceous, (2) floral, (3) pepperminty, (4) musky, (5) pungent, and (6) putrid. According to this theory each such smell fits like a key into the proper primary smell receptor, each particular molecule having the right key shape.

Social ethology: A name given by John H. Crook to a new approach to the study of social behavior in animals, in which the combined effects of innate tendencies, drives, or instincts, plus all conditions of the environment, all learned behavior, and every other possible influence, are studied as a whole to grasp the total picture of a given animal social

Figure B–12. Sexual dimorphism in the California quail. The female on the left is plainer than the strikingly marked male on the right. (James Gordon Irving)

264 / THE EXPLORER NATURALIST

species. It has proved very difficult to do a complete job, since so many
  sensory effects and producers are as yet hidden from us in most species
  studied.

Social feeding (trophallaxis): Best found in social insects, such as ants and
  bees, where adult insects transfer premasticated food to the larvae or
  to other adults, but it is also found among many birds who give premasticated food to their young. However, the insects by such feeding
  often transfer hormones from one to the other, which form a kind of
  communication we do not yet fully understand. See also *Communication*.

Social interaction and learning: Includes (1) *social stimulation or facilita-
  tion* (also contagious behavior), in which one animal performs and by
  so doing stimulates others to do likewise (as when one baboon starting
  to chase a young antelope stimulates others to take up the chase with
  him); (2) *observational learning*, especially strong when juveniles observe their parents' feeding behavior, flight, escape from enemies, etc.,
  but also found between adults, and less often when individuals of one
  species observe another species in action and learn from them; and (3)
  local enhancement, when one animal is attracted to a special locality
  by the activities of another animal in that locality.

Social systems, homology or analogy of: It is very difficult to look at two
  different species with similar behavioral patterns and determine
  whether these are homologous (derived from a common ancestor), or
  analogous (having no connection with the past, but derived from con-
  vergence of behavior in a similar habitat). An example of homology is
  found in a number of different species of cormorants that all nest in
  large colonies out on large rocks in the ocean, which is very likely to
  have derived from a common ancestor that started this practice long
  ago. An example of analogy in social behavior is the keeping of large
  harems of females by both sperm whale bulls in the ocean, and fur
  seal bulls on rocky beaches. These two very different sea mammals
  probably developed this behavior pattern entirely separately and not
  from any common ancestor.

Sociality: The state or quality of being sociable. This varies from animals
  just being together without any particular ties, to highly organized
  animal societies such as a termite city or a baboon troop in which
  discipline is maintained.

Sociobiology: The study of animal and plant social groups.

Sociophysiology: The study of the effects of social interactions between
  animals on the physiology of their bodies. An example is the fierce
  combative nature of a rogue elephant bull, or a rogue sperm whale
  bull, caused by his being expelled from his herd so he turns in anger
  on other living things. Much needs to be learned in this field.

Sound communication, territorial displays through: The songs of male
  birds often advertise to other males and females of the same species

that each singer holds a certain territory. The male moves about the boundary of the territory singing, and other males rarely cross this boundary. The male cricket also chirps to indicate it has a territory as well as to attract the female, as does the bull alligator when it roars from its part of the swamp. The drumming of male ruffed grouse is another territorial display.

Sounds, communication by: Sounds, both ultrasonic and those heard by the human ear, are used by many animals in communication, although the majority of invertebrates (with the exception of the Orthoptera, Homoptera, and some of the Hymenoptera among insects) use touch, sight, and smell, while reptiles are noted for little beyond a hiss for sound communication. Some fish make grunting noises with their swim bladders, while others make snapping noises, as do a number of shrimp and crabs. Most amphibians, mammals, and birds produce sound signals in the throat by the movement and vibration of air from the lungs, although the amphibian sounds of frogs and toads are mainly stereotyped mating calls. It is the mammals and birds alone that use a wide variety of sounds in communication, particularly the higher forms. Some of them use other ways to make noise, like the bill hammering of woodpeckers, the thumping or drumming of rabbits and grouse, the shrill wing noises of hummingbirds and snipe, and the chest beating of gorillas. Most of these sounds convey emotional meanings of various sorts, although man and possibly some of the whales can convey ideas with sounds.

Spacing behavior: Spacing is found mostly in territorial species, and how far the territories are spaced apart in size usually depends on a number of factors. Foraging patterns usually influence space, with predators almost always having larger territories than herbivores, while large predators have the largest territories of all. If food is plentiful, territories tend to be smaller in size partly because a small space is easier to defend and partly because plentiful food tends to limit aggressiveness. On the other hand starving conditions may limit territorial spacing simply because the animal has less energy for defending a territory.

Species common behavior: Behavior common to the whole species.

Species specific fixed motor pattern: Applies to a stereotyped behavior pattern or instinctive reaction to stimuli that is found in all members of a species or at least all of one sex, as for example the display of her swollen belly by the female stickleback fish at mating time in response to the male's displays.

Specific action potentiality: A newer term for *reaction-specific energy*, which means a reservoir of specific action potential energy is stored in the central nervous system ready to be let loose by the correct releaser or outside stimulus. Thus, a mouse hiding under a leaf and knowing

that a wildcat is stalking it crouches, with all its energy building for a
wild dash to its hole the instant it senses where the cat is.

Stereotyped motor pattern: Patterns of behavior that an animal does without previous learning; they are innate or instinctive. Thus, a baby
chick knows how to peck for food without having to be taught.

Stimulus generalization: When an animal is being trained to respond to a
certain stimulus by conditioning, when it becomes thoroughly conditioned, it will respond to another stimulus of generally the same
type. Thus, if it responds to a drum beat, a spoon banged on a plate
may give it the same stimulus, even though the sound is somewhat
different.

Stimulus input: The transfer of the outside stimulus into a message passing along the afferent nerve fibers to the central nervous system.

Sun-arc hypothesis of bird migration orientation: By something like an
inner sextant and an ability to judge distances in relation to the position of the sun in the sky, a migrating bird is supposed to be able to
gauge from the arc and position of the sun at noon where it is in flight
in relation to the nesting grounds towards which it is flying. If true,
the bird navigates homeward by innate response in somewhat the
same way a captain navigates his ship over the sea. If so, it is an
extraordinary feat, but it has not yet been proven to be possible.

Symbiosis: A close interrelationship between two or more different species,
including the following divisions (all described in this glossary): (1)
mutualism, (2) parasitism, and (3) commensalism.

Sympatric: Pertains to related species of animals found in the same geographic area, which are able to live together because they occupy different ecologic niches, just as hen water turkeys, great blue herons,
common egrets, and black-crowned night herons occupy different
levels for nesting in the treetops of a Tennessee flood plain forest.

Synchronization: Occurs when birds nest together at the same time in
large colonies, as sea birds do, or when a bird gives a signal and the
other birds of the group repeat the same signal at the same time, or
when an antelope flashes its white tail, which immediately causes all
neighboring antelopes to flash their tails and run in the same direction as the first signaler is running. There are many other examples of
synchronous behavior, all worth careful study to understand.

Taste (gustation): Taste reception on the tongue is generally much more
limited in its action than olfaction or smelling, but the two sometimes
interact together. Some creatures have taste buds in places other than
the tongue. The four major receptors are for sweet, salty, sour, and
bitter tastes.

Taxes: A taxis is a movement toward or away from some external
stimulus. Thus, an animal with a positive phototropic taxis moves towards light. Other types of taxes include moving towards or away

from warmth, height, dark, water, the smell of man (bed bugs move toward the smell but must do so in the dark, so have two taxes operating), and so forth. A taxis is not always quite this simple, as some moths prefer dim light, but not either darkness or bright light.

Temporal patterns: Temporary patterns of behavior, as when caribou spread out to feed during certain parts of the day, but come together in protective columns and groups when travelling.

Territorialism: Simply the marking off of a territory by sound, smell, visual display, or other means by an individual male or female, pair or group. In North America such territorialism happens mainly at certain times of the year, generally at the mating, nesting, or denning seasons, but group territorialism in some highly social animals such as the prairie dog may last all year around. Some species are territorial in both spring and fall, others in just one of these seasons, while still others may be territorial just in summer, as is the case with the California sealion and the fur seal in Alaska.

Thermoregulation, social: Many animals come close together in social aggregations in winter to conserve heat. Bees do this in their hives in winter, also fanning the air to dispel the cold. Penguins in the Antarctic winter, especially the huge emperor penguins (figure B–13), defy the worst cold and winds in the world by crowding closely together.

Thigmotaxis, positive: Said of animals, such as mice and rats, that like to keep their bodies in touch with the walls of tunnels.

Tradition learning: Generally found in animals of comparatively high intelligence whose young are raised and taught by their parents over a fairly long period. Thus, traditions of behavior are passed from gener-

P.T.

Figure B–13. The four-foot-tall emperor penguin demonstrates social thermoregulation when many crowd together on the ice during the Antarctic winter, giving mutual protection against cold and wind. (Phyllis Thompson)

ation to generation in wolf packs, caribou herds, baboon troops, and crow flocks. I even saw one flock of crows that had all the appearance of having a trial by judge and possibly jury, when one crow was delinquent in his duty of acting as sentinel and let a hawk attack a member of the flock without giving warning. He was killed, apparently by order of the court. This would be a tradition in this flock. However, although this is the way the trial appeared to me, a scientist has to be very careful not to accept this sort of thing as fact until backed by more evidence.

Transverse orientations: Such orientations are at fixed angles, such as at an angle of 90 degrees, oriented to the sun, which would be the source of external stimulus. This gives a bird orientation in flight, and the movement in flight in such orientations is different from straight toward or straight away from the source of stimulation, thus being transverse to it.

Trial-and-error learning: By trial and error an animal is conditioned to act in a way that will improve his well-being. Thus, a young toad tries hunting at night and finds his best luck occurs when he comes to where insects are attracted to a bright light. After a few experiences of this, he eagerly comes to the light at night because he has now learned, or is conditioned to expect, that at such a place he will find a good meal. See also *Operant conditioning*.

Ultrasonic communication: Bats, dolphins, shrews, and some cave-dwelling birds are noted for communicating in ultrasound, which means sound unheard by man. Man, however, can detect these sounds with microphones, tape recorders, and oscilloscopes.

Umwelt: A German term, used by ethologists to define the world as each kind of animal sees it. Thus, the umwelt of an eagle, whose sensations of the world are bound up almost entirely with his extraordinarily keen vision and his high flight, is very different from the umwelt of a bear, whose eyes are quite short-sighted and do not see very clearly any distance, but whose nose is extraordinarily keen, reading the world all about him by the many smells that come to him on the wind.

Vacuum activity: Activity that may occur when an animal is frustrated or prevented from receiving the normal stimulus to release his stored energy, such as hunger or sex, in which case he will go through the motions of eating even when there is nothing to eat.

Vestigial behavior: When an animal continues to use a form of behavior used by its ancestors even when this behavior is no longer of value to the species. Thus, the scavenger wasp (*Microbembix*) eats only dead insects or furnishes them for its young, but it still may sting them even as its predator ancestors used to sting live insects.

Vibration theory of smell: States that each type of smell molecule has a different range of vibration, which triggers an electric discharge in certain chemoreceptor cells in the nose.

Warning signals: Parents usually have special signals to warn their young of danger. Social animals often appoint sentinels that watch for and warn of enemies approaching. Some birds, like jays, are self-appointed warners of the whole woods when a predator approaches. In the jungles of Panama I observed how a special booming cry of the black howler monkeys warned of the coming of the jaguar, a big spotted cat.

Appendix C

SUGGESTED REFERENCES

Titles are arranged under the following categories, placed alphabetically:

Animal behavior
Animals in general
Birds
Climatology and weather
Conservation of Natural Resources
Ecology
Fish
Fresh water life
Geology and paleontology
Invertebrates in general
Mammals
Natural history in general
Naturalists, stories about
Photography and other special techniques
Plants
Plants—Primitive
Reptiles and Amphibians
Seashore life.

ANIMAL BEHAVIOR

Allee, W. C. *Cooperation Among Animals*. Rev. ed. 1951. Henry Schuman, New York.

Ardrey, Robert. *The Territorial Imperative* (A personal inquiry into the animal origins of property and nations). 1966. Atheneum, New York.

Callahan, Philip. *Insect Behavior*. 1970. Four Winds Press, New York.

Carthy, J. D. *Introduction to the Behavior of the Invertebrates*. 1971. Hafner Press, New York.

Crook, J. H., ed. *Social Behavior in Birds and Mammals*. 1970. Academic Press, New York.

Dimond, Stuart. *Social Behavior of Animals*. 1970. B. T. Batsford Ltd., London.

Ewer, R. F. *Ethology of Mammals*. 1969. Plenum Publishing, New York.

Fox, Michael. *Abnormal Behavior in Animals*. 1968. W. B. Saunders, Philadelphia.

Kikkawa, Jiro, and Thorne, Malcolm J. *The Behavior of Animals*. 1971. Taplinger Publishing, New York.

Lorenz, Konrad, and Leyhausen, Paul. *Motivation of Human and Animal Behavior: An Ethological View*. 1973. Van Nostrand-Reinhold, New York.

Nevin, J. A., and Reynolds, George S. *The Study of Behavior, Learning, Motivation, Emotion and Instinct*. 1972. Scott Foresman, Glenview, Ill.

Tinbergen, Niko. *The Animal in its World*. 1972. Harvard University Press, Cambridge.

Wallace, Robert A. *The Ecology and Evolution of Animal Behavior*. 1973. Goodyear Publishing, Pacific Palisades, Calif.

ANIMALS IN GENERAL

Breland, Osmond P. *Animal Life and Lore*. Rev. ed. 1972. Harper and Row, New York.

Brown, Vinson. *How to Make a Miniature Zoo*. 1957. Little, Brown, Boston.

———. *Knowing the Outdoors in the Dark*. 1972. Stackpole Books, Harrisburg, Pa.

Grunefeld, Gerhard. *Understanding Animals*. 1965. The Viking Press, New York.

Hancocks, David. *Master Builders of the Animal World*. 1973. Harper and Row, New York.

Hanson, Earl H. *Animal Diversity*. 2nd ed. 1964. Prentice-Hall, Englewood Cliffs, N.J.

Latimer, James. *Introduction to Animal Physiology*. 2nd ed. 1973. William C. Brown, Dubuque, Ia.

MacArthur, Robert H., and Connell, Joseph H. *The Biology of Populations*. 1967. John Wiley & Sons, New York.

Milne, Lorus and Margery. *The Senses of Animals and Men*. 1962. Atheneum, New York.

Murie, Olaus J. *Field Guide to Animal Tracks*. 1954. Houghton Mifflin, Boston.

Nathan, Peter. *The Nervous System*. 1969. J. B. Lippincott, Philadelphia.

Prosser, C. Ladd. *Comparative Animal Physiology*. 1973. W. B. Saunders, Philadelphia.

Snedigar, Robert. *Our Small Native Animals, Their Habits and Care*. Rev. ed. 1963. Dover Publications, New York.

Von Frisch, Karl. *Animal Architecture*. Trans. Lisbeth Gombrich. 1974. Harcourt Brace Jovanovich, New York.

BIRDS[1]

Bent, Arthur C. *Life Histories of North American Birds* (A series of several volumes). 1958. Dover Publications, New York.

Brown, Vinson, and Weston, Henry, Jr. *Handbook of California Birds*. 2nd rev. ed. 1973. Naturegraph Publishers, Healdsburg, Calif.

Forbush, Edward H. *Natural History of American Birds of Eastern and Central North America*. Revised and abridged by John Richard May. 1953. Houghton Mifflin, Boston.

Lockley, R. M. *Ocean Wanderers: The Migratory Sea Birds of the World*. 1973. Stackpole Books, Harrisburg, Pa.

Peterson, Roger Tory. *A Field Guide to the Birds: Eastern Land and Water Birds*. 2nd rev. ed. 1947. Houghton Mifflin, Boston.

———. *A Field Guide to the Birds of Texas and Adjacent States*. 1963. Houghton Mifflin, Boston.

———. *A Field Guide to Western Birds*. Rev. ed. 1961. Houghton Mifflin, Boston.

CLIMATOLOGY AND WEATHER

Day, John A., and Sternes, G. I. *Climate and Weather*. 1970. Addison-Wesley, Reading, Mass.

Griffiths, John F. *Applied Climatology, An Introduction*. 1966. Oxford University Press, Cambridge, Eng.

Trewartha, Glenn T. *Introduction to Climate*. 4th ed. 1968. McGraw-Hill, New York.

---

[1]See also Animal Behavior.

CONSERVATION OF NATURAL RESOURCES

Adams, Alexander. *Eleventh Hour: A Hard Look at Conservation and the Future*. 1970. G. P. Putnam's Sons, New York.

Clare, Patricia. *The Struggle for the Great Barrier Reef*. 1971. Walker, New York.

Dasmann, Raymond. *Environmental Conservation*. 1972. John Wiley & Sons, New York.

Plowden, David. *The Hand of Man on America*. 1973. Chatham Press, Riverside, Conn.

ECOLOGY

Allee, Warder C. *Principles of Animal Ecology*. 1949. W. B. Saunders, Philadelphia.

Ashby, Maurice. *Introduction to Plant Ecology*. 1969. St. Martin's Press, New York.

Dice, Lee R. *Natural Communities*. 1968. University of Michigan Press, Ann Arbor, Mich.

Hedgpeth, Joel W., and Ladd, Harry S. *Treatise on Marine Ecology and Paleo-ecology*. 2 vols. 1963. Geological Society of America, Boulder, Colo.

Macfadden, A. *Animal Ecology*. 1957. Sir Isaac Pitman & Sons, London.

Schafer, Wilhelm. *Ecology and Paleoecology of Marine Environments*. 1972. University of Chicago Press, Chicago.

Shelford, Victor E. *The Ecology of North America*. 1963. University of Illinois Press, Urbana, Ill.

FISH[2]

Breder, Charles M., Jr. *Fieldbook of Marine Fishes of the Atlantic Coast*. Rev. ed. 1948. G. P. Putnam's Sons, New York.

Eddy, Samuel. *How to Know the Freshwater Fishes*. 2nd ed. 1970. William C. Brown, Dubuque, Ia.

Fitch, John E., and Lavenberg, Rober J. *Deep Water Fishes of California*. 1968. University of California Press, Berkeley.

Herald, Earl. *Fishes of North America*. 1972. Doubleday, Garden City, N.Y.

Lagler, Karl F. *Freshwater Fishery Biology*. 1956. William C. Brown, Dubuque, Ia.

---

[2]See also Fresh Water Life and Seashore Life.

FRESH WATER LIFE[3]

Klots, Elsie B. *The New Field Book of Fresh Water Life*. 1966. G. P. Putnam's Sons, New York.

Needham, James G., and Paul R. *Guide to Study of Fresh Water Biology*. 5th ed. 1962. Holden-Day, San Francisco.

Pennak, R. W. *Fresh Water Invertebrates of North America*. 1972. Doubleday, Garden City, N.Y.

Usinger, Robert M. *Aquatic Insects of California with Keys to North American Genera and California Species*. 1956. University of California Press, Berkeley.

Vogt, Dieter, and Wermuth, Heinz. *Complete Aquarium*. 1963. Arco Publishing, New York.

GEOLOGY AND PALEONTOLOGY

Clark, Thomas H., and Stearn, Colin W. *Geological Evolution of North America*. 2nd ed. 1968. Ronald Press, New York.

Dunbar, Carl O., and Waage, Karl M. *Historical Geology*. Rev. ed. 1969. John Wiley & Sons, New York.

Kummel, Bernhard, and Raup, David. *Handbook of Paleontological Techniques*. 1965. W. H. Freeman, San Francisco.

Raup, David M., and Stanley, Steven M. *Principles of Paleontology*. 1970. W. H. Freeman, San Francisco.

Romer, Alfred S. *The Vertebrate Story*. 4th ed. 1959. University of Chicago Press, Chicago.

Schuchert, Charles. *Atlas of Paleogeographic Maps of North America*. 1955. John Wiley & Sons, New York.

Scott, Dukinfield H. *Studies in Fossil Botany*. 3rd ed., 2 vols. 1974. Hafner Press, New York.

Shimer, Harvey, and Schrock, Robert R. *Index Fossils of North America*. 1944. The M.I.T. Press, Cambridge.

Von Zittel, K. A. *Text-Book of Paleontology*. 3 vols. 1964. Hafner Press, New York.

INVERTEBRATES IN GENERAL[4]

Arnett, Ross H. *The Beetles of the United States*. 1971. American Entomological Institute, Ann Arbor, Mich.

Barnes, Robert D. *Invertebrate Zoology*. 2nd ed. 1968. W. B. Saunders, Philadelphia.

---

[3]See also Fish, Invertebrates in General, Reptiles and Amphibians, etc.
[4]See also Animal Behavior, Fresh Water Life, and Seashore Life.

Borror, Donald J., and White, Richard E. *Field Guide to the Insects of America North of Mexico*. 1970. Houghton Mifflin, Boston.

Brevoort, Harry F., and Fanning, Eleanor I. *Insects from Close Up*. 1965. Thomas Y. Crowell, New York.

Buchsbaum, Ralph. *Animals Without Backbones*. 2nd rev. ed. 1972. University of Chicago Press, Chicago.

Burch, John B. *How to Know the Eastern Land Snails*. 1962. William C. Brown, Dubuque, Ia.

Cousteau, Jacques H., and Diole, Philippe. *Octopus and Squid: The Soft Intelligence*. 1973. Doubleday, Garden City, N.Y.

Ehrlich, Paul R. *How to Know the Butterflies*. 1961. William C. Brown, Dubuque, Ia.

Evans, Howard Ensign. *Wasp Farm*. 1963. The Natural History Press, Garden City, N.Y.

Headstrom, Richard. *Spiders of the United States*. 1972. A. S. Barnes, Cranbury, N.J.

Helfer, Jacques. *How to Know the Grasshoppers, Cockroaches and Their Allies*. 1963. William C. Brown, Dubuque, Ia.

Hickman, Cleveland P. *Biology of the Invertebrates*. 2nd ed. 1973. C. V. Mosby, St. Louis.

Holland, W. J. *The Moth Book*. Ed. A. E. Brower. 1968. Peter Smith Publisher, Magnolia, Mass.

Howse, P. E. *Termites: A Study in Social Behavior*. 1970. Hutchinson University Library, New York.

Hoyt, Murray. *The World of Bees*. 1965. Coward, McCann, New York.

Jacques, Harry E. *How to Know the Beetles*. 1951. William C. Brown, Dubuque, Ia.

Jahn, I. *How to Know the Protozoa*. 1949. William C. Brown, Dubuque, Ia.

Klots, Alexander B. *Field Guide to the Butterflies*. 1951. Houghton Mifflin, Boston.

Klots, Alexander and Elsie. *Insects of North America*. 1971. Doubleday, Garden City, N.Y.

Lane, Frank W. *Kingdom of the Octopus: The Life History of the Cephalopoda*. 1974. Sheridan House, Yonkers, N.Y.

Lutz, Frank E. *Field Book of Insects*. 3rd ed. 1948. G. P. Putnam's Sons, New York.

Mackinnon, Doris L., and Hawes, R. S. *Introduction to the Study of Protozoa*. 1961. Oxford University Press, New York.

Savory, Theodore. *Spiders and Other Arachnids*. 1964. Crane-Russak, New York.

Schmitt, Waldo I. *Crustaceans*. 1965. University of Michigan Press, Ann Arbor, Mich.

Sudd, John H. *Introduction to the Behavior of Ants.* 1967. St. Martin's Press, New York.

Swan, Lester, and Papp, Charles. *The Common Insects of North America.* 1972. Harper & Row, New York.

Villiard, Paul. *Moths and How to Rear Them.* 1973. Funk & Wagnalls, New York.

Von Frisch, Karl. *Bees, Their Vision, Chemical Senses and Language.* 1971. Cornell University Press, Ithaca, N.Y.

Wheeler, William M. *Ants: Their Structure, Development and Behavior.* 1960. Columbia University Press, New York.

Wigglesworth, V. B. *The Life of Insects.* 1964. World Publishing, Cleveland, Oh.

Wilson, Edward O. *Insect Societies.* 1971. Harvard University Press, Cambridge.

Wright, C. A. *Flukes and Snails.* 1973. Hafner Press, New York.

MAMMALS

Andersen, Harald T., ed. *The Biology of Marine Mammals.* 1969. Academic Press, New York.

Bourlier, Francis. *Natural History of Mammals, A Field Outline.* 1961. Alfred A. Knopf, Westminster, Md.

Brown, Vinson. *Sea Mammals and Reptiles of the Pacific Coast.* 1976. Macmillan, New York.

Burt, William H., and Grossenheider, R. P. *Field Guide to the Mammals.* 2nd ed. 1964. Houghton Mifflin, Boston.

Cousteau, Jacques-Yves, and Diole, Philippe. *The Whale—Mighty Monarch of the Sea.* 1972. Doubleday, Garden City, N.Y.

Ingles, Lloyd G. *Mammals of the Pacific States.* 1965. Stanford University Press, Stanford, Calif.

Norris, Kenneth S. *Whales, Dolphins and Porpoises.* 1966. University of California Press, Berkeley.

Stenuit, Robert. *The Dolphin, Cousin of Man.* 1968. Sterling Publishing, New York; 1970. Bantam Books, New York.

Van Lawick-Goodall, Jane. *In the Shadow of Man.* 1971. Houghton Mifflin, Boston.

NATURAL HISTORY IN GENERAL

American Wildlife Region Series. A series of volumes produced by Naturegraph Publishers, Healdsburg, California 95448, each picturing and describing the mammals, birds, reptiles, amphibians, common plants, and often the common fish of natural wildlife regions of America. This series so far covers the following regions: Californian, Sierran, Pacific Coastal, Cascades and Siskiyou Mountains, Inter-mountain West, Northern Rockies, Southern Rockies, and (in preparation) Great Plains and Prairies.

Brown, Vinson. *The Amateur Naturalist's Handbook*. 1948. Little, Brown, Boston.

De Laubenfels, David. *Geography of Plants and Animals*. 1970. William C. Brown, Dubuque, Ia.

Hillcourt, William. *Field Book of Nature Activities and Conservation*. Rev. ed. 1951. G. P. Putnam's Sons, New York.

Milne, Lorus J. and Margery. *The Balance of Nature*. 1960. Alfred A. Knopf, Westminster, Md.

Palmer, E. Lawrence. *Fieldbook of Natural History*. 1949. McGraw-Hill, New York.

Watts, May T. *Reading the Landscape*. 1957. Macmillan, New York.

NATURALISTS, STORIES ABOUT

Adams, Alexander B. *Eternal Quest: The Story of the Great Naturalists*. 1969. G. P. Putnam's Sons, New York.

California Academy of Sciences. *A Century of Progress in the Natural Sciences: 1853–1953*. 1955. California Academy of Sciences, San Francisco.

Ewan, Joseph. *Rocky Mountain Naturalists*. 1950. University of Denver Press, Denver.

Gabriel, Mordecai L., and Foge, Seymour, eds. *Great Experiments in Biology*. 1955. Prentice-Hall, Englewood Cliffs, N.J.

Thomson, Sir J. Arthur. *The Great Biologists*. 1932. Books for Libraries Press, Freeport, N.Y.

PHOTOGRAPHY AND OTHER SPECIAL TECHNIQUES

Angel, Heather. *Nature Photography, Its Art and Technique*. 1973. Morgan and Morgan, Dobbs Ferry, N.Y.

Klinne, Russ. *The Complete Book of Nature Photography*. 2nd ed. 1971. American Photographic Book Publishing, New York.

Larach, Simon. *Photoelectronic Materials and Devices*. 1965. Van Nostrand, Reinhold, New York.

Maye, Patricia, ed. *Fieldbook of Nature Photography*. 1973. Charles Scribner's Sons, New York.

Walker, M. I. *Amateur Photomicrography*. 1972. Chilton Book Co., Reading, Pa.

Warham, John. *The Technique of Bird Photography*. 3rd ed. 1973. American Photographic Book Publishing, Garden City, N.Y.

PLANTS—ADVANCED (FERNS TO SUNFLOWERS)

Abrams, Leroy, and Ferris, Roxana S. *Illustrated Flora of the Pacific States*, 4 vols. 1960. Stanford University Press, Stanford, Calif.

Britton, Nathaniel L., and Brown, Addison. *Illustrated Flora of Northern United States and Canada*. 2nd rev. ed., 3 vols. 1974. Peter Smith Publisher, Magnolia, Mass.

Brown, Vinson. *Reading the Woods*. 1969. Stackpole Books, Harrisburg, Pa.

Cobb, Boughton. *A Field Guide to the Ferns*. 1956. Houghton Mifflin, Boston.

Corner, E. J. H. *The Life of Plants*. 1964. World Publishing, New York.

Correll, Donovan S. *Manual of the Vascular Plants of Texas*. 1970. Hafner Press, New York.

Cronquist, Arthur, et al. *Intermountain Flora, Vascular Plants of the Intermountain West*. 1972. Hafner Press, New York.

Davis, Ray. *Flora of Idaho*. 1969. Brigham Young University Press, Provo, Utah.

Gleason, Henry A., and Cronquist, Arthur. *The Natural Geography of Plants*. 1964. Columbia University Press, New York.

Grimm, William C. *The Book of Trees*. 2nd ed. 1962. Stackpole Books, Harrisburg, Pa.

Harrar, Ellwood S., and George, J. *Guide to Southern Trees*. 1962. Dover Publications, New York.

Hitchcock, C. Leo, and Cronquist, Arthur. *Flora of the Pacific Northwest, an Illustrated Manual*. 1973. University of Washington Press, Seattle, Wash.

Hutchinson, John. *Families of Flowering Plants*. 3rd ed. 3 vols. 1972. Oxford University Press, New York.

Kuchler, A. W. *Vegetation Mapping*. 1967. Ronald Press, New York.

Mason, Herbert L. *Flora of the Marshes of California*. 1957. University of California Press, Berkeley.

Munz, Philip A., and Keck, David. *California Flora & Supplement*. 1973. University of California Press, Berkeley.

Petrides, George A. *A Field Guide to Trees and Shrubs of North Central and Northeast United States and Southeast and South Central Canada*. 1972. Houghton Mifflin, Boston.

Radford, Albert E. *Manual of the Vascular Flora of the Carolinas*. 1973. University of North Carolina Press, Chapel Hill, N.C.

Rendle, Alfred B. *The Classification of Flowering Plants*. 12 vols. 1967. Cambridge University Press, Cambridge, Eng.

Rydberg, Per A. *Flora of the Prairies and Plains of Central North America*. 1965. Hafner Press, New York.

———. *Flora of the Rocky Mountains and Adjacent Plains*. 2nd ed. 1954. Hafner Press, New York.

Seymour, Frank C. *Flora of New England*. 1969. Charles E. Tuttle, Rutland, Vt.

Shreve, Forrest, and Wiggins, Ira. *Vegetation and Flora of the Sonoran Desert*. 1964. Stanford University Press, Stanford, Calif.

Small, John Kunkel. *Manual of the Southeastern Flora*. 2 vols. 1972. Hafner Press, New York.

Steyermark, Julian A. *Flora of Missouri*. 1963. Iowa State University Press, Ames, Ia.

Tidestrom, I. *Flora of Utah and Nevada*. 1969. Hafner Service, New York.

Weaver, John. *Native Vegetation of Nebraska*. 1965. University of Nebraska Press, Lincoln, Neb.

Wooton, Elmer O., and Standley, P. C. *Flora of New Mexico*. 1971. Hafner Press, New York.

PLANTS—PRIMITIVE

Clements, Frederic, and Shear, Cornelius L. *Genera of Fungi*. 1965. Hafner Press, New York.

Conard, Henry S. *How to Know the Mosses and Liverworts*. 1956. William C. Brown, Dubuque, Ia.

Dawson, E. Yale. *How to Know the Seaweeds*. Rev. ed. 1956. William C. Brown, Dubuque, Ia.

Gaeumann, E. *The Fungi*. 1974. Hafner Press, New York.

Grout, A. J. *Moss Flora of North America, North of Mexico*. 3 vols. 1972. Hafner Press, New York.

Guberlet, Muriel. *Seaweeds at Ebb Tide*. 1956. University of Washington Press, Seattle, Wash.

Harthill, Marion P. *Common Mosses of the Pacific Coast*. 1975. Naturegraph Publishers, Healdsburg, Calif.

Kleijn, H. *Mushrooms and Other Fungi*. 1974. Doubleday, Garden City, N.Y.

Morris, Ian. *Introduction to the Algae*. 1967. Hutchinson University Library, New York.

Prescott, George W. *How to Know the Freshwater Algae*. 3rd ed. 1970. William C. Brown, Dubuque, Ia.

Robinson, R. K. *Ecology of the Fungi*. 1967. Crane-Russak, New York.

Smith, Alex V. and Helen. *How to Know the Non-gilled Fleshy Fungi*. 1973. William C. Brown, Dubuque, Ia.

Stevenson, G. *Biology of Fungi, Bacteria and Viruses*. 1970. American El' sevier Publishing, New York.

Taylor, William R. *Marine Algae of Florida*. 1967. Hafner Press, New York.

———. *Marine Algae of the Northeastern Coast of North America*, 2nd rev. ed. 1957. University of Michigan Press, Ann Arbor, Mich.

REPTILES AND AMPHIBIANS

Brown, Vinson. *Reptiles and Amphibians of the West*. 1974. Naturegraph Publishers, Healdsburg, Calif.

Carr, Archie. *So Excellent a Fishe—A Natural History of Sea Turtles*. 1973. Doubleday, Garden City, N.Y.

———. *Handbook of Turtles*. 1952. Comstock Associates, Ithaca, N.Y.

Conant, Roger. *A Field Guide to Reptiles and Amphibians of Eastern and Midwestern North America*. 1958. Houghton Mifflin, Boston.

Gans, Carl, ed. *Biology of the Reptiles*. 1970. Academic Press, New York.

Stebbins, Robert C. *A Field Guide to Western Reptiles and Amphibians*. 1966. Houghton Mifflin, Boston.

SEASHORE LIFE

Miner, Roy Waldo. *Field Book of Seashore Life*. 1950. G. P. Putnam's Sons, New York.

Morris, Percy A. *Field Guide to the Shells of Our Atlantic and Gulf Coasts*. Rev. ed. 1951. Houghton Mifflin, Boston.

———. *A Field Guide to the Shells of the Pacific Coast and Hawaii*. Rev. ed. 1966. Houghton Mifflin, Boston.

Ricketts, Edward F., and Calvin, Jack. *Between Pacific Tides*. 4th ed. Ed. Joel Hedgpeth. 1968. Stanford University Press, Stanford, Calif.

Appendix D

NATURAL HISTORY SUPPLIERS

American Biological Supply Co., 1330 Dillon Heights, Baltimore, Maryland 21228.

Arthropod Specialties Co., Box 1973, Sacramento, California 95809.

Combined Scientific Supplies, P.O. Box 125, Rosemead, California 91770.

Turtox Cambosco, Macmillan Science Co., Inc., 8200 South Hoyne Avenue, Chicago, Illinois 60620.

Ward's Natural Science Establishment, Inc., 3000 Ridge Road East, Rochester, New York 14609.

Wind, Cleo, 827 Congress, Pacific Grove, California 93950.

Appendix E

SCIENTIFIC PERIODICALS

American Midland Naturalist, University of Notre Dame, Notre Dame, Indiana 46556.

American Naturalist, publication of the American Society of Naturalists, University of Chicago Press, 5801 Ellis Avenue, Chicago, Illinois 60637.

American Zoologist, official publication of the American Society of Zoologists, University of Arizona, Tucson, Arizona 85721.

Animal Behaviour, quarterly publication of the Association for the Study of Animal Behaviour and Animal Behaviour Society, BAILLIERE Tindall, 7–8 Henriette Street, London W.C.2, England.

Annals of the Entomological Society of America, 4603 Calvert Road, P.O. Box AJ, College Park, Maryland 20740.

Auk (The), published by the American Ornithologist's Union, National Museum of Natural History, Smithsonian Institution, Washington, D.C. 20560.

Behavioral Science, University of Louisville Health Science Center Library, P. O. Box 1055, Louisville, Kentucky 40201.

Biotropica, quarterly publication of the Association of Tropical Biology, Department of Biology, George Mason University, Fairfax, Virginia 22030.

Bulletin of the Entomological Society of America, 4603 Calvert Road, P.O. Box AJ, College Park, Maryland 20740.

Canadian Entomologist, 1320 Carling Avenue, Ottawa, Ontario, Canada K1Z 7K9.

Canadian Field Naturalist, Box 3264, Postal Station C, Ottawa, Canada, K1Y 4J5.

Castanea, Southern Appalachian Botanical Club, West Virginia University, Morgantown, West Virginia 26506.

Condor, Cooper Ornithological Society, Inc., Oakland Museum, Natural Sciences Division, 1000 Oak Street, Oakland, California 94607.

Copeia, the official organ of the American Society of Ichthyologists and Herpetologists. Send inquiries to Division of Reptiles and Amphibians, National Museum of Natural History, Washington, D.C. 20560.

Ecological Monographs, Duke University Press, Box 6697, College Station, Durham, North Carolina 27708.

Ecology, Duke University Press, Box 6697, College Station, Durham, North Carolina 27708.

Explorer (The), quarterly magazine of the Cleveland Museum of Natural History, University Circle, Cleveland, Ohio 44106.

Gastropodia, journal for original papers on mollusks, Kutztown State College, Kutztown, Pennsylvania 19530.

Herpetologica, Department of Biology, San Diego State University, San Diego, California 92182.

Journal of Animal Ecology, publication of the British Ecological Society, Blackwell Scientific Publications Ltd., Osney Mead, Oxford CX20EL, England.

Journal of Herpetology, University of Texas Graduate School of Biomedical Sciences, Box 20334, Houston, Texas 77025.

Journal of New York Entomological Society, American Museum of Natural History, 79th Street and Central Park West, New York, New York 10024.

Malacologia, international journal of malacology, Institute of Malacology, Academy of Natural Sciences, 19th and the Parkway, Philadelphia, Pennsylvania 19103.

Nautilus (The), Delaware Museum of Natural History, 11 Chelton Road, Havertown, Pennsylvania 19083.

Ontario Field Biologist, semiannual journal of Toronto Field Naturalist's Club, 49 Craighurst Avenue, Toronto, Ontario, Canada M4R LJ9. (Most Canadian provinces have similar natural science journals.)

Pacific Insects, Department of Entomology, Bishop Museum, Box 6037, Honolulu, Hawaii 96818.

Sea Pen (The), P.O. Box 10512, Bainbridge Island, Washington 98110. For members of the Marine Science Society of the Pacific Northwest, Inc.

Studies in Natural Sciences, The Natural Sciences Research Institute, Eastern New Mexico University, Portales, New Mexico 88130.

Systematic Zoology, quarterly journal of the Society of Systematic Zoology, National Museum of Natural History, Washington, D.C. 20560.

Note: There are a number of other periodicals dealing with natural history that you can find out about at your nearest university, college, or other large museum.

INDEX

(*Note:* Names used in the two glossaries in this book, Appendix A (Ecology) and Appendix B (Ethology), are not repeated in this index unless they are used elsewhere in the book.)